The Culture of Conflict

The Culture of
Conflict

Interpretations and Interests in

Comparative Perspective

Marc Howard Ross

Yale University Press

New Haven and London

Designed by James J. Johnson.
Set in Melior Roman and Optima types
by Rainsford Type, Danbury,
Connecticut.

Printed in the United States of America
by BookCrafters, Inc., Chelsea,
Michigan.

The paper in this book meets the
guidelines for permanence and
durability of the Committee on
Production Guidelines for Book
Longevity of the Council on
Library Resources.

*Library of Congress Cataloging-in-
Publication Data*

Ross, Marc Howard.
The culture of conflict : interpretations
and interests in comparative
perspective / Marc Howard Ross.
p.   cm.
Includes bibliographical references and
index.
ISBN 0-300-05273-1

1. Political anthropology. 2. Conflict
(Psychology)—Cross-cultural
studies. 3. Ethnopsychology.
4. Intergroup relations—Cross-
cultural studies. 5. Conflict
management—Cross-cultural
studies. I. Title.
GN494.5.R66   1993   92-41994
306.2—dc20

A catalogue record for this book is
available from the British
Library.

10 9 8 7 6 5 4 3 2 1

To Katherine

with love

Contents

Preface

Ordinarily, neither textbook discussions of research methods nor descriptions of individual projects like the current study provide insights into the twists and turns research takes as ideas are developed, discarded, sharpened, and refined; yet anyone who has engaged in serious scientific or social scientific research knows that the process is far less linear than the coherent finished product suggests. In this spirit, this preface offers a few comments about some assumptions critical to my study of patterns of conflict in preindustrial societies that are not raised in the body of the text. Several leaps of faith—temperamental and intellectual—have been essential, and without them this book would never have been written.

At the most basic level is my naïve conviction that human societies can learn to deal with conflict more constructively than they have done in the past. Of course the capacity to engage in destructive conflict can diffuse across societies, but a key goal of this project is to consider how successful conflict management practices can spread. Conflict itself, in my view, is not necessarily a bad thing nor something we can eradicate; rather, the problem is ineffective conflict management, with resulting high social and human costs.

It is not surprising that an American would be looking far and wide for insights into constructive conflict management, for this is a domain that American society has not handled well. During my lifetime the United States has fought four major wars, engaged in dozens of other minor conflicts, and financed one side (and sometimes both) in many other disputes. Within our country, violent self-help tactics and a legal system which is most accessible to the rich and famous are the two preferred modes of conflict management. Our citizenry is armed to the teeth, and, not surprisingly, our homicide rate is far and away the highest in the industrial world. Our popular culture, whether we consider professional football, movies, television, or music, is just as violent. In contrast, joint problem solving by disputants and the use of mediation and negotiation are often seen as signs of weakness. Is it any wonder that I want to believe that there must be societies which can teach us something about conflict management?

This inquiry is also dependent upon my naïve willingness as a political scientist to examine conflict cross-culturally using ethnographic field data and then to develop explanatory mechanisms which draw heavily on social and psychoanalytic theory. There are considerable potential risks in the effort to make connections between fields. Yet there is also an excitement in the exploration of new linkages and in the union of theories and data that had previously remained apart. It is stimulating to find new (and perhaps improved) answers to old questions. It is also challenging to persuade people in one field that work in another field is relevant to their agenda.

The argument advanced by anthropologist Max Gluckman and economist Ely Devons (1964) justifies such an endeavor by suggesting that naïve assumptions which ignore or oversimplify the research base of other disciplines are essential for the effective delineation of many complex problems: "If a social scientist is to set himself a manageable aspect or field for study, about which he can say significant things, he may often have to make assumptions which will appear to be distorting or even false to the practitioners of other disciplines. We go so far as to say that he has a duty to be naive in this way about his 'outside' assumptions, and a duty to avoid attempting to deal with aspects of reality which can only be adequately handled by some discipline other than his own" (166).

Economists, for example, make simplistic assumptions about psychological processes of choice making when they construct microeconomic models and pay no heed to the relevant work in the field of psychology. There is no problem with such naïveté, Gluckman and Devons argue, provided that the naïve assumptions do not affect important conclusions drawn about the primary problem a researcher is investigating. "A fair test is to ask whether the analysis would stand if different naive assumptions were adopted" (1964:168). If the answer is yes, then the naïveté, in their view, is justifiable.

As I became increasingly involved in this project, I found that the intellectual naïveté so comforting in Gluckman and Devons's argument became a luxury I could no longer afford. If I had continued to make naïve assumptions about data and theories from anthropology, sociology, and modern psychoanalysis, my understanding of conflict and conflict management could not have advanced. I could not accept simplifying assumptions about data and theory that had become central to my concerns. For example, using ethnographic reports effectively as primary data meant learning more about the role of anthropological fieldwork in various intellectual traditions and historical periods. In order to be able to evaluate psychocultural hypotheses connecting socialization experiences and adult conflict behavior in an informed manner, I attended a psychoanalytic institute for a year and have tried since to keep up with the field to better understand its core assumptions about conflict behavior and their implications for conflict management.

All of this, of course, took far more time than I originally anticipated when in 1978 I decided to spend a few months examining a sample of preindustrial societies as a first step toward writing a general text on political anthropology. That book has not been written and eventually my interest in conflict and then conflict management displaced it in my priorities. As I concentrated on conflict behavior, the focus of my analysis shifted as well. Initially my goal was to choose between competing predictions derived from alternative theories of conflict; yet the clearer the details of various theories and the results of my data analysis became, the more I began to emphasize the complementary aspects of the theories. Social structural conflict theory, I now argue, can primarily explain who one's friends and foes will be when conflict develops, whereas psychocultural conflict theory best predicts a community's overall level of conflict. The theories are not mutually exclusive; rather, each focuses on a different aspect of conflict and, taken together, they offer a more useful theory of conflict than either one alone.

When in 1990 I finished a draft of this book, it was almost 600 pages long and contained not only much of the material in the present volume but also six chapters developing the conflict management implications of the culture of conflict theory. It subsequently became clear to me that establishing the essential linkage between conflict and conflict management did not have to be done in a single work. This volume thus focuses on the question of conflict in cross-cultural perspective, and a second book, *The Management of Conflict* (also published by Yale University Press), develops the issues of conflict management. Although the two books are highly interdependent, each volume is self-contained and may be read independently.

All of this is a way of saying that the process of scholarship is filled with unanticipated zigs and zags and often motivated by critical concerns which are rarely spelled out in publications. Scholarship requires both careful consideration of the relation between data and theory and a willingness to move beyond accepted formulations of existing problems in order to think about how we understand action in new ways. I hope that in this project I have demonstrated both, analyzing data on conflict in small-scale societies and conceptualizing the question of conflict and conflict management in a new way.

Over the years I have received widespread encouragement and support for this endeavor. Bryn Mawr College granted me several sabbatical leaves and provided research support and facilities since I began this project. The Anthropology Program of the National Science Foundation provided crucial support for the data collection (BNS82–03381) in 1982–83. The Harry Frank Guggenheim Foundation provided generous support in 1989–90 for completing the data analysis and writing.

More than a few individuals have been particularly helpful to me in this project. Don Campbell, Bea Whiting, and John Whiting have all, in different ways, been teachers, mentors, and colleagues over the years. Each encouraged me to explore politics in a wide variety of settings and to ask rigorous questions about the relationship between theory and data. They have always been generous with their time and energy and offered me models of intellectual curiosity, integrity, and commitment.

Maria Cattell, Cindy Konecko, and Camille Paglia, all students at Bryn Mawr at the time, coded the ethnographic data for this project during the summer of 1982. Each of them worked carefully and thoughtfully on the project, raising important questions and objections and at times redirecting our efforts in more productive directions. I am grateful to them not only for their commitment but also for the high quality of their work. Gina Granelli did a first-rate job of collecting and analyzing existing studies of Norway and Northern Ireland.

Colleagues in the Society for Cross-Cultural Research, a small association whose meetings are always stimulating and enjoyable, helped me in many ways. Raoul Naroll unceasingly encouraged systematic research even when it led to rejection of one of his favored hypotheses or methods. Carol Ember and Mel Ember have provided tremendous encouragement and many specific comments and suggestions over the years. Carol read and commented on an earlier version of this manuscript and many papers that preceded it, offering countless insightful suggestions for improvement. Tom Weisner provided important ideas about the reorganization of my argument for which I am very grateful. Mike Burton and Malcolm Dow have made important methodological suggestions to me over the years. Joel Aronoff has helped clarify my thinking about the challenge of using personality-based arguments to explain societal-level behaviors. A number of years ago, Phil Kilbride made the useful suggestion that I use the term dispositions, not personality, in connection with psychocultural characteristics, and he has contributed much to my understanding of the connections between psychological and cultural processes in discussions with me on a number of occasions. Michael Weinstein made many substantive and methodological suggestions during the early phases of this project. Bob Mulvihill persuaded me that the general model proposed here could offer important insights into the conflict in Northern Ireland. Lou Kriesberg, as a reader for Yale University Press, made a number of specific suggestions that I found very helpful in clarifying my argument, especially concerning the relationship among the major theoretical approaches. Noreen O'Connor, the manuscript editor for Yale University Press, provided many detailed ideas about how to clarify and streamline my argument for which I am very grateful.

Earlier versions of parts of chapters 6, 7, and 10 have been published in *Political Psychology, The Journal of Conflict Resolution, Anthropological Quarterly,* and in Silverberg and Gray's *Aggression in Humans and Other Primates* (Oxford University Press, 1992) and are reprinted with permission.

Kimberly, Aaron, Kristin, and especially Ethan have spent a number of years watching me work at the computer, never fully understanding my underlying motivation. Scholarship must seem the slowest thing in the world to them—except maybe to Ethan, who, when informed that this book was about to be published, told his mother "Oh, I thought he finished that a *long* time ago."

Katherine Conner, my wife, has, more than anyone else, shared every stage of this entire project with me. She patiently discussed with me its conceptualization, the details of the data collection, the ups-and-

downs of the analysis, and the hard questions which come up in com-
mitting one's understandings to paper. Her keen mind and sharp insights
shaped the book in important ways. I am grateful that she never hesitated
to offer her thoughts and reactions to what I was doing or saying, even
when they were not necessarily what I wanted to hear at the time. I will
always be appreciative for the way she could be counted on to focus her
energies on my pressing questions, even when her life was filled with
other, more acute matters. Katherine read every draft and revised draft
of every chapter and continually fiddled with my sometimes opaque
prose until she thought it was just right. Because Katherine's effort was
truly a labor of love, I dedicate the book to her.

1

Why Are Some Societies More Conflictual Than Others?

Despite the fact that political conflict and violence are among the most pressing issues of the twentieth century, their dynamics are only partially understood. We do a better job of describing particular disputes than of understanding the underlying general principles. This is not due to a lack of effort, however, for the production of theories of conflict has occupied all the social sciences for quite some time.

Our incomplete understanding of conflict behavior has serious consequences for our ability to manage conflicts constructively. It restricts the help given to adversaries seeking effective solutions and makes it particularly difficult to create arrangements limiting the escalation of conflicts before they get out of hand. The fragmented character of approaches to conflict is a central impetus for this book, which proposes to integrate previously distinct theories.

Complex social and political conflicts invariably have multiple roots. Conflict is about the concrete interests adversaries pursue and, at the same time, about their interpretations of what is at stake in a dispute. Much of the time the issue in dispute is the focal point for underlying differences of which the antagonists may be only partially aware and which, if ignored, are likely to resurface later. Managing a conflict effectively, then, usually means not only doing something about the issue in contention but also addressing deeper concerns. Conflicts become intense not just because of the value of what is being fought over but because of the psychological importance of winning and losing.

I explore these themes by inquiring into how particular societies develop characteristic patterns of disputing. The answers I offer here are different from what I expected when I started considering why some societies have far more conflict and violence than others do. Initially I stressed the contrasts between what I call structural and psychocultural theories. As I worked to make sense of my empirical results, however, I found myself emphasizing ways in which these theories drew attention to different, but not necessarily opposing, factors. That one was right did not mean that the other was therefore wrong. Each offered partial answers; coming to understand how the two theories complement, rather than compete with, each other has been particularly important.

My approach is broadly comparative, utilizing data from a worldwide sample of preindustrial societies typically studied by anthropologists. These data provide an opportunity to examine ideas about conflict developed in settings very different from urban, industrial ones. The process can provide insights that help us distinguish more clearly between behavior patterns found across human societies and those that are products of a particular cultural, economic, or political organization.

The argument I propose is that the culture of conflict—a society's particular constellation of norms, practices, and institutions—affects what groups and individuals fight about, the culturally approved ways to pursue their goals in disputes, and institutional resources that shape the course and outcomes of the conflicts (Avruch and Black 1991). Cultural dispositions about conflict are rooted in early developmental experiences, while a society's structural features identify who the targets of conflict behavior are. While conflict is played out around concrete interests, the interpretations of the participants are equally important in establishing whether conflict develops and whether it can be managed constructively. Understanding the origin, course, and management of a conflict requires consideration of both structural and psychocultural factors.

Two Contrasting Cases

Conflict is a ubiquitous feature of behavior within and between human groups. Problems of theft, murder, unpaid debts, sexual assault, jealousy, and anger are human universals in that there are virtually no communities where they are unknown (Nader and Todd 1978). At the same time, there is great variation from society to society in both the amount of conflict and what people do when it occurs. Consider two well-described preindustrial societies which are very different from our own: the Yanomamo of southern Venezuela (Chagnon 1968, 1983) and the Mbuti pygmies of the Zaire rain forest (Turnbull 1961, 1978). Why is conflict a key element in the daily life of the Yanomamo but much less central among the Mbuti? A brief examination of these two cases illustrates several answers that organize this book.

Yanomamo

The Yanomamo, a small-scale horticultural people, live in dispersed, mutually hostile villages of 40 to 250 persons in an isolated jungle area crisscrossed by rivers and streams.[1] Members of a village consist of related males, their wives, and their children.

A militant ideology and the warfare associated with it are the central reality of daily existence among the Yanomamo. Interpersonal relations are tension laden, and there is a preoccupation with attacks from supernatural forces directed by one's enemies as well as ever-present concern with actual enemy raids. Villages are continually planning attacks on, fearing attacks from, or carrying out attacks on one another. One village, Chagnon (1983:183) reports, was raided 25 times during his initial 15 months of field work in the mid-1960s, and he estimates that about a fourth of Yanomamo men die violently.

The capture of women and the achievement of autonomy through overt violence are, according to Chagnon (1968), the primary goals of intervillage fighting. The extreme militancy and hostility toward neighbors, especially in the more densely populated core regions of Yanomamo territory, are associated with efforts to protect village autonomy. Dependence on cultivated crops means that the location of a village is predictable to enemies, however, and although villages move regularly, preparation of new sites takes at least a year.

Villages regularly develop intervillage alliances which involve giving refuge in time of need, sharing gardens if one group is uprooted from its home, and providing active military aid during raiding periods. These alliances are very tenuous, however. Host groups exact a high price (typically in terms of women) from weaker allies, and there are times when a village will turn on an unsuspecting ally in a "treacherous feast" or other opportune situation. Marriage alliances, which might be expected to solidify intercommunity bonds, are inherently unstable be-

1. Throughout the book I use the ethnographic present, the time of the anthropologist's field research, to describe a society which may be quite different today.

cause of "the reluctance that each group displays in ceding women to others and the aggressiveness with which the demands for women are made" (Chagnon 1968:123). The preferred form of marriage—bilateral, cross-cousin exchanges within the village (in which a man marries the daughter of his father's brother or his mother's sister)—means that social links which might extend political alliances are very narrow indeed.

Even within the village many of the same pressures for autonomy are present. The weak emotional significance of kinship ties means that in larger villages narrow sublineage-based factions with their own interests develop within the more extended lineage. In addition, even in smaller groups there is often high tension among closely related males. Although they are dependent upon one another for mutual support in feuds and military activities, brothers and patrilineal male cousins are also in competition for the same women, who are always seen as in short supply. There are times when intravillage tensions become so severe that fighting breaks out within the village. Larger villages, Chagnon reports (1968), often divide as a result.

In the Yanomamo view, the world is a dangerous place. Enemies, both human and supernatural, are everywhere, and the support of allies is never certain. Autonomy, for the village and the individual, becomes the unattainable solution to this dilemma. It is sought in what Chagnon calls the *waiteri* complex, a fierce political and personal stance in which groups and individuals behave aggressively to forestall dependency and to communicate to others the probable high cost of their own aggression.

The inculcation of fierceness is a dominant theme in socialization, especially for boys. Parents encourage displays of aggression in young boys and taunt those who fail to use physical force in the many situations in which it is considered appropriate. As boys grow older, they are expected to practice the skills of fighting they will need as adults in club fights, chest-pounding duels, and spear fights. Aggressive adult role models abound, and reinforcement for appropriate expressions of aggression in youth is easy to obtain.[2]

Male-female relationships among the Yanomamo are distant and aggression-laden with male hostility regularly directed against wives and other females. Strong ambivalence also characterizes mother-son relationships. While mothers are the main source of nurturance and pro-

2. Although male aggression is the main focus of Chagnon's analysis, his writing and films also provide some examples of female aggression.

tection, boys see women in general, and their mothers in particular, being devalued and physically abused. Becoming a successful adult male requires not only breaking the bond to one's mother but behaving aggressively toward all females. Young boys learn this from an early age, for aggressive behavior toward girls is encouraged.[3]

From Chagnon's rich case material it is easy to generate several hypotheses about the roots of Yanomamo conflict and violence. Most obvious is the absence of well-established social and political bonds among individuals in different communities, which might limit the intensity of conflict and create pressures for the peaceful resolution of disputes when they occur. Even within the communities where such bonds exist, they are weak and apparently easily set aside when disputes begin to escalate. Alternatively, the absence of institutions and practices that discourage violence as a favored method of conflict management might be attributed to the relatively low level of complexity of the Yanomamo socioeconomic system, with its weak differentiation among communities and the lack of any overarching political authority that might effectively address the ever-present intergroup aggression. Finally, high conflict seems to be rooted in the Yanomamo world views and psychocultural dispositions promoted from earliest childhood. Their socialization emphasizes toughness and physical aggression, especially for males; there is little expression of warmth and affection, particularly in father-child interactions. Male-female relationships are marked by hostility and distance. All these elements are critical in the development of the waiteri complex, with its emphasis on low social trust and the need for autonomy. They foster Yanomamo suspiciousness and aggression, contributing to the perpetuation of violence and the failure to develop viable ways to manage conflicts constructively.[4]

3. Male children provide continual reminders of their fathers and husbands invoking feelings of fear and danger at times. Responses to these emotions probably decrease a young child's sense of trust and security and reinforce the idea of the tenuous nature of social relationships. In addition, from a psychoanalytic viewpoint, the relationship between mothers and daughters probably has strong ambivalence as well.

4. Ferguson (1992) suggests that the extensive warfare among the Yanomamo that Chagnon describes is best understood in terms of the extensive contact-related changes that affected the region prior to Chagnon's arrival. He argues that "the occurrence and patterning of warfare . . . among the Yanomami is a result of antagonistic interests regarding access to or control over Western manufactured goods" (1992:201). The unequal availability of goods such as steel

Mbuti

Chagnon's portrait of the Yanomamo is consistent with a Hobbesian view of small-scale societies, whereas Turnbull's writings on the Mbuti present a very different picture. If there is a human propensity toward violent conflict, or if the smallest and technologically simplest societies are more prone to unmanageable conflict than other peoples, the Ituri rain forest where the Mbuti live ought to be filled with violence; it is not.

The Mbuti live in small hunting and foraging groups deep in the rain forest. As Turnbull portrays them, the Mbuti are at peace with themselves and with their environment. The forest is a source not only of sustenance but also of the deepest emotional support. Each camp consists of a number of kin groups living together, but the group's composition frequently changes because of individual decisions to spend time with other relatives or close friends and seasonal differences in the organization of foraging and hunting tasks.

There are no formal leaders in an Mbuti band, and the only real division of labor is by age and gender, although even here the boundaries are far less rigid and their emotional significance less charged than in many other societies. Cooperation in hunting is essential for subsistence, and Turnbull describes how community members coordinate their actions to capture and kill the swift, and sometimes large, game. When a hunt is successful, all band members share the meat. That it might belong to a single hunter or that a member of the community could go hungry while there is food for others is unthinkable to the Mbuti.

A striking feature of Mbuti life is its social density. In the settlement, people live very close to one another, and the concerns of any

---

axes and machetes in the region, Ferguson argues, affected patterns of local trade, marriage exchanges, village location, social cohesion, and warfare.

Although Ferguson's argument is interesting, particularly for understanding the overall level of conflict in the region, it does not contradict the argument that Yanomamo social organization and world views encouraged hostility and aggression even prior to extensive western contact. In addition, Ferguson reminds us that the impact of western cultures tends to be felt earlier than we often believe and that there are important indirect effects, as well as direct ones. Ferguson's strong argument that all Yanomamo warfare can be explained in terms of conflict over western goods is obviously not consistent with Chagnon's published materials. Ferguson plans to document it in a future publication.

one or two individuals easily become matters involving everyone. If, for example, someone complains about another's actions, a third person is likely to join in the conversation, which soon can involve all those present. At times, tempers flare and people scream or even toss burning logs at each other. Occasionally a third party needs to step between disputants to restore order.

Turnbull suggests that most of the time, however, even in situations where feelings are intense, community discussion of a dispute leads to a solution acceptable to all concerned. Critical to this process is the fact that disputes are "generally settled with little reference to the alleged rights and wrongs of the case, but chiefly with the intention of restoring peace to the community" (Turnbull 1961:188). Assessing penalties for past wrongs is far less important than clearing the air so that future relations will be harmonious. Sometimes this means the separation of disputants while tempers cool down.

In his portrait of Mbuti nonviolence, Turnbull (1978) places great emphasis on ways in which the community is a critical source of support and nurturance at each stage of the life cycle. An Mbuti mother-to-be gently sings to her unborn child. Following the birth, the parents and all others in the community welcome the infant and feel a collective responsibility for its physical and spiritual well-being. Security and dependence are essential Mbuti values that work against the open expression of aggression. Individuals may tease and laugh at each other, but the result is not frustration, for underneath these actions they apparently find tremendous security through links to others.

Mbuti rituals express the importance of the community as a source of nurturance. Solemn rituals affirm the connections of each person to the forest and to other Mbuti, living and dead. Less sacred rituals make the same points in a different tone. For example, Turnbull describes a ritual tug-of-war between adult men and women that initially expresses the very real tension between the sexes. Yet as the men begin to win, one of them adjusts his clothing, sings out in a falsetto voice, and joins the women. When the women start to do better, one of them will go to the men's side. Soon the composition of each team is completely reversed. "Each person crossing over tries to outdo the ridicule of the last, causing more and more laughter, until when the contestants are laughing so hard they cannot sing out any more, they let go of the vine rope and fall to the ground in near hysteria" (1978:205). Laughter serves to unite people, emphasizing their interdependence and shared norms. Differences are not so much denied as put in a larger social perspective.

Aggressive role models are uncommon among the Mbuti. Individual achievement at the expense of another is likewise disapproved, and a real effort is made to emphasize the equality of all. Only inner competition, not competition with others, is approved. Adult men, for example, are obviously the physically strongest members of the community and the hunters on whom everyone depends for meat. At the same time, their physical power is offset by a negative moral judgment concerning the dangers hunting and killing bring to the forest. Men are reminded of their impurity and the need to be properly cleansed and feel the striking contrast between their physical strength and moral power.[5]

In their dealings with Bantu peoples who live in neighboring villages at the edge of the forest, the Mbuti are far more cautious than they are with one another. The villagers seek to control the Mbuti both economically and emotionally. The Bantu need the products of the forest—meat, wild mushrooms, and so on—but have no desire to enter it to acquire them. The Mbuti resist Bantu domination in a number of nonviolent ways, protecting their autonomy and capacity to keep the villagers away from the forest. They regularly acquire goods from the village and, at the insistence of the villagers, participate in a range of rituals and occasional work activities. To the Bantu this binds the Mbuti to them, while for the Mbuti this is the price paid for maintaining the safety of the forest.

As with the Yanomamo, it is possible to build several alternative explanations for Mbuti conflict behavior. For Turnbull, the critical explanatory factors are psychocultural. He emphasizes the importance of the Mbutis' warm, supportive social relationships in the development of trusting, secure individuals. For the Mbuti, profound dependence upon others is a source of support, not threat. Their attention to social relationships emphasizes a shared fate which limits overt aggression and guides conflict management in constructive directions. It is also possible to build a persuasive interest-based explanation for Mbuti conflict patterns by identifying elements in their social organization which

5. Although both men and women participate in hunting, because the men kill the animals they raise a more troubling moral dilemma than the women, whose role in the hunt is to chase the game toward the men and their nets.

create a greater interest in cooperation than competition. Most obviously, one can point to the need for high levels of cooperation in hunting and the powerful social sanctions invoked when anyone violates these norms (Turnbull 1961). In addition, strong links among Mbuti living in different camps make it easy for people to move among groups. Finally, no sizable material wealth provides a motive for one group in the society to seek domination over another.

Overview of the Argument

As illustrated in the examples of the Yanomamo and the Mbuti, interests and psychocultural dispositions provide the bases for very different explanations of societal differences in conflict behavior. They identify dissimilar sources of conflict, offer strikingly different accounts of why conflicts escalate, and point toward alternative mechanisms for effective conflict management. I begin by focusing on the dissimilarities in these two theoretical approaches to emphasize the extent to which each one is plausible. Gradually, building on data from a sample of 90 preindustrial societies, I bring the two theories together to offer a cross-cultural theory of conflict and an explanation for variations in the culture of conflict in these societies.

In the most general terms, the psychocultural dispositions rooted in a society's early socialization experiences shape the overall level of conflict, while its specific pattern of social organization determines whether the targets of conflict and aggression are located within a society, outside it, or both. Because structural and psychocultural explanations for conflict behavior are so different, it is easy to view them as incompatible alternatives. Yet each set of factors explains different aspects of conflict behavior, making sense of something the other cannot fully explain. The fears and threats identified in the psychocultural explanation account for the intensity of feelings involved, but only the structural explanation can speak to why actions are taken in a particular direction.

The importance of psychocultural factors in conflict is worth emphasizing for several reasons. One is that the empirical results so clearly show that a society's early socialization is intimately associated with patterns of conflict and violence. Psychocultural effects cannot be reduced to structural conditions explained in terms of simple interests. As a result of the long-standing bias against psychological explanations in the social sciences, this theoretical orientation may be unfamiliar to many readers and will be explained in some detail. In this view, interest-based rational-choice arguments are not so much wrong as far more limited than many of their proponents suggest. Interests matter, I agree, but psychocultural forces are crucial in determining how these interests are defined and what actors do to defend them (Wildavsky 1991, 1992).

Early childhood is when cultures establish orientations, such as trust, security, and efficacy, toward the self and others in one's social world. Early social relationships provide the foundations for the model of social behavior (what I call psychocultural dispositions) one carries throughout life. In particular, the socialization of warmth and affection, the harshness of childrearing, and male gender-identity conflict all affect societal conflict patterns. But early childhood is not the only formative time for interpretations of the world that shape conflict behavior. A wide range of a society's institutions and practices reinforce important psychocultural dispositions through the values and behaviors that are encouraged or discouraged, through cultural definitions of group identity (we versus they), and through culturally approved responses to perceived aggression.

How actors interpret events is central in shaping a group's actions, especially in the situations of ambiguity and high stress that characterize many conflicts. Deeply held dispositions are significant elements in determining how participants interpret conflict and how these interpretations affect the actions they take (Northrup 1989). Psychocultural dispositions shape how groups and individuals process events and the emotions, perceptions, and cognitions the events evoke. Dispositions link particular events to culturally shared threats to self-esteem and identity. I use the term *psychocultural*, as opposed to psychological, because it emphasizes assumptions, perceptions, and images about the world that are widely shared with others and not idiosyncratic (Wildavsky 1987).

Conflict is interpretive behavior and psychocultural dispositions serve as a filter through which actions are understood. Dispositional patterns are culturally learned and approved methods of dealing with others. Although disputants have little trouble citing "objective" bases for conflict—"She (or he) took my toy" (land, water, women, cows)—what is striking to an observer is the number of different cultural patterns of response to the same supposedly provocative action. This distinction means that objective situations alone do not cause conflict; *interpretations* of such situations also play a central role.

An emphasis on psychocultural dispositions does not require excluding other explanatory forces. Specifically, social groups pursue and defend interests which structural explanations for conflict infer from the organization of society. My analysis identifies two sources of these interests relevant for understanding conflict behavior. First, societies vary greatly in the extent to which people with common interests in one domain also have common interests in others. When social organization reinforces a single dominant cleavage, conflicts escalate because few overlapping interests reinforce mutual interests; when lines of cleavage cross-cut each other and ties among the parties are well established, the same precipitating incident often has far less severe consequences.[6] Where there are strong links among various groups, common interests are forged through interaction and exchange. The results of cross-cultural analysis show that when cross-cutting ties are strong, interests tend to limit the severity of conflict within a society, while conflict with outsiders is more likely.

A second set of interests is associated with a society's particular level of socioeconomic and/or political complexity. At each level of organization, specific interests become salient. Less complex societies have fewer valuable resources, but they also possess weaker capabilities of defending what they do have. Simpler societies, in one view, have a lower incidence of conflict because there is less resource concentration and hence there are fewer motives for groups to attack each other. In contrast, others point to the absence of centralized authority as making conflict more likely. The data analysis supports neither position with respect to internal conflict. I suggest that political differentiation may limit political conflict through direct control—the peacemaking function of the state—while socioeconomic complexity, with its increasing accumulation of resources, inequality, and military capability, increases it. External conflict is a different story, however, and the evi-

6. Yngvesson (1978), for example, describes an isolated, factionalized Atlantic fishing community in which taking items belonging to another person is called theft when it is done by an outsider but borrowing when it is done by a member of the group. In New Guinea, Koch (1974), Meggitt (1977), and others have described the differences in responses to transgressions within the clan, between members of clans of the same phratry, and between phratries.

dence is that more complex societies have higher levels of conflict with outsiders.

In preindustrial societies, internal and external conflict are positively correlated, as is the case in modern nations. Yet conflict within a society and conflict with outsiders have common psychocultural but different structural roots. Both internal and external conflict are higher in societies in which socialization is relatively low in warmth and affection, harsher, and higher in male gender identity conflict. In societies with strong cross-cutting ties, hostile action is more likely to be directed at external targets, whereas when cross-cutting ties are weak the differentiation between internal and external targets of conflict is weak.

Although any society's culture of conflict has unique features, the analysis here focuses on a small number of general patterns. Variations in each suggest how culture affects conflict and also show that conflict is usefully viewed as cultural behavior reflecting what people in a society value, their socially shared definitions of friends and foes, and the means groups and individuals use to pursue their goals (Avruch 1991; Avruch and Black 1991).

The theory offered here has important consequences for understanding the effectiveness of steps participants and conflict managers take to settle disputes. It is necessary to recognize the importance of interests rooted in social structure as well as psychocultural dispositions in understanding conflict management outcomes. Because structural and psychocultural theories attribute the primary source of conflict to very different forces, they implicitly suggest very different strategies for resolving conflict successfully. Structural theory gives a primary role to conflict-limiting strategies involving altering incentives, payoffs, or—most fundamentally—the organization of society. Divergent interests, in this view, are hard to bridge; therefore, there is an emphasis either on unilateral action or on third parties. In contrast, psychocultural theory points to the need to alter the dominant metaphors surrounding a dispute or the interpretations of the parties in conflict (Ross 1993).

Yet the argument presented here suggests that any culture of conflict has typical patterns of escalation, redefinition, extension to new parties, and termination that have both structural and psychocultural components. Because interests and perceptions matter, conflict management strategies will succeed only to the extent to which they pay attention to both. In fact, the intensity of psychocultural factors often is so high that until they are addressed, differences in the structurally rooted interests separating adversaries cannot be bridged. And some cultures are better at doing this than others.

Plan of the Book

My central concern is the question of why the world's preindustrial societies differ so greatly in levels and patterns of conflict and violence. The next three chapters offer a theoretical approach to the cross-cultural study of conflict. In chapter 2 I present the concepts of conflict and culture and key elements of a cross-cultural investigation. In chapter 3 I discuss social-structural theory and internal and external conflict and violence, developing a series of hypotheses to be tested cross-culturally. In chapter 4, psychocultural theory is examined in the same way.

The cross-cultural analysis of data to test the structural and psychocultural theories of conflict begins with chapter 5, which outlines the methods used in the study, defines the key conflict measures, and describes the culture of conflict in four preindustrial societies. In chapter 6 I present the tests of the major hypotheses, showing partial support for both structural and psychocultural hypotheses. In chapter 7 I turn to the question of the relationship between internal and external conflict and identification of two different cultures of conflict—one in which there is great differentiation between the levels of internal and external conflict, and a second, more common one, in which there is generalization in the levels of conflict across domains. The data in these chapters support the idea that a society's overall level of conflict is determined by its psychocultural features while the targets of conflict are most related to its social organization. In chapter 8 I then consider variations in the general model, exploring cases in the sample that fit the model least well and suggesting contextually specific variations in the culture of conflict.

In chapter 9 I extend the analysis, using the model developed from examination of conflict in preindustrial societies to explain the protracted conflict in Northern Ireland and the relatively low level of conflict in modern Norway. In chapter 10 I integrate the findings through a discussion of the mechanisms of interests and interpretations that underlie structural and psychocultural explanations. In the final chapter I return to the integrating theme of the culture of conflict and suggest two important extensions of the argument—the development of a model of a low-conflict society in which constructive conflict management is common and the important implications of the cross-cultural theory of conflict for the development of effective conflict management.

2

Conflict, Culture, and the
Cross-Cultural Method

Because of strong negative cultural assumptions about conflict in western cultures, we do not easily distinguish among different forms or levels of conflict or among different motives of disputants. Yet it is important to keep in mind that conflict in and of itself is neither undesirable nor desirable. Just as there are cases where it is easy to suggest that the costs of conflict for individuals and the wider society are too high, in other situations the absence of conflict is also costly, as in authoritarian regimes where all dissent is ruthlessly repressed. Judgments about any conflict involve not only considering the goals of each side but also asking if there might have been less costly ways to achieve them.

This chapter explores the concepts of conflict and culture and suggests that conflict is usefully viewed as cultural behavior. Among the world's preindustrial societies, there is wide variation in the intensity of internal and external conflict and the forms each takes as a result of biological and social evolution and the interaction of each society with a specific environment. Cross-cultural analysis of conflict emphasizes ways in which social and psychocultural differences among societies can account for this variation. Using Axelrod's analysis of the evolution of cooperation as an example, I discuss how investigations at the individual and societal levels of conflict or cooperation can offer important insights into how cultural practices and institutions affect behavior—insights that are easily neglected in analyses at a single level. Finally, I suggest that a society's culture of conflict defines what people value, appropriate ways to obtain it, responses to others seeking the same things, and institutions and practices that help determine the course of disputes over objects of value.

Conflict: A Descriptive Definition

Conflict occurs when parties disagree about the distribution of material or symbolic resources and act because of the incompatibility of goals or a perceived divergence of interests.[1] Both behavioral and perceptual elements of conflict are important. Considering behaviors alone ignores the motivations underlying an action, while asking only about perceptions fails to distinguish among situations in which similar perceptions lead to sharply divergent behaviors.

Not all conflict is violent, but physical violence is one form political conflict takes. No society is without violence or threats of its use. In some societies, violence may be a normatively sanctioned method for dealing with a situation, as it is among the Jale of New Guinea, who permit killing any member of a different clan who has murdered one of its own members (Koch 1974). Often violence is not authorized and is

---

1. Most definitions of conflict focus on behavior. According to Morton Deutsch, for example, conflict exists "whenever incompatible activities occur [and] ... an action that is incompatible with another action prevents, obstructs, interferes, injures or in some way makes the latter less likely to be effective" (1973:10). Underlying Mack and Snyder's (1957) definition of conflict is the notion of scarce resources in a zero-sum situation, where the actions of one party are intended to produce gains for itself and losses for others. Other theorists place less emphasis on behavior and focus on differences in goals or perceptions. Bernard states, "Conflict arises when there are incompatible or mutually exclusive goals or aims or values espoused by human beings" (1953:38), whereas Kriesberg suggests, "A social conflict exists when two or more parties believe they have incompatible objectives" (1982:17). Pruitt and Rubin are most explicit in the perceptual emphasis, suggesting that "conflict means perceived divergence of interest, or a belief that the parties' current aspirations cannot be achieved simultaneously" (1986:4). Focusing on behavior—what people actually do—emphasizes a component that needs to be understood and certainly simplifies methodology by avoiding the difficult question of the subjective states which precede action. The perceptual approach, by suggesting that differences in interest are subjective, leaves open the question of the extent to which interests are actually incompatible, pointing out a key mechanism by which seemingly intractable conflicts can be resolved. These definitions emphasize that conflict is a process, not a static condition, and that an important element involves the change in perceptions during the course of a dispute.

a sign that conflict management involving joint problem solving or third-party decision making has failed.

The conflicts of concern here are collective actions (not individual intrapersonal or interpersonal actions) which parties engage in when faced with divergent interests or incompatible goals.[2] Confronted with an unacceptable situation, an aggrieved party may undertake unilateral action; two or more disputants may partake in joint problem solving to search for a mutually acceptable outcome; or a dispute may be brought before a third party who is asked to render a binding decision. Of course, many complex social conflicts involve a combination of one-, two-, and multiparty actions.[3] One-party action (self-help) can take the form of exit, avoidance, noncompliance, and unilateral steps ranging from verbal statements to physical violence. In joint problem solving the control over outcomes rests with the disputants, who communicate (not always directly) with each other, sometimes with the help of a third party who acts as a go-between, mediator, or arbitrator. Third-party decision making is seen in judicial or bureaucratic processes when the community imposes its judgment upon disputants and can invoke sanctions to secure compliance with a decision.

Although the term conflict often connotes an event, it is more useful to think about a process, involving the disputants' sequence of responses to each other.[4] Describing conflicts in terms of a set of stages (Gulliver 1979) means identifying different actions and perceptions associated with particular phases. One way to compare conflict behavior in different societies is to investigate the relative importance of one-, two-, and multiparty actions at specific phases or in certain kinds of disputes.

2. Conflict can be examined on a number of levels. The emphasis here is on the societal level. Intrapsychic and intrapersonal conflict are no less important but are not central to my concerns here. Similarly, the course of specific disputes is discussed only briefly here. For more elaboration of this topic see Ross (1993).

3. For a more detailed description of conflict management through one-, two-, and multiparty action see Ross (1993).

4. Conflict can be distinguished as the more basic and often highly diffuse differences between two or more parties, whereas a dispute is a particular issue over which one or more parties takes action. In practice, however, the boundary between the two is not always clear and inevitably the two terms are used somewhat interchangeably.

Conflict Within Versus Conflict Between Groups

How is conflict within groups related to conflict between them? Theoretically, this relationship can be described in two ways. One draws on the psychological principle of generalization and emphasizes how individuals or groups prone to contentious behavior or violence in one area of their lives (or with one set of actors) behave in similar ways in other domains. The second model emphasizes strategic factors and suggests that actors cannot engage in conflict with too many other parties at the same time. Differentiation becomes a crucial strategy for survival as groups or individuals distinguish among possible allies and opponents in their environment and behave accordingly toward each. Each perspective yields different predictors about the relationship between internal (within-group) and external (between-group) conflict. Generalization emphasizes continuity across boundaries, suggesting that behaviors learned in one domain will be transferred to others. Differentiation focuses on ways in which the forces in each domain create opposing pressures: internal divisions make concerted action against an outside enemy more problematic, while internal unity makes coordination easier. Similarly, external peace can provide space for internal differences to flourish, while an external threat can serve to minimize them. The evidence from preindustrial societies, presented in chapter 7, suggests that some societies are conflict generalizers and others are differentiators, with generalization more common than differentiation. The challenge is to understand why.

Conflict and Social Evolution

The human capacity for conflict and violence is closely connected to an evolved human propensity to form and a capacity to live in social groups. Evidence for the human ability to form groups quickly and easily and for groups to influence their members' behavior is widespread. The elaborate laboratory and natural experiments of Sherif and his collaborators, particularly the Robbers Cave, show dramatically how individuals previously unknown to each other can develop named groups, the capacity for cohesive action, and a strong sense of in-group identity (Sherif et al. 1988).[5] Even more striking evidence for a readiness to form

5. This study raises thought-provoking questions: e.g., how might the

groups is found in the minimal group experiments of Henri Tajfel and his colleagues (Brown 1986; Tajfel 1981). In these experiments, individuals are assigned to named groups for arbitrary and unimportant reasons, such as whether they prefer a painting by Klee or Kandinsky. In spite of the fact that they never meet others with whom they share the group label, people systematically make in-group-biased judgments when asked to evaluate work supposedly done by members of one group or the other.

In-group identification is an adaptive social-cognitive process that makes such pro-social relations as social cohesion, cooperation, and influence possible (Turner 1988:67). Groups are the central mechanism for providing individuals with their identity; rather than holding that individuals "sacrifice" part of their identity when they are part of a group, the perspective adopted here sees positive individual identity as possible only in the context of secure group attachments. Hence the effectiveness of social ostracism as a mechanism of social control (Gruter and Masters 1986); expulsion or exclusion from the group and its activities is terrifying, not only because of the physical threat to individual security but because the emotional separation is intolerable.[6] The notion of the individual apart from the group is a product of western thought, not of the general human experience.

The evolution of conflict and cooperation can be thought of in terms of how each affects survival in small kin-based groups of hunters and gatherers. Groups that coordinate subsistence activities and share resources and knowledge should be more successful than those who do not. Similarly, in-group cooperation should enhance a group's ability to defend itself against predators and other groups. Bigelow (1973) argues that the capacity for out-group aggression has evolved along with an ability for increased in-group cooperation. Yet the capacity for cooperation and conflict is quite different than their presence. Since the ethnographic evidence shows the great variation in levels and forms conflict can take, we are still left with the question

---

pattern of in-group formation and out-group hostility followed by cross-group cooperation have been similar (or different) if the participants in the experiment had been female instead of male? Adults rather than eleven-year-olds? Racially heterogeneous? Non-Americans?

6. See, for example, Turnbull's description of this mechanism among the Mbuti of Zaire (Turnbull 1961; 1978).

of how to understand the conditions under which conflict occurs. Yet the knowledge that humans have a capacity for aggression tells us little about the forms or level of aggression unless we know more about the particular context.

Biological and social evolution can both promote in-group co-operation and out-group conflict, but they can work at different rates, operate through different mechanisms, occur at different levels, and sometimes work in opposite directions. Biological evolution is Darwinian (based on blind variation and selective retention); social evolution is often Lamarckian (based on purposive innovation and selected retention) (Goldschmidt 1976). As a result, biological evolution is often slow, whereas social evolution can be rapid. In addition, the consensus among evolutionary biologists is that whereas the unit of selection in biological evolution is the individual gene, group selection can occur in social evolution (Campbell 1983; Boyd and Richerson 1985; Barkow 1989). Consequently, on biological grounds alone we might expect cooperation to develop only in very small groups of closely related persons, whereas powerful social and cultural processes may lead to far larger effective units of cooperation. Not only can social and cultural processes define larger in-groups than biological relatedness can, but social and cultural institutions which inhibit biologically evolved propensities can develop (Ross 1991). In this sense, cultural evolution can work "against" biological evolution (Barkow 1989; Boyd and Richerson 1985).[7] As a result of social evolution, then, humans have developed a number of institutions that encourage cooperative behavior among a wider range of groups and individuals than biological selection alone would permit. For example, Campbell (1975; 1983) argues that religious institutions and norms enhance cooperation and inhibit conflict among non-kin.

Due to the complex interaction of biological and cultural evolution and of each process with particular environments, human societies exhibit a tremendous range of cooperative and conflict behaviors. In preindustrial societies, the main focus of concern here, evolved capacities make possible many different behaviors. Trying to understand the order underlying this variation is, of course, a central concern of this inquiry.

7. Barkow (1989) explicitly discusses "maladaptation," cultural practices which seem to override what would be favored on biological grounds alone.

Conflict as Cultural Behavior

Conflict and cooperation occur in specific cultural settings. Culture is the particular practices and values common to a population living in a given setting.[8] It is a shared, collective product that provides a repertoire of actions and a standard against which to evaluate the actions of others (Avruch and Black 1991; Wildavsky 1987, 1989). Culture is often manifest in the shared symbols and rituals which invoke common responses and easily link the interests and actions of individuals to those of the larger collectivity (Laitin 1986; Kertzer 1988). Viewing conflict as cultural behavior helps explain why disputes over seemingly similar substantive issues can be handled so dissimilarly in different cultures.

The culture of conflict refers to a society's specific norms, practices, and institutions associated with conflict.[9] Culture defines what people value and what they are likely to enter into disputes over, suggests appropriate ways to behave in particular kinds of disputes, and shapes institutions in which disputes are processed. In short, a culture of conflict is what people in a society fight about, whom they fight with, and how they go about it.

8. This broad definition of culture, not unlike Tylor's famous one, specifically includes both beliefs and norms about action and behaviors and institutional practices. As a political scientist, I would rather not enter into a complex discussion of a core concept of another discipline. I therefore refer the reader to Kroeber and Kluckholm (1952) and more recent anthropological writings on the subject. For more on culture and conflict see Avruch (1991) and Avruch and Black (1991).

9. There are those who believe that the last thing the social sciences need is another concept, especially one which is so global that it can, at times, seem to explain both everything and nothing. The controversy surrounding the concept of the culture of poverty is instructive in this regard. When Lewis (1966) described the culture of poverty in *La Vida*, the reaction of social scientists included rejection of his condemnation of the poor for a situation not of their own making or choosing—all the while ignoring larger uncontrollable forces that maintained the levels of poverty (Valentine 1968).

My use of the notion of the culture of conflict is different than Lewis' deployment of the concept of the culture of poverty in several ways. Most important, I have emphasized the cultural patterns of more autonomous communities, whereas Lewis described a minority culture within a larger society. Second, the culture-of-poverty literature not only described a cultural pattern but also condemned it as pathological. Although I generally view low levels of conflict as preferable to high levels, this is not always the case and I have tried carefully to separate analysis from such judgments.

Culture shapes what people consider valuable and worth fighting over, investing particular goods, statuses, positions, or actions with meaning. Although economists are fond of translating diverse values into a common standard of reference, a cultural analysis is more likely to move in the opposite direction, asking why particular objects or positions take on the value they do in particular settings (Wildavsky 1991, 1992). An inquiry into actors' strategic choices divorced from the cultural settings in which they are made cannot account for why and how individual and group interests are established. Cultural differences can explain why people in one setting feel their interests are threatened by a certain event while in another place, individuals confronted by what appears to be a similar event do not feel that their interests are in danger.

Culture affects conflict behavior when it sanctions specific ways to pursue individual or group interests and disapproves of others. Anthropologists have learned that intertribal warfare, for example, takes highly stylized form in most settings. The same is true of other forms of conflict. Most cultures have clear expectations about what a party should do when grievances arise, to whom it can turn for help, and if and when it is appropriate to involve the wider community. A physical attack on a kinsperson, for example, may result in physical retaliation in one culture, a community meeting to discuss the situation in another, and an appeal to the authorities in a third. Practices for managing conflict within and outside of existing institutions reflect basic cultural values.

Cultural assumptions underlying conflict are revealed in the communication among the parties embroiled in a dispute (Gulliver 1979). Sometimes the messages exchanged are interpretable because disputants share a common cultural frame of reference. Certain messages may seem quite cryptic to outsiders, but their cultural meanings are, in fact, obvious to disputants. Conflict occurs not only within a common cultural frame of reference, but also between groups and individuals who come from different cultures and with few shared assumptions. Here conflicts can escalate as each side relies on its own understanding of events, sometimes reading unintended meanings into a situation (Cohen 1990; 1991).

The impact of culture on conflict behavior appears at many levels. At the societal level it is seen in the diverse norms, practices, and institutions found in societies throughout the world. At the level of individual disputes, culture shapes the disputants' choice of strategies and tactics. In addition, culture can determine disputants' different assumptions about each other's actions or intentions. Emphasizing societal-level differences in conflict, as I do here, suggests that comparative frameworks which make little or no use of the idea of cultural variation can be significantly improved when cultural differences in values or practices are integrated into their conceptual approach. This framework not only permits testing theories cross-culturally but also points out ways in which culture affects patterns previously seen as invariant.

Studying Conflict Cross-Culturally

Political scientists have rarely concerned themselves with examining conflict in small-scale societies typically studied by anthropologists. Yet there are important reasons for redressing this neglect. First, a worldwide sample of preindustrial societies permits an inquiry into widely varying behaviors, utilizing cases which represent ways in which humans have lived for a great proportion of our evolutionary history. Second, it allows the examination of theories of intragroup and intergroup conflict with new evidence. As Friedrich and Horwitz argue, "Any broadly comparative theory of politics needs to make all possible use of the kind of data concerning primitive societies which anthropology is able to furnish" (1968:545). To date, however, despite occasional calls for political analysis to include data on traditional societies (Easton 1959; Friedrich with Horwitz 1968), few of these examinations have occurred (Scott 1972; Bates 1983; Masters 1964; Barkun 1968). Theories that are supported by data from a sample of cases that differs from that on which they were originally based will gain credibility. Other theories will need to be modified or seen as relevant only in certain contexts. Lastly, I have always been impressed by the anthropological belief that studying what seems most removed from our daily world allows us to better understand parts of ourselves, and this premise seems particularly applicable to thinking about conflict.

The underlying logic of cross-cultural investigation uses the diverse experiences offered by the world's societies as a natural laboratory to investigate diversity. Cross-cultural research, like anthropology more generally, is interested in documenting the tremendous range in human beliefs and behaviors but also seeks to understand underlying patterns of variation. A cross-cultural study of conflict and violence, therefore, must not only describe conflict behavior in different societies but also ask why conflict takes diverse forms and occurs at different levels from society to society.

Cross-cultural studies can provide hypotheses about conflict and ideas for conflict management relevant in many other settings. For example, research in legal anthropology concerned with systems of mediation, negotiation, and patterns of conflict management has profoundly influenced the alternative dispute resolution movement in the United States and Western Europe. I suggest that the theory developed here has relevance for contexts beyond preindustrial societies and could be applied to intragroup and intergroup relations in modern, industrial societies.

Societal and Dispute Levels of Analysis

Cross-cultural research compares societies, in contrast to studies in which the unit of analysis is the individual, the social group, or a particular kind of behavior (for example, warfare). Conflict, of course, can fruitfully be studied at several levels. The focus of a societal-level analysis is why some societies are more prone to conflict (or at least certain forms of it) than others. In contrast, attention to the dispute level accounts for why particular conflicts take the forms they do and considers the dynamics of individual incidents, the strategies used by different parties, and the specific sequence that unfolds (Swartz, Turner, and Tuden 1966; Kriesberg 1982; Pruitt and Rubin 1986). One type of analysis is not necessarily better than the other. The societal approach emphasizes forces which dispose a community to characteristic forms and levels of conflict; the dispute-level approach tells how specific conflicts actually came about. The "best" explanation depends on the question one wants answered. One need not choose between the two; on the contrary, at some point they must be connected. Societal-level forces provide the context in which a dispute occurs and shape the actions of the parties. At the dispute level, a society's resource level, institutions, norms, and values shape outcomes.

Frequently the language of societal- and dispute-level theories of conflict makes it appear that they share few concerns. This is unfortunate, because the opposite is more often the case. Although different mechanisms work at each level, there are cross-level influences as well. One emphasis here is on psychocultural processes, which have been described most elaborately at the individual level but which I explore in terms of societal-level differences. In a study of conflict management which builds on the theory developed here, I discuss ways in which these societal-level propositions about conflict can be restated and evaluated at the dispute level (Ross 1993). Cross-level theoretical elaboration and empirical investigation go hand in hand, and each contributes to improved understanding of specific conflicts and to improved methods of constructive conflict management.

Interests and Interpretations as Mechanisms

The discovery that two or more phenomena are related only sometimes reveals the reason why. Consider the relation between exposure to sick people and the chances of becoming sick. In the case of contagious diseases like chicken pox, the correlation is high, whereas with heart disease it is nonexistent. The reason is that people contract chicken pox from germs which are easily transmitted by contact, while heart disease does not develop in the same way. The mechanism by which people contract these two diseases is different in each case.

Explanations for social or political phenomena similarly need to identify the mechanism underlying an observed relationship. What if we find that the more centralized the political system, the lower the level of internal political protest? Is this because more centralized regimes are better able to distribute widespread benefits to their citizens, as Bates (1983) and Service (1975) suggest, or because they are more effective at repressing dissent, as Fried (1967) argues? Each argument identifies a different underlying mechanism consistent with an observed relationship, but only empirical analysis can reveal which one actually operates in a given situation.

Individual or group interests are a widely invoked mechanism linking social, political, or economic organization to action. Two assumptions underpin this view: one is that interests are clearly associated with social location, and the other is that a great deal of action can be explained in terms of such interests. The core postulate of microeconomic theory, for example, is that self-interest is a central motive for individuals and firms acting to maximize profits. Interests are widely cited as underlying individual and collective beliefs and behaviors ranging from preferences for family size and structure to defense of property to voting choices, including cultural practices which seem incomprehensible to outsiders viewing them from their own cultural assumptions (Harris 1974).

My objection to interest theories is not that they are wrong but that they often try to explain more than they can (Wildavsky 1991). Economic action, for example, may often be central to human behavior but rarely suffices to explain it. Although many behaviors are consistent with assumptions of interest maximization, other motives, sometimes inconsistent with a narrow definition of interests, also operate. In addition, while microeconomic theories and many rational-choice theories derived from them (including sociobiology) emphasize self- (or individual) interest, there is good reason to see group interests as sometimes more powerful and as leading to different behaviors than self-interest assumptions (Caporael et al. 1989; Mansbridge 1990). Finally, interests are a cultural product only partially shaped by economic factors (Wildavsky 1992). Effective use of the concept of interest as a mechanism, then, requires investigating what interests groups and individuals try to maximize in particular cultural settings rather than assuming a priori what they are.

Psychocultural interpretations—a very different kind of mechanism than interests—link individual and group action first by shaping shared perceptions and frames of reference in a community and then by directing collective action. Psychocultural interpretations are important because humans do not simply act; they also process actions, and this processing can have important effects on subsequent behavior. Psychocultural dispositions give rise to motives and perceptions which affect decision making in conflict situations. The roots of these mechanisms are found in the social relationships at the earliest stages of life where templates are developed for later relations with authority and with other people and for dealing with conflicts. Object-relations theory (Greenberg and Mitchell 1983) suggests that crucial processes include attachment, identification, repression, projection, externalization, and displacement. These processes establish a framework for the *interpretation* of events which links culture and the individual and which places the concepts of perception and interpretation at the center of a cross-cultural theory of political conflict. Interpretation is especially important in matters of high cruciality and where the meanings of actions are ambiguous for individuals. Cruciality produces engagement while ambiguity is associated with anxiety and the invocation of inner world-views. Political conflict often has these characteristics; this explains both the intensity of action and its collective nature within closed communities.[10]

10. The Whitings identify illness and religion as two domains where

Psychocultural conflict theory, I shall argue, provides powerful ways to understand conflict behavior. Like interests, however, it is not able to adequately account for some important aspects of conflict, and it fails to explain some crucial elements of conflict behavior. Psychocultural conflict theory may point to a human propensity for cooperation or contention with others but rarely suggests who such friends or foes are likely to be. To say, for example, that a group's own hostile impulses are frequently projected onto outsiders tells us too little about which outsiders are most or least likely to be selected. Another limitation to interpretations as mechanisms underlying conflict behavior is that while psychocultural dispositions are relatively constant in a society, at least in the short and medium run, outbreaks of conflict are far more sporadic. What, we might wonder, links interpretations to conflict in one situation but not in another?

Investigating Mechanisms Cross-Culturally: Axelrod's Study of the Evolution of Cooperation

As is the case with many concepts, interests and interpretations are mechanisms that operate on and can be investigated at several levels. In fact, it is important to recognize that although many theories are developed at one level of analysis, examining them at other levels can provide important evidence for their validity (Naroll 1983).[11] To illustrate a cross-cultural examination of a theory developed at another level, I will use one of the most-cited studies of the past decade, Axelrod's (1984) work on the evolution of cooperation, which poses a vexing political problem: how and why cooperation develops in a world with no central authority.[12] His framework is broadly comparative—any frame

---

projective behaviors can be investigated. My argument is that aspects of political life involving authority, conflict, and community often fit in the projective domain as well (Whiting 1980).

11. Campbell and Fiske (1959) describe validation through multimethod and multitrait tests of a theory. The notion of cross-level tests is fully consistent with their argument.

12. Axelrod's game-theory framework allows him to avoid asking many analytic questions about the concept of cooperation itself, which is simply defined by his payoff matrix. In fact, cooperation is complex and difficult to define. If, for example, actions are taken out of individuals' self-interest, then we hardly need the concept of cooperation (or altruism, to borrow an example from socio-

work that discusses bacteria and nations in the same chapter must be—but it is not explicitly cross-cultural. His attention is devoted to individual actors (which may be genes, people, or computer programs) and the strategies they use in playing the prisoner's dilemma game. Adding a cross-cultural dimension to the discussion illustrates how this level of analysis can add new insights.

Axelrod's study of cooperation begins with a round-robin computer tournament in which the contestants are programs playing the prisoner's dilemma game. The basic structure of the game is quite simple (figure 2.1), although there can be numerous variations. Two players must independently choose whether or not to cooperate with each other and the size of their gains and losses depends on both their own and their opponent's choices. The dilemma is that although during any single move, the greatest gain for any player can be achieved through non-cooperation (cells 2 or 3), the greatest collective gain is achieved through joint cooperation (cell 1). There is no individual gain registered when one player cooperates but the other does not. Thus, cooperation is risky and can produce high joint totals but not the highest individual gain. To win Axelrod's tournament, the player must accumulate the highest point total over a number of rounds.

Figure 2.1
The Prisoner's Dilemma

	Player A	
	Cooperate	Defect
Cooperate	A = 3, B = 3 Mutual cooperation 1	A = 5, B = 0 Payoff to A for defection 2
Player B Defect	A = 0, B = 5 Payoff to B for defection 3	A = 1, B = 1 Punishment for mutual defection 4

The winner of this tournament turns out to be the simplest program, Tit-for-Tat, consisting of four statements. Its decision rules are

biology) to explain them. It is important to view cooperation as not necessarily the opposite of conflict. Each of these is a separate phenomenon whose relation with the other varies. In the discussion below, I do not question the nature of cooperation itself but rather try to use it as Axelrod does and suggest how cross-cultural analysis may further our understanding of cooperation in his terms.

very simple: cooperate on the first move and then reciprocate every move thereafter. Tit-for-Tat never has the highest score in any single round—it can't—but it has the highest total score across rounds. Axelrod published his results and then held another tournament with even more entrants and, once again, Tit-for-Tat emerged victorious.

What insights do the examination of this idea in a cross-cultural framework yield? First, we see that Axelrod's definition of winning—highest point total after a number of rounds—is clear, but hardly free of cultural assumptions (Wildavsky 1991). His definition is certainly un-American, rather like saying the baseball team that scores the most runs in a season or a series is the champion, irrespective of their total victory. In 1987 the Minnesota Twins were outscored by their opponents during the season, but they won the World Series. In 1960 the New York Yankees outscored the Pittsburgh Pirates 55–27 in the World Series but lost four games to three. In contrast, winners in Axelrod's contest have the highest absolute point totals even though they do not win individual rounds and their relative totals may not be much higher than others'. Winning by a score of 400–395 is better in his game than a final tally of 375–300. However, it's not clear that when presented with such choices, all humans in all cultures would define winning as Axelrod does.[13]

Second, a cross-cultural question leads us to focus on the role of perceptions. In explaining why Tit-for-Tat does so well, Axelrod tells us it is "nice," "reciprocal," "forgiving," and "clear." All of these are motives inferred from actions of an opponent that, in fact, depend on psychological and cultural frameworks. There is good reason to see the validity of inferences about such motives as variable, and, hence, there is a need to inquire further into how real players come to draw inferences about these motives which will shape future behavior on the basis of past actions. Jervis, Lebow, and Stein, for example, when considering deterrence in international relations, remind us that behaviors which may be intended as nice, reciprocal, forgiving, and (especially) clear are often subject to systematic misperception (Jervis 1976; Lebow 1981; Jervis, Lebow, and Stein 1985).

What causes this misperception and when is it most likely? Jervis,

13. Snidal (1992) does not discuss cultural variation in a preference for relative versus absolute gains. He does, however, offer a provocative discussion of the consequences of assumptions of relative and absolute gains for theories of international conflict.

Lebow, and Stein emphasize the impact of domestic political pressures. Another reason for misperception is cultural context. The Yanomamo (and other societies) operate in what they consider an unfriendly world where they cannot assume either the spirits, deities, or other humans to be nice. One must be ever vigilant; there are treacherous feasts during which murderous attacks are made and dangerous spirits and people lurking, waiting for the chance to take what one has. Among the Mbuti or !Kung, different assumptions about the world lead to different inferences and a far more "benevolent misperception" (Deutsch 1973).

Third, a cross-cultural question enriches the discussion of the implications of Axelrod's study. When he asks how to increase the likelihood of cooperation, his first answer is "Don't be envious." I understand this in one of two ways: follow the example of Mother Theresa and change one's moral outlook on life; or, true to the cross-cultural approach, think about institutions and practices which increase the likelihood of low incidence of envy in interpersonal and intergroup relations. Envy, I must note, is closely tied to the psychology of identification. Increasing common identification among members of a community should, in the language of Axelrod's prisoner's dilemma game, make absolute gains more important than relative ones. What sorts of institutional arrangements and practices make this more likely? Cross-cultural analysis offers cases which can provide the basis for testable hypotheses as well as suggesting new ones.

Envy may be lower when there is a great deal of cooperation in subsistence activities and what is available is shared, as among the Mbuti and other foragers, but also pastoralists like the Maasai, Kipsigis in East Africa, or even the Kurds. Lack of direct competition between individuals and strong social pressures against those who excel or boast serve as leveling forces and may reduce envy. Both the Navajo and Norwegians believe that the mean is desirable and personal achievement is not.

Envy may also be rarer when there is relatively broad political participation and reluctance to grant independent authority to individual leaders, as among the Semai in Malaysia or native American groups like the Apache or Comanche during peacetime. In these settings, participation builds commitment to decisions and loyalty to the community (Ross 1988a). Societies whose socialization practices emphasize warmth, trust, and father involvement with children and offer little sense of the world as an arbitrary and capricious place, as among the Trobriand islanders or Papago Indians, may also have less incidence of envy.

If these and other hypotheses are correct, we ought to find significant variations in how people from different cultural settings respond both to Axelrod's prisoner's dilemma game and to other situations requiring a choice between cooperation and conflict. Cross-cultural analysis can test and extend such ideas, illuminating not only the results but also the underlying mechanisms.

An important limitation of Axelrod's analysis of Tit-for-Tat as a strategy for achieving cooperation is that he pays too little attention to the structural and psychocultural contexts in which the strategy is employed. Although the specific sequence of moves involved in Tit-for-Tat can indeed be described without any reference to culture or cultural differences, the assumption that individuals or groups make or respond to moves irrespective of their cultural location needs evaluation. An understanding of how culture affects responses to the choices in the game suggests a powerful extension of Axelrod's argument.

Axelrod's analysis of cooperation stimulated much interest, in great part because of the applicability of his core concepts to many different settings and levels of analysis. Whether his ideas about Tit-for-Tat are correct or not is of less concern here than how insights can be gained when an idea is examined in multiple contexts. I shall emphasize how theories of social organization and psychocultural development further our understanding of conflict cross-culturally. Furthermore, cross-cultural tests of theories are particularly useful ways to consider relationships previously examined at other levels. Finally, worldwide societal-level comparisons emphasize both the diversity of human cultures and ways in which they are patterned.

Conclusion

The evolved human capacity for both communal coexistence and conflict, combined with adaptation to specific environmental conditions, has produced the tremendous diversity of human cultures. Conflict regularly occurs within and between these groups but is manifest in diverse forms and at many degrees of intensity. At the most basic level I examine how cultural differences in the organization of society and in psychocultural dispositions affect a society's patterns of conflict. Conflict can be defined as the actions of two or more parties who contest control over scarce material or symbolic resources. Likely actions and responses depend upon a number of factors including the prior relationship between the parties and the cultural meanings of the actions. Culture defines what resources are considered scarce, sanctions strategies by which parties can seek to acquire or control them, and creates particular institutions to manage conflicts when they occur.

Analysis of societal-level differences in patterns of conflict offers an opportunity for cross-level examination of theories that are often considered in only a single cultural setting. Similarly, cross-cultural findings about conflict can apply to other levels of analysis. This requires employing the same concepts across levels and suggesting how insights from one level can be applied to a different one. I shall suggest that interests and interpretations which are critical in explaining cross-cultural differences in conflict can also be fruitfully employed both to understand the dynamics of particular disputes and to suggest effective strategies for constructive conflict management in a variety of settings (Ross 1992, 1993). First, however, it is necessary to examine the specific roots of the culture of conflict as spelled out in social structural and psychocultural theories of conflict.

3

Political Conflict and the Structure of Society

The structure of society provides a ready source of explanations about political conflict and conflict management, some so self-evident that we give them little thought. We explain conflict in Israel in terms of incompatible interests of Jews and Palestinians or in Northern Ireland as a struggle between Protestants and Catholics. But such explanations ignore the fact that in other parts of the world, or at other times in history, Jews and Moslems or Catholics and Protestants have lived together without severe conflict.

Other social structural explanations for conflict are more sophisticated. Turner (1957), in a masterful analysis, shows how the principles of virilocal residence (postmarital residence with the husband's kin group) and matrilineality (tracing lineage or inheriting property through one's mother) are a source of continual stress and conflict in Ndembu (of Zambia,) marriages, kinship groups, and communities. Matrilineality means that Ndembu men succeed to village political positions held by their mother's brothers and that they need their sister's sons to build a following. This can occur, however, only if a man's sister and her sons are living in the man's village not in the sister's husband's, and this is only possible if she is divorced or if she and her husband come from the same village (which is unlikely for other reasons). Turner shows that cross-pressures in Ndembu society lead to a high divorce rate and frequent village fission counterbalanced by strong ties between villages. As a response to stresses (of whose source the Ndembu themselves are not fully aware), Turner finds a high level of ritual action, which he argues focuses the attention of the Ndembu on shared norms rather than unsolvable, divisive contradictions.

Underlying a structural theory of conflict like Turner's is the idea that the organization of society creates specific interests which determine who disputes and who cooperates. Among the Ndembu, for example, brothers share a common interest in political succession and depend upon each other and upon their sisters' sons for their following. As a result, Turner reports, brothers are likely to live together, and when a village splits, most often a group of brothers (with their sisters, if possible) move together. Although any single principle of social organization can direct behavior in a particular direction, from the point of view of conflict theory, in almost no setting is only one principle relevant at a time. Turner's analysis, for example, shows that the interests defined by residence and those defined by inheritance pull people in opposite directions simultaneously, while ritual groups serve to unite individuals who may be divided on the basis of other principles.

Social structural conflict theory argues that common positions in the social structure produce common interests among individuals, but the argument linking social and economic organization to political conflict can be made in several ways.[1] Cross-cutting ties theory explains conflict and conflict management in terms of the links between different members of a society. Complexity theory, in contrast, accounts for conflict behavior primarily through competing group interests associated with a society's level of socioeconomic and political organization. Whereas attention to cross-cutting ties focuses on common interests formed through interaction and exchange, complexity theory emphasizes the competing incompatible interests and tensions resulting from the same forces. If cross-cutting ties theory stresses the benefits of interdependence, complexity theory draws our attention to ways in which group-based inequalities of power and resources characterize exchanges and sow the seeds of conflict. Structural conflict theory, especially useful in explaining the particular targets of aggressive actions, is thus a differentiating theory which emphasizes the choice of

---

1. I use the term social structural conflict theory to refer to a large number of hypotheses which explain conflict behavior in terms of the interests social groups pursue. Cross-cutting ties and complexity theories are treated as two different formulations of the general argument. Within each of these theories I then identify specific hypotheses. I use the singular form to maintain the parallel between social structural theory and psychocultural theory.

one target over another. For example, forces that increase group cohesion and limit conflict may also make aggression against an outside group more likely.

In this chapter I shall spell out the logic underlying structural conflict theory and then discuss cross-cutting ties theory and complexity theory as sources of testable hypotheses about societal differences in conflict behavior. The final section of the chapter suggests several ways in which the connection between social organization and action can be limited additional factors the theory does not consider.

Social Structure and Conflict

Social structural conflict theory does not seek to explain the outbreak of any particular incident of violence or conflict; rather, it directs attention to forces which can make a society more or less prone than another to particular levels and forms of conflict and violence. From this perspective, the same sorts of precipitating incidents—livestock theft, land disputes, or tension over the exercise of power—occur in many settings. In some cases these events unleash an escalating pattern of violent conflict, while in others the conflict is limited. The organization of the society determines which outcome is most likely.

Social structural conflict theory has two goals. First, it uses the structure of society to understand who is likely to initiate conflict with whom, based on a society's pattern of subsistence, its rules of marriage and residence, its organization of authority, and the strength of religious and other ritual organizations, if any are present. Such factors as how, where, and with whom people spend their time and share common resources shape their interests and the actions they take to further them. Second, social structure offers an explanation of how conflicts, once started, develop. The relationship between the original disputants and the extent to which it reinforces other societal divisions determine whether or not a dispute is likely to escalate rapidly, and, if it expands, how different groups are likely to be aligned.

Theories connecting the organization of society and the nature of political conflict are among the most common social science generalizations, yet there is little agreement on the specific nature of such relationships. Materialists emphasize the connection between the organization of production and the structure of societal conflict; social anthropologists focus on kinship to explain patterns of conflict; and political and social analysts identify different patterns of conflict in communities based on the extent of cross-cutting ties.[2]

Although social structural hypotheses about conflict differ in their particulars, they share some common elements, beginning with the observation that daily living, even in the smallest communities, produces some division of labor, sometimes based only on age and gender. Not all differences have equal political importance, however. Merton (1957) distinguishes three levels of organization: *category*, people who happen to share a characteristic (left-handedness or brown hair, for example); *collectivity*, people with something in common who are aware of others with the same characteristic; and *group*, people who share a characteristic who engage in common action based on that characteristic.[3] Structural conflict theory is about the behavior of groups, as Merton uses the term, and the ways they pursue common interests (not necessarily consciously) based on their shared characteristics.[4]

Crucial to structural conflict theory, but often unstated, are assumptions about interests shared by groups and individuals in the same social structural positions. According to this theory, interests of individuals, such as a concern with security, material resources, or power, are easily equated with those of groups. In this view, individuals prosper when their groups do well, although we can certainly think of situations where group and individual interests are at odds. Members share group interests for two reasons: because their own fate is tied to the fortune of the group and because a common position in the social structure builds shared perceptions and understandings which facilitate joint action in the name of the group.

2. My view is that most of these theories are right in some situations but not others. Their proponents simply emphasize those cases which fit the theory and de-emphasize those which do not. Structural theories are often implicitly contingent or interactive, although they are rarely presented as such.

3. J. K. Ross (1975) further distinguishes between groups that engage in action to improve the position of the group and its members and those that seek to weaken the boundaries dividing the group from others.

4. Awareness of group identity and self-consciousness about the pursuit of common interests is not an important concern to many structural theorists, who, for the most part, are more focused on an organization's effect on action than on self-consciousness.

Figure 3.1
A Structural Theory of Conflict

	A		B	
economy / mode of production	→	social structure [interests]	→	conflict / conflict management

A simple structural theory of conflict (figure 3.1) asserts that the economic organization of a society influences its social structure, in the sense of kinship and residence patterns, settlement patterns, and political organization (link A), which then shapes conflict patterns (link B).

In this theory, economic organization, in part shaped by the natural environment, sets constraints on social organization; anthropologists have identified forms of organization characteristic of hunter-gatherers, pastoralists, sedentary agriculturalists, and industrial societies (Murdock 1949; Harris 1979). Materialists like Harris (1979) argue that each form of economic organization produces pressures favoring different forms of social organization. Hunter-gatherers, for example, characteristically live in small communities whose size varies seasonally, do not have well-developed corporate kin groups, own little or no private property, and tend toward a relatively egalitarian and participatory political organization. Sedentary agriculturalists, in contrast, tend to live in larger communities, to be patrilocal and patrilineal in kinship structure, to have a more formal and hierarchical political organization, and to have a greater division of labor and greater social inequality.[5]

The second link in the theory, in which the social and economic organization point toward characteristic sources and patterns of intense conflict in a society, emphasizes that groups and individuals sharing positions in the social structure possess common interests, opposing others in different positions. For example, territorially based communities in a region where population pressure is high develop an interest in defending their land and perhaps in acquiring more from their neighbors (Meggitt 1977). Where corporate descent groups (groups organized on the basis of descent) are important they are likely to define common

5. But see Ember (1978a), who points out that myths about hunter-gatherers overstate some of these generalizations. For example, many are peaceful, but almost two-thirds have a war at least every two years. While hunter-gatherers are less likely than sedentary agriculturalists to be patrilocal, a majority of them are.

property interests. Marxist theory describes the common interests workers in industrial societies develop vis-à-vis capitalists.

Social Structural Hypotheses about Conflict

Social structural conflict theory is often persuasive because of its common-sense basis and its broad applicability. Yet a potential weakness arises from the wide-ranging elements of social structure posited as affecting conflict. Therefore, evaluating social structural hypotheses about conflict requires identifying specific elements of social organization associated with variations in internal and external conflict in preindustrial societies in order to investigate how the organization of a society affects who cooperates and who fights. In addition, how does social structure affect the forces which encourage internal versus external conflict? To explore these questions, I present a set of testable hypotheses about societal differences in conflict behavior derived from the theories of cross-cutting ties and complexity.[6]

Cross-cutting Ties Theory

Cross-cutting ties theory emphasizes how the strength and configuration of economic, social, political, and affective bonds among mem-

---

6. Elsewhere (Ross, 1986a) and in notes 7–22 which follow I offer a more detailed review of this literature which may be of passing interest to most readers. Because my main concern is conflict behavior in preindustrial societies, the hypotheses discussed here draw most extensively on the work of anthropologists who have studied these societies. In addition, I cite the works of some international relations theorists, recalling the argument of Masters (1964), Barkun (1968), and Worsley (1986) that there is a structural similarity between the stateless societies anthropologists study and the international political order. Many anthropological and international relations studies I draw on focus on warfare and armed combat. Although my concerns include other types of conflicts, these studies are helpful in that there is no reason to assume that war is qualitatively different from other forms of conflict; rather, warfare is the escalation of conflict using violent means (Howard, 1983; Koch, 1974). The argument that warfare is one end of a continuum and has the same roots as nonviolent conflict will be discussed in greater detail in chapter 5. I agree with Koch (1974) and others that the distinction between feuds, armed raids, warfare, and other forms of organized group violence, which has preoccupied some anthropologists, is not always useful theoretically or empirically.

bers of a society affect the origin and expansion of conflicts and make their peaceful resolution more or less likely (Coleman 1957; Gluckman 1955; Colson 1953). Consider two different patterns, one in which an individual's multiple social roles reinforce one another and a second in which the same affiliations compete (LeVine and Campbell 1972:43–59).[7] Given *reinforcing* ties, an individual's kin group, residence, age group, ritual group, and political affiliations place the person within a core group of people who share those roles. In contrast, given *cross-cutting* ties, an individual shares different affiliations with different people.

The way conflict is managed depends on whether the society has a reinforcing as opposed to a cross-cutting social structure. In societies with a reinforcing social structure, conflict is expansive and difficult to resolve for several reasons: the mobilization of others in one's core group is relatively easy, there are few people whose interests hinge on the resolution of the dispute, and conflict may persist unless a common external foe forces disputants to resolve their differences. In contrast, individuals in cross-cutting ties societies cannot count on a large, loyal core group who share the same interests, because people mobilized on the basis of one shared characteristic, like kinship, can oppose each other over another, such as residence or ritual affiliation. Ties among members of the same community and among different communities limit the severity of overt conflict and promote dispute settlement through shared interests. Each community has individuals with links to parties on all sides of a dispute who will take steps to see that the dispute is resolved. Where overlapping loyalties connect diverse and often dispersed members of a society, it is difficult to convince coalitions of persons and factions to be at odds with others for extended periods of time, as bonds across social units produce less suspicion, more trust, and greater cooperation (Coleman 1957; LeVine and Campbell 1972:53).[8]

7. LeVine and Campbell (1972) label these two types "pyramidal-segmentary" and "cross-cutting" and use the term "loyalty structures" with regard to each. Although their discussion is consistent with the argument presented here, I avoid the term "loyalty," which focuses on perceptions, as the emphasis in cross-cutting ties theory is on interests, not feelings.

8. A related but not fully parallel hypothesis is Gluckman's (1955; 1969) suggestion that the nature of the relationship among disputants affects conflict. He suggests that in communities where multiplex ties (those which connect the same individuals in many ways) are predominant, a greater use of negotiation

Although cross-cutting ties can limit the expansion of conflict within a community or society, these same ties can promote rapid and successful mobilization against outsiders. Societies with powerful cross-cutting ties develop a strong, positive sense of group identity and common interests more easily than societies with reinforcing ties. When alliances and other forms of cooperation with neighbors are easy to establish, attacks against outsiders are more likely. LeVine and Campbell (1972) suggest, for example, that such groups frequently exhibit higher levels of ethnocentrism and become more brazen when confronting outsiders.

Cross-cutting ties affect who fights with whom, the severity of conflicts, and the steps taken to manage disputes. There is little consensus, however, as to which specific ties (or their absence) matter. Important ties range from kinship, age, or ritual ties to marriage and residence rules to the strength of local power groups to economic exchanges affecting conflict behavior. Within each of these areas I shall identify specific hypotheses to test regarding the effect of cross-cutting ties on conflict.

Multiple-reference groups. In no society do people have a single social identity. Social differentiation—based at the least on age and gender—is universal. In some societies, formal or quasi-formal organi-

---

or mediation between the parties leads to compromise outcomes, whereas in societies where the disputants have simplex (single-interest) ties, conflicts will more often involve adjudication or arbitration and result in win-or-lose decisions (Nader and Todd 1978:13). The multiplex-simplex distinction is not the same as the difference between reinforcing and cross-cutting ties. Gluckman refers to the number of strands between the members of any dyad, whereas the theories I discuss describe the nature of ties across the dyads in a system. In practice, however, we expect to find important overlaps between the two frameworks. Multiplex ties, according to Gluckman and Nader and Todd, encourage negotiation and compromise for many of the same reasons cross-cutting ties do—the value they place on future interactions within a system of strong interdependence. When multiplex ties exist, parties in a conflict continue to value (or at least want to preserve) their relationship, which goes beyond the issue at hand. They are, consequently, less likely to worry only about past wrongs and more likely to focus on the continuing need to live together in relative harmony, which encourages the use of joint problem solving and compromise solutions in which each side can take some solace (Gulliver 1979). When simplex ties are common, conflict management places a greater emphasis on righting past grievances, as opposed to re-establishing an ongoing relationship. Third-party decision making, like adjudication, becomes important in such situations, as is self-help.

zation based on such principles of social organization as kinship, age, and ritual may come into play. Each of these links brings together somewhat different groups of people, and the existence of such multiple-reference groups[9] usually makes intrasocietal conflict less severe and less expansive by providing a potential mechanism for resolving disputes in a peaceful manner. An age-based organization, for example, brings together individuals who are in different kinship groups. In situations where a dispute develops between a person's age-mate and a kinsman, the individual and others with the same multiple loyalties are more likely to facilitate an end to the dispute than if they had strong ties to only one or another of the disputants. The stronger multiple-reference groups are in a society, the greater the emphasis on establishing and maintaining good relations between groups and in the peaceful management of conflicts which develop.[10] If strong multiple-reference groups inhibit in-group conflict, however, they can, at the same time, increase the likelihood of external hostility, making it easier to achieve greater cooperation and coordination of groups against outsiders.

Marriage and residence. Preferences for marriage outside the local community can build cross-cutting ties which limit conflict between groups within a society and may enhance the ability to construct alliances to oppose outsiders.[11] Postmarital residence rules can also affect

9. I use the term "multiple-reference groups" rather than "cross-cutting membership groups" to avoid the confusion which would result from using the same term to refer to the larger hypothesis and to this specific form.

10. Colson (1953) is widely cited but also see Coleman (1957), Gluckman (1954), Guetzkow (1955), and LeVine and Campbell (1972).

11. Although this functionalist view of marriage ties sounds plausible, just because fighting with close kin is potentially disadvantageous does not mean it does not occur. Alliances and exchanges create their own tensions, as mother-in-law jokes in western society clearly reveal. After all, statistics from our own society show that the vast majority of violent crimes are committed among family members and close friends. The literature on societies where it is said, "We marry who we fight" (Meggitt, 1977), disputes this view of marriage. In one study in New Guinea, Hayano (1974) found that fighting and marriage took place between the same villages. Rather than a deterrent to fighting, he suggests, marriage patterns may more usefully be seen as a reaction to the tension of warfare (1974:289). In addition, women seized in warfare can be desirable marriage partners because a kin group does not have to give up any of its own females in return. Although this pattern of taking enemy women as wives clearly occurs, it remains to be determined how widespread this is as a source of marriage partners. The "we marry who we fight" hypothesis also lacks any sense of how

conflict behavior. Matrilocal residence disperses related men and inhibits internal conflict which would pit related males against each other but increases the likelihood of external conflict, as alliances among local communities in a society are relatively easy to build. In contrast, patrilocality produces the opposite effect and promotes internal and inhibits external conflict.[12] Polygyny (which is far more likely in patrilineal societies) can independently affect internal conflict because it creates local male groups with common, but narrow, interests in obtaining women from other neighboring communities.[13]

Local power groups. The fraternal interest group is created through reinforcing ties of kinship and residence which unite coresident related males in politically uncentralized societies who pursue common interests through autonomous, and often violent, action.[14] These interests can involve control of such material interests as land and livestock as well as control over women and their offspring.[15] The existence of fraternal interest groups is associated with internal conflict and feuding

---

marriage and fighting affect each other. It is quite plausible that marriage bonds lower the intensity of intergroup conflict but do not end it altogether.

12. Murphy (1957) and LeVine (1965) argue that matrilocal or uxorilocal residence disperses males, thereby inhibiting conflict among communities of the same society which would pit kin against each other while promoting the unity which makes external fighting more likely. Other studies that have found the same pattern do not agree on why this is the case. Thoden van Velzen and van Wetering (1960) contend that there is less internal conflict in matrilocal societies because organized power groups are not present, whereas Murphy's explanation, and LeVine's application of it, in contrast, give a crucial role to psychodynamic as well as structural factors in the choice of targets for aggression. See also Ember and Ember (1971), Divale (1974) and the response from Ember (1974).

13. In fact, Otterbein (1968) finds that polygyny is a better predictor of internal warfare than patrilocality.

14. Fraternal interest group theory is first spelled out in Thoden van Velzen and van Wetering (1960). Otterbein (1968; 1977) tests a number of their propositions using cross cultural data. For a more sophisticated elaboration of the theory see Paige and Paige (1981).

15. Paige and Paige (1981) propose that the strength of fraternal-interest groups is dependent upon the capacity of coresident males to act collectively, as seen in the ability to make marriage agreements with other groups, in an ideology manifest in their reckoning of descent through the patriline, and in their overall size. Such groups are found, they hypothesize, in uncentralized societies where the resources males protect are significant, nonmobile, and stable (1981:61–67).

in politically uncentralized societies,[16] making joint actions against external foes difficult.[17]

Economic exchanges. The functionalist school in international relations suggests that the exchange of persons and goods tends to reduce warfare among nations (Haas 1964). The ethnographic literature agrees, emphasizing the cooperation which can grow out of economic exchanges (Harner 1972; Meggitt 1977). Interdependencies among communities of the same society, in this view, inhibit overt fighting and encourage the development of peaceful mechanisms for managing disputes when they arise. Where economic links among communities in the same society are strong, internal conflict will be diminished.

Complexity and Conflict

Complexity theory associates particular levels and styles of conflict and conflict management with different forms of socioeconomic and political organization and supports the argument that clearly defined groups with divergent interests exist at each level of complexity. Although socioeconomic and political complexity are associated, the different ways in which each affects conflict behavior are worthy of separate discussions.

Socioeconomic complexity. Social scientists and philosophers tend to be divided between a Hobbesian view, that social life prior to the emergence of western civilization was filled with violence and conflict, and a Rousseauian view, that life in most primitive societies was peaceful, nonmanipulative, and self-actualizing (Fabbro 1978). Yet available studies show that the technologically simplest societies are no more prone to violence than more complex societies, although there may be important variations in the form conflict takes (Knauft 1988). Cross-cultural studies reveal no clear pattern (Ember and Ember 1992; Otterbein 1973; Russell 1972).[18]

---

16. See Otterbein (1968) and Otterbein and Otterbein (1965). Fraternal-interest group theory has focused on the role these groups play in internal, not external conflict.

17. When Otterbein examined the relationship between fraternal-interest group strength and external warfare, he found none at all (1970).

18. Fried (1967) offers an excellent example of a problematic study in this area, identifying four levels of political organization (bands, tribes, chiefdoms, and states). He then describes the key defining features of each, and sug-

The different views of the simplest societies perhaps depend on what the source of conflict in such societies is assumed to be. Materialists like Leacock (1982) attribute harmony in band societies, those in which the local band is the highest level of social and political organization, to the absence of private property, differential access to resources, or control one group in the population exercises over another. Materialists argue that social and economic differentiation fosters internal conflict as more diverse and competing interests and greater material resources produce more frequent disputes. But this view is not unchallenged, for it is not clear that greater complexity produces higher conflict levels. After all, greater conflict potential is not the same thing as actual conflict. Parallel to the advance in socioeconomic complexity is an increase in political coordination and control (Ross 1981), which limits or channels conflict in order to maintain a stable social order, permitting those with the largest share of the valued goods to keep it (Fried 1967). In addition, complex systems are more capable of distributing benefits to their members, who are thus rewarded by the maintenance of order (Bates 1983; Service 1975).

The effect of socioeconomic complexity on external conflict seems more straightforward. There is general agreement that from an evolutionary point of view, success in external conflict has been necessary for survival, and groups that have been more belligerent and victorious in warfare have displaced others lacking these traits (LeVine and Campbell 1972:72–77). Conflict, therefore, has been functional from the point of view of human evolution and groups that successfully engaged in external conflict also evolved more sophisticated means of internal coordination (Bigelow 1973).[19]

---

gests ways in which simpler societies give way to more complex forms. Fried's book is curiously vague in a number of ways. First, he says virtually nothing about the sources of data for the many undocumented generalizations he freely offers. Second, he does not clearly distinguish sequences in the transition between stages he discusses, so the reader is often left to wonder what the primary change factors are and what are their correlates. Finally, and most important, Fried's construction of ideal societies at each level of political complexity never suggests the real variation which cross-cultural analysis has thoroughly documented within each form, for he emphasizes only constants, never patterns of variation.

19. International relations theorists have also spent a good deal of time on this question. Reviewing the literature on modern states, Zimmerman (1980) finds three competing hypotheses—that violence is greatest in the least developed

Political complexity. Political complexity has received more attention than socioeconomic complexity as a correlate of conflict and warfare. More highly centralized systems have both greater capacity and more motivation for attacking, and more vulnerability to being attacked by, internal and external enemies. The available data, especially with respect to warfare, agree that as political complexity increases, so does violent conflict, but the factors underlying the relation are still uncertain. It may be that increasing political complexity results in increasingly unequal distribution of resources in a society. Some theorists point out that internal conflict concerns internecine battles for control over the instruments of political authority and the right to distribute resources. Others emphasize that political complexity increases the capacity to attack outsiders and to control domestic enemies or assert that it is inherent in the nature of the state itself.[20]

It is also plausible that political complexity has an indirect, rather than direct, effect on conflict and violence, such that although complexity does not affect the level of conflict, the correlates of conflict will be different at each level of complexity. In uncentralized societies, for example, the existence of fraternal-interest groups is positively associated with feuding and internal war, but this is not the case in centralized societies, where political authority is exercised outside the local community.[21] This suggests that even if structural factors affect conflict in

---

nations (Lipset, 1959; Feierabend, Feierabend, and Nesvold, 1969), that the relationship will be curvilinear (Hibbs, 1973), and that different forms of conflict (protest versus rebellion, for example) relate to complexity in different ways.

20. Also adopting an evolutionary perspective, Wright (1942) finds that increasing technology and civilization are associated with a parallel rise in the severity of warfare. Using the same data, Broch and Galtung (1966) also find a correlation between complexity and belligerence. Looking at modern nations, Haas (1965) finds a modest tendency for more developed nations to have higher levels of external conflict.

21. Wright's (1942) analysis identifies a shift in the type and severity of warfare according to political complexity, and Broch and Galtung (1966) see political organization as a crucial factor in increased belligerence. Swanson's warfare measure is positively correlated with political centralization in a sample of forty-five cultures (Textor, 1967). Midlarsky and Thomas' analysis of sixty-five preindustrial nations suggests that political complexity has a clearer positive impact on warfare than does socioeconomic complexity (1975). Other theorists point to the same connections with different underlying mechanisms. Spencer (1961) suggests that the development of military leadership produces political

centralized and uncentralized political systems, different structural features are likely to be involved and there may be few structural roots of conflict common to both.[22]

Specific Hypotheses

The cross-cutting ties theory of conflict focuses on the distribution of people across social roles in order to understand patterns of conflict and conflict management, whereas complexity theory links conflict behavior to the group interests associated with specific forms of socioeconomic or political organization. What is striking about the theories is not that they necessarily conflict with each other, but that they are so often proposed in isolation that their underlying mechanisms are rarely compared. Specific hypotheses derived from each appear in table 3.1, and I shall discuss the evidence for the individual hypotheses in chap-

---

leaders and subsequent centralization. Materialist interpretations of the rise of the state argue that the development of social stratification and wealth create the need for a military to protect privileged interests against internal and external predators (Fried, 1967). According to theories that consider the state a mechanism of conquest, the growth of military sophistication is a way to control neighboring peoples and resources (Adams, 1966). A less-frequently argued perspective suggests that even if centralized systems are militarily more sophisticated, the concentration of political power in a few hands leads to greater control over the outbreak of violence. This view emphasizes the role of the state as a conflict inhibitor through its control over violence (Service, 1975). If the state is effective in controlling the overall level of violence as well as its targets, then political centralization will be associated with lower violence both internally and externally.

22. While Otterbein (1968; 1970) and Otterbein and Otterbein (1965) do not find direct effects of political centralization on internal or external conflict, they maintain that centralization is a crucial variable. Otterbein (1970) finds that more centralized societies adopt more sophisticated military strategies, have higher casualty rates, and engage in war more frequently. Although there is no direct effect of political centralization on their measures of warfare, the relation between military sophistication and warfare holds at both levels of centralization. Similarly, looking at modern nations, Wilkenfeld (1973) and Wilkenfeld and Zinnes (1973) suggest that the political structure of a state does not necessarily determine the overall conflict level, yet it does seem to have an impact on patterns across time and on the correlates of conflict. They suggest that different explanations are needed for what they call centrist, personalist, and polyarchic states. LeVine and Campbell (1972:57) also argue that different explanations for violence are needed for uncentralized and for centralized societies.

Table 3.1
Summary of Social Structural Hypotheses about Conflict

Independent variable	Internal conflict	External conflict
Cross-cutting ties theory		
Multiple-reference groups	−	+
Local marital endogamy	+	−
Matrilocality	−	+
Patrilocality	+	−
Polygany	+	+
Fraternal-interest group strength in uncentralized societies	+	?
Intercommunity trade	−	
Complexity theory		
Socioeconomic complexity	?	+
Political complexity	− or indirect	+ or indirect

+ relation is expected to be positive
− relation is expected to be negative

ter 6. Finally, it should be noted that predictions for internal versus external conflict for virtually all of the structural variables are in the opposite direction for internal and external conflict, raising the question of the relationship between the two, the topic of chapter 7.

Some Limitations of Social Structural Conflict Theory

The usefulness of structural conflict theory lies in the clear way it portrays group interests and the actions groups take to pursue them as functions of the organization of society. Yet structural theory can be problematic at times. The conclusion that many alternative bases of conflict are possible is less useful than specifying which ones are likely to be critical in particular situations. In addition, important questions remain about the concept of interests: how are interests identified and defined in actual situations, what is the sometimes uncertain relationship between group and individual interests, what role does consciousness have in group action, and how are potential interest conflicts translated into action. Each of these issues can be viewed as limiting the connection between the structure of a society and the organization of action—the critical assumption underlying structural conflict theory.

Structural theory can be concerned with individual level interests, like versions of the multiple-loyalties hypothesis, or may focus on collective group interests, like fraternal-interest group or class-conflict hypotheses. Social structural hypotheses disagree about which particular interests are the most important, and too often advocates of a specific point of view simply offer examples that fit their theoretical predilections. Sociobiology, for example, defines interests in terms of long-term inclusive fitness (survival of individual genes); materialists emphasize tangible assets such as land, wealth, or animals (Harris 1979; Ferguson 1984); others posit prestige, titles, ethnic group legitimation, or even salvation as interests pursued. Yet there is too little effort to understand the relative importance of alternative interests or to identify the cultural conditions related to the importance of each (Wildavsky 1987).

The problem of defining interests in a nontautological way is not unique to social structural theory. Most of rational-choice theory, like modern microeconomics, too easily assumes that interests are self-evident and often just infers them from behavior. The nature and origin of interests and how they are shaped by culture is too complex to be assumed, however (Wildavsky 1987; 1992). The process by which individuals develop certain interests is intimately shaped by their social world and the priorities it sets. Presuming that individual action is based on self-interest and necessarily reveals clear preferences ignores individuals' variation in awareness of interests, how this affects actions, and the ways in which actions can be inconsistent with the self-interest hypothesis.[23]

Social structural theory too easily equates individual and group interests, presuming that by pursuing the interests of the group, individuals further their own interests. Although there are certainly situations where this is the case, there are others in which collective and individual interests diverge. The problem is especially acute in large groups where members do not believe that individually they can have a great impact on group behavior, and yet if everyone adopts this position the effectiveness of the group to engage in collective action disappears (Olson 1965). Groups variously use coercion, ideology, and selective incentives to minimize the divergence between individual and group

23. In this regard, Harris (1979) is to be commended. Although he is clearly a partisan of cultural materialism, he suggests ways in which propositions in his theory may be tested in a systematic manner alongside those deriving from rival theories.

interests. The existence of such mechanisms is, in fact, evidence for the gap between individual and group interests, a distinction which is insufficiently acknowledged in social structural conflict theory.

Structural conflict theory often says little about the process by which people sharing structural interests develop a common consciousness. The question is a critical one, for the ways in which feelings of identification translate into action cannot be taken for granted, especially in situations where individuals draw on multiple sources of identity. Although some structural theories such as cultural materialism or sociobiology assume that certain attachments will be primary, data on this question show that the reality is far more complex and that structural explanations for conflict patterns are less general and more ad hoc than their proponents suggest. The process of identifying major structural units in a community and deducing their common interests is only part of the analytic task. To adequately answer the question of how interests are converted into political action or inaction, one must also evaluate the emotional meaning of these observed social bonds.[24]

Finally, the presence or absence of collective action is often used as evidence for the strength of group interests. Such an approach fails to define the two separately and ignores the role of other forces which can encourage or inhibit action in particular situations.[25] In an authoritarian society with a centralized political structure, the cost of dissent may be great for groups opposed to those in power. An example of this is the recent vigorous articulation of latent ethnic interests in the former Soviet Union. Similarly, action against an external opponent can be inhibited if the opponent is seen as particularly powerful. In neither case is the lack of action necessarily evidence for the weakness or ab-

24. Understanding interests from the point of view of social groups is contrary to some structural theories, particularly neo-Marxist ones, which define interests without reference to culture or perceptions. When people fail to behave according to these theories, a concept such as false consciousness must be invoked.

25. An obvious example is the differential rate with which workers vote for socialist or other left-leaning parties whose policies are likely to favor them. In one comparative analysis, Verba, Nie, and Kim (1978) found notable differences between Austria, where workers were most likely to vote for parties of the left, and the United States or Japan, where this was least likely to occur. The conversion of structure into action is far from automatic, and structural theory often poorly spells out other intervening conditions.

sence of structurally based interests; rather it is only testimony to why the translation of interests into action is not always direct, or even possible.

Conclusion

Structural conflict theory is compelling, despite its imprecise identification of interests and of the complex linkage between interests and action. Structure is crucial, I have argued, in determining the targets of aggressive behavior. Yet there are limitations to the explanatory role of structural factors as well, depending in part on other conditions of society. In this regard, a structural theory of conflict alone is as incomplete as one based solely on a psychocultural approach, the topic of the next chapter.

4

Conflict and Psychocultural Dispositions

Structural explanations for conflict, violence, and warfare focus on how the organization of society shapes action, whereas psychocultural explanations look to the actors themselves and how they interpret the world. Psychocultural explanations account for cross-cultural differences in conflict behavior in terms of motives for action rooted in culturally shared images and perceptions of the external world. These dispositions form the basis of an interpretive framework that strongly influences how individuals and groups understand and respond to each other's actions.

The use of the term "psychocultural dispositions," though cumbersome, is intentional. Psychocultural refers to processes rooted in human psychology, specifically those whose patterns and content are pervasive within a culture (Whiting and Whiting 1975a). Obvious examples include widely shared norms concerning how to respond to infants or how to discipline disobedient children. A more abstract but still pertinent example comes from Volkan's (1988) discussion of ethnicity and nationalism, in which he describes the primordial nature of culturally shared targets of ethnic hostility. Psychocultural dispositions are culturally shared response tendencies acquired through mechanisms spelled out in both psychodynamic and social learning theory from the earliest stages of life (LeVine 1973:6–8). Dispositions are fundamental orientations vis-à-vis the self and others and include culturally learned and approved methods for dealing with others both within and outside one's community.

Individuals draw on their psychocultural dispositions to deal with the powerful emotions stressful and ambiguous situations produce

51

and this affects how participants in a conflict come to interpret the actions and motives of opponents. Shared interpretations relieve both anxiety and ambiguity and infuse conflicts with intense social and political meanings. Shared interpretations offer guides to action and, at the same time, are a source of cognitive and perceptual distortion because the desire for certainty is often greater than the need for accuracy. Psychocultural dispositions help us understand action from particular cultural points of view and their importance reminds us to be cautious when imposing external assumptions about interests or motives on a situation.

Though social structural explanations rooted in group interests are easy to accept, psychocultural ones which explain conflict or co-operation in terms of shared, deep-seated fears or threats to identity are sometimes far less intuitively appealing. One reason is a continuing social science rejection of older psychological models of collective action, such as Freud's, which paid no attention to social and cultural processes beyond the family. Another is psychology's tendency to focus on pathology more than on normal functioning. Finally, there is continuing acceptance of the Durkheimian injunction that social facts must be explained by other social facts, not psychological ones. Yet arguing that collective phenomena cannot be explained fully in terms of forces at the individual level need not mean that psychological factors have no role in our understanding of social action.

Psychocultural conflict theory provides a strong challenge to this antipsychological view. First, it addresses the intensity of some conflicts, a factor that cannot simply be explained in terms of the objective differences between disputants. Second, psychocultural theory, more social in orientation than the early psychological formulations, views society as more than the family writ large it was for Freud, addressing the development, maintenance, and use of particular orientations toward the world. Third, the interest in interpretive approaches in the social sciences has made us aware of the importance of understanding how intrapersonal and cultural frameworks, not just objective conditions, shape social action. Psychocultural conflict theory provides a vital addition to this perspective and articulates an essential set of connections between individual developmental processes and collective action.

In this chapter I shall argue that culturally shared interpretive frameworks are grounded in individuals' earliest social relationships. I first discuss the idea of a psychocultural model of conflict behavior because the language of contemporary psychoanalytic theory is important in understanding the social character of development and not necessarily familiar to political scientists, anthropologists, or others interested in conflict behavior. I then develop three distinct psychocultural hypotheses about cross-cultural variation in conflict behavior: that conflict is related to the harshness of socialization; that it is related to the absence of warmth and affection in early social relationships; and that it is dependent upon the severity of male gender-identity conflict. Underlying these hypotheses is the view that early psychosocial experiences shape a person's models of the self and of others in his or her social world, and these shared representations later guide collective (adult) actions.

A Psychocultural Model of Behavior

Psychological theories about individuals do not necessarily make for good theories about societal behavior. When Freud, late in life, wrote about collective behavior, he viewed the collectivity, whether it was the army, the church, or the nation, as the family writ large and suggested ways in which the Oedipal paradigm explained behavior in each institutional domain. Civilization, in his view, could curb individual impulses (which he increasingly saw as biological) but could never fully repress them. Hence Freud's pessimism in his famous exchange with Einstein about war (Freud 1932).

The Freudian paradigm was central to the cultural and personality studies of the World War II period, including the national character studies which received much attention and criticism. These efforts to understand modern nations convinced many that psychoanalytic concepts could have little role in serious social science explanations of cross-cultural differences (Wallace 1962; Inkeles and Levinson 1968). As LeVine notes:

The wide public attention received by these studies, the support of the United States government for some of them, and the impression they gave that a diluted version of psychoanalysis could solve the major international problems of our time (in the name of social science!) called forth an indignant reaction from many social scientists, who found themselves engaged once more in arguing for institutional complexity and autonomy against attractive, oversimplified psychological explanations. (LeVine 1973:viii)

LeVine argues, however, that not all efforts to account for the role of psychological processes in collective behavior are as reductionist as Freud's or as simplistic as Mead's or Gorer's.[1] Linton, Hallowell, Beatrice and John Whiting, Edgerton, LeVine, and others have suggested important ways in which personality and cultural processes interact, rather than completely overlapping or fully determining each other.

In J. Whiting's (1974) and B. Whiting's (1980) model, many behaviors of both children and adults are prescribed by a society's social organization, and established roles, clear expectations, and task assignments often severely limit individual or cultural choices. B. Whiting (1980) calls such behaviors mundane, or everyday, interpersonal behavior. The learning mechanisms involved in the acquisition of mundane behaviors are identified in social learning theory (Bandura 1973), especially trial and error and direct tuition, but modeling and imitation are important, too. Situations in which only modest levels of learning-associated affect are present are crucial to learning mundane behaviors (B. Whiting 1980:97). To the extent that conflict behavior is mundane, it is best explained by structural forces, such as those considered in the previous chapter.

B. Whiting (1980) identifies a second group of behaviors: expressive and projective ones. Religious behavior or beliefs about illness are typical here, but so might be political domains such as conflict or authority. Cross-cultural studies have illustrated a wide range of ways in which expressive beliefs and behaviors are related to early socialization (Levinson and Malone 1980; Whiting and Child 1953). One example shows that the severity of child discipline is associated with the harshness or benevolence of a culture's supernatural figures (Swanson 1960).

According to the Whitings, both mundane and projective behaviors are culturally patterned, but in different ways. Mundane behaviors are directly shaped by environmental, contextual factors, whereas projective behaviors are less directly affected by these forces and are more directly a function of early social relationships and concern domains of action that are more ambiguous, less structured, and involve intense emotions. The mechanisms underlying projective behaviors are those associated with psychoanalytic theory, as discussed below. The Whitings' formulation is significant for this study of conflict behavior for

1. LeVine (1973) offers a fine overview of approaches to the field.

several reasons: first, it shows the importance of considering the social context in which behavioral dispositions are shaped; second, the distinction between mundane and projective behaviors rejects the idea that a single factor like personality development alone can adequately account for complex social behaviors.[2]

Interestingly, psychoanalytic theory, too, has for several decades become more concerned with social context. At the same time, without necessarily rejecting earlier concerns, like Freud's emphasis on psychosexual development, there has been increased attention to the preoedipal and adolescent stages of the life cycle and to the many new ideas which have arisen from these concerns. Similarly, psychoanalysis developed a relational language to describe many of these phenomena, which has largely replaced the older drive-based terminology of orthodox Freudian theory (Greenberg and Mitchell 1983; Mitchell 1988). The result is socially rooted psychoanalytic formulations which offer a theory and a rich vocabulary to talk about psychocultural dispositions in cross-cultural terms.

The Psychocultural Construction of Social Worlds

By paying attention to social interaction from the first days of life, current psychoanalytic formulations emphasize different factors than earlier views. The infant is far more than a creature fighting to fulfill a host of physical cravings which society seeks to limit and redirect. Psychoanalytic thinkers from Melanie Klein and British object-relations theorists onward have emphasized the importance of the inner worlds constructed in the pre-verbal period as a template for later relationships and actions. Stern (1985), synthesizing a great deal of data from infant observations, argues that from birth the infant is an interactive processor of stimuli.

Some of the most exciting recent behavioral science research has shown, often in dramatic fashion, the social judgment skills of even very

2. B. Whiting points out ways in which mundane behaviors, once established, can, at times, produce generalized effects similar to those sometimes associated with projective behaviors. For example, she reports that the experience of nurturing young children increases a child's likelihood of being nurturing with noninfants (1980:102).

young infants. Three-day-old babies can accurately pick out their mother's smell; a short time later they accurately link sounds and images and make other cross-modal transfers of information. Infants seek out sensory stimulation: they pick out human faces and prefer looking at them to other objects, and at five to seven months they can remember a week later a picture of a face they have seen for just one minute. They also have a temporal sense, and they develop a capacity for self-regulation (Stern 1985).

This research, Stern points out, runs counter to the older psychoanalytic view of early infancy, which sees a lack of differentiation between the infant and mother. Freud spoke of a stimulus barrier enveloping the newborn; Mahler termed the first months of life the autistic phase, to indicate the lack of interest in the world beyond the mother; few early theorists would use the concept of a sense of self to describe humans in the first year of life (Lichtenberg 1983).[3] According to Stern, these views are not warranted by the data, for "The infant engages in the same kind of active regulatory traffic with the external world as does anyone at any age" (Stern 1985:233).

Instead of viewing the infant as initially fused with the mother and gradually separating from her physically and psychologically, Stern suggests that the sense of the self is developed earlier than had been previously thought and that the construction of social and emotional bonds to others is as crucial a part of the first stage of development as differentiating the self from others. Stern draws on the work of Bowlby (1969; 1973), an ethnologically informed psychoanalyst, to emphasize the importance of bonding and attachment from birth. Although language acquisition makes it more visible, the building of social bonds is well underway before the child begins to speak. And it is a process with many internal and external manifestations.

One of the most interesting ideas about how social attachments are formed and changed comes from Winnicott's concept of transitional objects—physical objects such as teddy bears, blankets, or pieces of

3. Although Lichtenberg (1983), like Stern (1985), explores the implications of the boom in infant observational research, mainly by academic psychologists, he is much more timid in the conclusions he draws. In particular, he is more hesitant to reject many established views and emphasizes a need for their modification. Moreover, his reconceptualization of the first eighteen months of life is less radical than that of Stern, who is willing to talk about a sense of self from the earliest months. Lichtenberg applies the idea of a "self" only after the first year.

cloth which children invest with great emotional significance. The reason they do this, Winnicott (1953) tells us, is that although at one level the young child knows that his mother (or another significant person) is safe and sound and continues to exist when she is not physically present, at another level there is some lingering doubt. The transitional object, invariably soft and snuggly, represents the absent valued person and therefore provides real comfort to the child, a connection between the inner and outer worlds. The "fantasy friends" that many children have are a parallel example of a child's need for mastery and ability to construct relationships based on real needs. Although all individuals have personal objects to which they attach both positive and negative affect, Volkan (1988) points out that members of a culture invariably come to hold certain of these objects in common. He argues that in adolescence, in fact, the peer group, rather than the initial familial unit, provides the crucial objects in this process of defining individual and group identity.

Linking Psychocultural Dispositions and Conflict Behavior

There is ample evidence that humans are predisposed to establish social bonds from birth and that strong ties to others have important adaptive significance. Volkan (1988) argues that the way in which this central task is completed is part of a universal process of the definition of allies and enemies—friends and foes.[4] An individual's external experiences provide the raw material for the construction of his or her internal world which will contain primordial models of human interaction involving nurturance, conflict, authority, power, community, and other core concepts which have significance throughout life.

These dispositions are internal configurations that have significance for external action. In the conflict domain, we want to know not only who the allies and enemies are, but also how they can be expected to behave and what constitutes appropriate action toward them. Identifying psychocultural dispositions related to conflict and violence

4. Volkan also dates the roots of the process to the first months of life and cites the importance of both the mother-infant bonds and stranger-anxiety reactions of the first year of life as evidence for the universality of the we-they differentiation process.

requires the specification of mechanisms linking early learning to personality formation and adult behavior. I have found particularly useful psychodynamic mechanisms in object-relations theory: attachment and individuation, identification, repression, projection, externalization, and displacement (Greenberg and Mitchell 1983).

Attachment refers to the ways in which a young child develops or fails to develop bonds to others. Early deprivation and lack of nurturance severely impair the capacity to develop strong affective bonds later in life in both human and nonhuman primates (Bowlby 1969; Harlow and Harlow 1962, 1965; Stern 1985). Mahler, Pine, and Bergman (1975) describe the process of separation and individuation in the second year of life. The secure child is capable of differentiating itself from its mother (or father) when the child's internalized image of the parent is positive and sufficiently secure so that separation does not produce overwhelming tension and anxiety (1975:109). Winnicott (1965) uses the term "good enough mother" to refer to the caretaker who provides a child with early experiences resulting in a positive sense of self and trust and openness toward others. In contrast, if early relationships are negative and threatening, psychological growth remains at an early stage and bonds to others cannot develop. Attachment to others is crucial for an individual's ability later in life to form intimate relationships or to join others in socially cooperative activities.

Identification is the process of developing bonds to an object and altering one's actions because of these attachments (Bronfenbrenner 1960; Schafer 1968). Much of psychoanalytic theory has emphasized the ways in which identification with frustrating objects results in destructive actions (for example, A. Freud 1937; S. Freud 1922). But S. Freud also wrote about another, more positive form of identification, involving identification as a function of loss of love (Freud 1914, 1917; Bronfenbrenner 1960:16; Slater 1977:20). When the object of identification is benign, Schafer says the child derives a sense "of mastery, competence, or independence . . . [and] there is an atmosphere of precious intimacy surrounding these identifications—a glow of well-being that is also seen in fond embraces" (1968:154).

Identification and the development of a superego which monitors behaviors and feelings is a normal aspect of psychological maturation. Individuals come to repress impulses which are too frightening to hold at a conscious level. Although *repression* is a normal part of psychological functioning, it is necessary to distinguish the various degrees to which repression occurs in the individual and the consequences of these differences. When a superego is overly harsh, repression is severe, and the pent-up feelings can be highly destructive for the individual or those around him or her. Aggressive identification and severe repression are the raw material for the expression of violence. In some cases they are turned inward (Spotnitz 1976), while in others one's own aggressive feelings are displaced onto available targets (Adorno 1950).

Externalization and projection remove unpleasant self-images, feeling states, thoughts, and impulses which cannot be integrated with the image of the self by attributing them to the external world, whereas *displacement* is the investment of feelings about one object in another (Volkan 1988:18–20). From a psychodynamic point of view there are significant differences in these processes. I shall focus on what they have in common, the transfer of feelings from one object (either the self or another object) to a different one.[5] These processes can result when an object (such as the image of one's mother) is split into two parts, the good and the bad. The good part may then be retained and the bad one externalized—that is, given to another. Suitable targets for externalization, Volkan argues, are frequently shared in a community through the definition of common enemies and allies. Projection appears in Fornari's (1975) Kleinian psychodynamic theory of war in which conflict is seen as a defense against inner fears and persecution fantasies projected outward. For Fornari, the psychological roots are in the loss of love objects (felt prototypically as the child begins to differentiate him- or herself from the caretaker), which can be terrifying when accompanied by profound feelings of guilt and self-blame. As a defense against this inner terror, individuals develop strong identifications with their own group and project the hostile guilt feelings onto outsiders who are then unconsciously blamed for the original loss.

The most enigmatic aspect of this system would seem to be its desire to control the uncontrollable by translating internal psychotic anxieties into real danger. I have called paranoid elaboration of mourning that group of maneuvers ... emerging in the form of a sense of guilt for the death of the love object ... The experience of mourning then becomes not sorrow for the death of the loved person, but the killing of the enemy who is falsely thought to be the destroyer of the loved object. (Fornari 1975:xviii)

5. Volkan's discussion clarifies the differences in these processes which are not my major concern (1988:18–20).

Fornari's theoretical explication suggests sources of social and cultural variation in outcomes. Early relations with the environment provide a template for resolving conflicts later in life (Fornari 1975:101). Highly hostile cultures ought to create the highest levels of guilt, outwardly projected hostility, and violence.

Freud (1930), of course, saw a clear connection between individual repression in response to societal demands and the displacement of aggression onto external targets. Displacement occurs when individuals cannot express their feelings toward the original object, because it is too powerful, unavailable, or because the idea of such a confrontation is too frightening. Displaced hostility onto groups and individuals can be crucial in the escalation of conflict.

Specific Hypotheses

Findings from research on infants and recent psychoanalytic writing are relevant for their emphasis on psychological development as a social process, not just a physiological one. This work focuses on social relationships as shaping dispositions which provide the basis for adult psychocultural behaviors, rather than the innate drives that older thinking considered crucial (Greenberg and Mitchell 1983:20). Early learning experiences affect cognition as well as deeper motivations, preparing individuals for patterns of conflict and cooperation in society and providing key conceptual tools for interpreting their social worlds. Variations in development are understood in terms of different kinds of early social relationships. I shall use this perspective to develop three specific hypotheses about cross-cultural variation in conflict behavior.

Harsh Socialization

Harsh socialization makes it difficult to establish bonds with others later in life and is likely to be associated with low levels of trust in social relations and exaggerated emphasis on social (or political) attachments as a compensatory mechanism. Harsh physical and emotional experiences induce powerful feelings of guilt and anxiety which are then repressed or externalized and projected onto others. As both Volkan (1988) and Fornari (1975) suggest, out-groups and individuals connected to such negative representations can easily become socially approved targets of aggression.[6]

A large number of existing studies provide data consistent with modern psychoanalytic formulations. Several approaches—orthodox psychoanalytic theory (and the authoritarian personality work derived from it), social learning theory, and frustration-aggression theory—associate severe child training practices with later aggressivity. Although the mechanisms underlying each of the theories vary, the predictions are similar (Zigler and Child 1969). For example, psychoanalytic and frustration aggression theory connect severe physical punishment of children with later displacement onto out-groups, whereas social learning theory explains a connection in terms of imitation, modeling, and reinforcement. In all three cases, however, harsh socialization experiences produce adults who are aggressive and engage more readily in overt conflict.[7] Finally, a number of cross-cultural studies report a positive association between harsh socialization practices and physical aggression, bellicosity, and warfare (Levinson and Malone 1980:249).

Warmth and Affection

The healthy psychosocial development of the individual in terms of early object relations (internalized representations of others) and se-

6. For Durbin and Bowlby (1939), the key mechanism is identification with the state as a consequence of individual repression of private feelings. "War is due to the transformed aggressiveness of individuals" (1939:41). Another obvious process at work here is Anna Freud's "identification with the aggressor" (1937).

7. Gurr's work on political violence (1968; 1970; Gurr and Duvall 1973) offers an explanation in terms of relative deprivation and frustration-aggression theory (also see Feierabend and Feierabend 1971). But if Gurr's theory is psychological his data are not; he uses measures of social and economic conditions in a sample of nations as a basis for inferring psychological states (Zimmerman 1980:211–12). Muller (1972) criticizes Gurr's explanation of political violence as inadequate because it does not provide any individual-level data. Muller then offers survey data showing support for the hypothesis that propensity for political violence is more related to political trust than to relative deprivation. In a second study he finds that a "just desserts" measure of frustration is a better predictor of political violence than other relative deprivation measures (Muller 1980: 80–81).

cure ties to parental figures prepares the way for socially cooperative experiences later in life (Winnicott 1965; Guntrip 1968, 1971; Fairbairn 1954). Sociality is emphasized in warm and affectionate social relationships that provide the infant with secure bonds to others, and which paradoxically ease the process of separation and individuation, making object loss a less salient fear and facilitating attachment to others (Trevarthen and Logtheti 1989). When externalization, projection, and displacement occur, they are less likely to be charged with hostility and in some cases may even attribute positive feelings or motives to outsiders.

Affectionate, warm, and loving child-rearing practices are not simply the opposite of harsh socialization;[8] they have independent effects on aggressive behavior. The distinction is perhaps parallel to the difference between permissiveness and punishment in the socialization of aggression, which according to Sears, Maccoby, and Levin (1958) have independent effects on aggressive behavior. More open expression of affection toward children, greater emphasis on values such as trust, honesty, and generosity, and closer father-child ties, for example, are all practices which encourage individuals to develop the social skills needed to resolve conflicts without violence.

Montagu's (1978) profiles of seven small-scale societies, all low in internal conflict and aggression (including the Mbuti discussed in chapter 1), provide good ethnographic examples of this pattern and a sense of the specific socialization practices involved. In these societies, affection is frequently directed toward the child, whose overall feelings of security are reinforced. Overt expression of aggression is discouraged but not through physical punishment. When children are aggressive, they are often quickly removed from a situation. Children have multiple affectionate caretakers; there is continued surveillance of behavior; gender differentiation and sexual tension are low; and sharing is highly valued. Finally, these societies lack models of highly aggressive persons whom the child can imitate. Warmth and affectionate socialization produce lower conflict both within one's society and in dealing with outsiders. Internal images of others are relatively supportive, trusting, cooperative, and responsive. Where expectations are mutual, reinforcing

8. For example, in independent factor analyses, including the one cited in Appendix A, variables measuring harsh socialization practices load on different factors than indicators of warmth and affection (Russell 1972; Steward and Jones 1972).

sequences develop and, once begun, maintain low conflict patterns. Finally, this hypothesis does not suggest important distinctions between internal and external targets.

Male Gender-Identity Conflict

The widely cited hypothesis of male gender-identity conflict views a good deal of aggressive action as compensatory behavior arising out of male gender-identity confusion.[9] Although its origin is in classical Freudian theory, it can be connected to preoedipal processes as well. Male problems with attachment and identification produce high levels of projection, externalization, and displacement of intense hostility onto out-groups and increase the levels of overt conflict both within a community and with neighboring societies. In this view, in cultures in which male gender-identity conflict is common, disputes escalate rapidly and resolving them is difficult as long as individuals continue to see the outcomes of disputes as intimately related to issues of identity and self-worth.

In male-dominated cultures where fathers are distant and aloof from their children, frustration develops when young boys, who grow up with especially strong bonds to their mothers, must sever these bonds to meet the societal expectations of adult male behavior. A second source of frustration is maternal ambivalence. Women living in patrilocal, polygynous societies have neither strong ties to their natal families nor strong affective bonds with their husbands, a situation Slater and Slater (1965) call "diluted marriage." Women in these settings develop strong bonds with their children but also take out frustration on them. "The male child was alternatively seduced and rejected" (Slater and Slater 1965:242). The result is that males in these cultures develop ambivalent feelings toward females and fear intimacy;[10] in addition, narcissistic personalities—preoccupied with early developmental tasks, pride and self enhancement, and prone to aggressive actions—are common (Slater

9. The Whitings use the term "protest masculinity" to refer to the pattern which links uncertainty concerning gender identity to overt aggression (Whiting 1965; Whiting and Whiting 1975a). Also see Ember (1978b), who finds support for this hypothesis in an analysis of cross-cultural differences in men's fear of sex with women.

10. Herdt (1987) discusses male repression of the part of themselves which is associated with identification with females as a consequence.

and Slater 1965; also Kernberg 1975; Spotnitz 1976). Cultural attempts to deal with male gender ambivalence through initiation rites, including circumcision ceremonies (Munroe, Munroe, and Whiting 1981:614–616),[11] are only partially successful. Compensatory behaviors like bellicosity, aggressive display, and fighting occur frequently.[12] Although several critics have suggested that the same data may be better explained by other theories (for example, Young 1965; Paige and Paige 1981), the male gender-identity conflict hypothesis is widely supported.[13] Koch (1974b), for example, argues that the protest masculinity model provides a useful framework for understanding pervasive conflict and warfare in New Guinea, which he says is marked by the absence of third-party intervention, an outgrowth of the early socialization patterns the Whitings describe.[14]

11. J. Whiting, Kluckhohn, and Anthony (1958) link male circumcision rites and both a long post-partum sex taboo between husband and wife and exclusive mother-infant sleeping arrangements.

12. Herdt (1987) illustrates many of these points.

13. The male gender-identity conflict hypothesis suggests that distant father-child ties promote aggressivity, whereas close, affectionate bonds are associated with low levels of overt conflict (Ember 1980:561–62; Whiting and Whiting 1975a; West and Konner 1976). Herdt (1989), discussing the question of ritual homosexuality in Melanesia in terms of Whiting's protest masculinity hypothesis, says that father absence is less associated with aggressivity than the presence of a highly ambivalent father-son relationship. Fathers are present but not emotionally accessible to the young child or to their wives. "The boy's basic dilemma in Lowland ritual homosexuality societies is that he feels close to his father but *cannot consistently* influence his father's behavior. He finds it hard to catch and hold his father's attention" (Herdt 1989:352). Lacking responsive interaction, the son can neither master the father's role nor distance himself from his father emotionally. Adorno et al. (1950) contend that distant fathers produce children (particularly sons) who are insecure in interpersonal relationships and are more ready to engage in open aggression against out-groups. B. Whiting (1965), reviewing detailed data from the Six-Culture study, shows that low adult male salience in early life was most marked in the two cultures with the highest rates of physical assault and homicide. She also notes the correlation frequently found between father absence and juvenile delinquency in western settings.

14. Whiting and Whiting (1975b) report that distant fathering is associated with training boys to be warriors, and West and Konner find a clear relationship between lack of father-child closeness and high levels of warfare (West and Konner 1976:203). Whiting and Whiting (1975a), reporting the results of detailed observations of children in six cultures, find that household structure,

Conflict as Interpretive Behavior

Psychocultural conflict theory is centered on the idea that because conflicts evoke deeply held emotions in situations which are highly ambiguous and often unstructured, an important component of conflict behavior is interpretation. Although participants in any dispute think they can tell someone exactly what the conflict is about, this precision is often illusory. Different parties do not always agree on what a conflict is about, when it started, or who is involved (Northrup 1989).[15] As Schattschneider (1960), Coleman (1957), and many others note, the substance of conflicts, the disputants, and their goals change over time. A conflict is less a one-time event than an evolving phenomenon. Many disputes, whether between families or nations, involve parties with long histories, which, of course, include accumulated grievances to which newer ones can be added as conditions change. Gulliver (1979:234–252), for example, describes a dispute between two Arusha neighbors over the ownership of a newly vacant farm located between them: sixteen distinct issues were raised in joint negotiations. Labor disputes, often

particularly the role of the father, differentiates cultures on their sociable-intimate versus authoritarian-aggressive behavior dimension. In societies where the children's behavior is more authoritarian and aggressive, the extended family is common, the father has a smaller role in child rearing and is present less, the level of overt husband-wife conflict is often higher, and the level of child-father contact is lower (1975a:120–23). Alcorta (1982) finds support for the hypothesis that close father-child ties are associated with lower aggressivity and conflict among both human and nonhuman primates. Stress among infants (particularly males) and subsequent aggression decreases noticeably the more adult males are involved in child rearing.

15. I find unsystematic but interesting support for this position in a regular assignment I have given the students in my conflict and conflict management class for more than ten years. Their task: find a local conflict and study it. The instructions are deliberately vague and my only ground rule is that the students have to utilize ethnographic methods involving face-to-face contact with the disputants. In the early phase of the research they invariably report: "I thought I knew what the conflict was about, but now I'm lost"; "I'm confused—I don't think I have a conflict to study anymore"; "Everyone's telling me something different—no one can tell me what the conflict is about." Only later, when they realize that researchers have to process data actively and develop interpretations based on what they have observed, can they proceed. Similarly, it is seldom self-evident that a conflict can be about both a substantive interest and a symbolic issue (like self-esteem or integrity).

presented to the public as disagreements over wages, may include hundreds of agenda items. In fact, one of the most important steps in resolving such conflicts is for the parties to agree on which issues to discard and which ones to take seriously.

A striking feature of many conflicts is the emotional investment parties have in matters which often seem trivial to outsiders. Once positions are invested with emotional significance, however, they are no longer trivial. Horowitz (1985) describes intransigent ethnic disputes characterized by threats to group self-esteem and legitimation. Only when these issues are addressed can any progress on the "substance" of the dispute be made. The same dynamic can be observed when parties who perceive themselves as threatened place identity issues at the top of their concerns. Of course, when both sides feel the equally intense emotions, it is often difficult for them to recognize what assumptions they may, in fact, share. For example, although both Protestants and Catholics in Northern Ireland see their own group as a threatened minority, neither can view the other that way. One party's emotional concerns may be difficult for another to accept, especially when its own action may be the cause.

The psychocultural view of conflict emphasizes the role of such interpretation in the disputing process. Because of the ambiguity and emotional investment in many conflicts, actors need to make sense of a situation. This may lead to cognitive and perceptual distortion because the need for certainty is often greater than the desire for accuracy. Not only are individuals likely to make systematic errors in interpretation, but the homogeneous nature of most social settings often reinforces self-serving mistakes. Interpretations of a conflict offer a coherent account which links discrete events and actors. Central to these interpretations is the attribution of motives. Once identified, the existence of such motives makes it easy to "predict" another's future actions, and through one's own behavior to turn such predictions into self-fulfilling prophecies. The infusion of events with meaning makes it especially likely that processes of externalization and projection involved in the construction of interpretations will involve a group's inner needs as well as external events. In this sense, rather than believing that particular events cause conflicts to escalate, we ought to determine which interpretations of these events are associated with escalation of conflict and which ones are not.

Finally, interpretive behavior is neither irrational nor unaffected by external events. Making sense of one's world is adaptive. If some interpretive efforts are more successful than others or if systematic errors enter the process, this is not evidence that interpretation is foolish. The inner worlds that are the basis for an understanding of events are themselves, in part, the product of earlier relationships and experiences. Psychocultural theory suggests how individuals and cultures interpret their world in order to survive in it.

Some Limitations of Psychocultural Conflict Theory

Psychocultural conflict theory provides a rich and appealing approach to understanding the intensity of conflicts and why they can be so difficult to manage once they begin to escalate. It offers a link between the ways in which groups and individuals perceive social action and the larger cultural setting in which behavior occurs. At the same time, there are some important limitations to psychocultural accounts of conflict.

One limitation is that while dispositions may be important in shaping conflict behavior, a psychocultural theory needs to address why particular dispositions are invoked in situations where alternative ones, directing behavior in other directions, are possible. Psychocultural accounts, much like psychoanalytic ones, usually offer a plausible explanation for an outcome once it has occurred, but they cannot necessarily predict, even at a very general level, which particular dispositions are likely to be invoked or how. If prior to a conflict a group is seen as both suspicious toward potential enemies and capable of pragmatic cooperation with outsiders, for example, then a post hoc explanation that simply confirms one pattern or the other is not very persuasive.

Another criticism is that psychocultural accounts, even if they have some merit, ignore proximate causes of conflicts in favor of more remote ones. Consideration of long-term developmental forces seems unnecessary when much more obvious causes of a conflict are clear. This objection is not so different than Whiting's (1980) distinction between mundane and projective behaviors and has real merit. Frequently situational factors rooted in institutional patterns offer a sufficient (if simple) explanation for the origin or continuation of a conflict. A psychocultural explanation can be most useful, therefore, in circumstances where institutional forces are weakest, precedents are most unclear, and levels of stress and ambiguity are highest (Greenstein 1967; Whiting 1980).

A final important limit to psychocultural conflict theory is its lack of precision in identifying targets of hostile or cooperative impulses. Various authors emphasize that hostility is projected on to outsiders and that this provides a rationale for attack, yet too little attention is paid to the questions of who is defined as an outsider, or, from among the many outsiders available, which ones become targets for specific hostile actions. Once again, psychocultural accounts are better at post hoc explanations of why a particular target group is appropriate given the group's dispositions, rather than the identification and selection of one group over another.

Conclusion

Psychocultural theory explains why some societies have more conflict than others in terms of deeply held dispositions that affect how social actions are understood. This approach emphasizes how early social relationships affect the development of world views and the organization of actions later in life. Unlike earlier psychoanalytic explanations for social behavior, a psychocultural approach emphasizes the common aspects of dispositional learning and ways in which this sharing helps groups and individuals deal with the high levels of anxiety and stress produced by conflict.

Psychocultural conflict theory directs attention to how actors interpret their social world, how they are likely to react to particular events or behavior, and how actors' beliefs about the motives of others shape their own actions. Although it borrows more explicitly from psychoanalytic theory than do those interested in social interpretation, psychocultural conflict theory shares some goals with each approach. There is a common interest, for example, in the cultural context of action, as well as in the understanding of how actors' construction of social reality provides a basis for subsequent action. Important differences include my interest in examining behavior cross-culturally, in contrast with many interpretationists, particularly in anthropology, who want to render an account only of individual cases and profess no interest in generalization.

The strength of psychocultural theory is its identification of general dispositions toward conflict, yet it cannot predict with accuracy the particular dispositions likely to be evoked in diverse situations or the targets of aggression. Interestingly, this limitation of psychocultural theory is one of the obvious strengths of social structural theory. For this reason the two theories complement each other and each contributes to an integrated cross-cultural theory of conflict which is stronger than an approach based on either on its own. Before making this argument in detail, I shall test the specific hypotheses derived from each theory using a sample of ninety preindustrial societies.

5

Investigating Conflict Cross-Culturally: Sample and Measures

The cross-cultural method is a powerful tool for systematic testing of the social structural and psychocultural theories presented in the two preceding chapters (Ember and Levinson 1991). This approach is appropriate for investigating what forms of conflict occur in preindustrial societies, in what ways different forms of conflict are related to each other, and whether a society's pattern of internal conflict is more likely to be related to bellicose or peaceful relations with its neighbors. To answer these questions, I employ data from a worldwide sample of preindustrial societies frequently used by cross-cultural researchers. The basic data come from the ethnographic reports of anthropologists, missionaries, and others who have written about the societies in the sample. Quantitative methods are used to make comparisons and test the hypotheses.

In this chapter I describe the sample of preindustrial societies, explain the coding of conflict behaviors from the ethnographic data, present the distribution of conflict behaviors among the societies in the sample, and offer profiles of four societies with distinctive patterns of internal and external conflict, showing how the culture of conflict is deeply rooted in a society's institutions, practices, and norms. In chapter 6 I examine the social structural and psychocultural hypotheses about societal differences in internal and external conflict and in chapter 7 offer the empirical basis for a theory of conflict which suggests that psychocultural factors shape a society's overall level of conflict whereas structural factors determine the targets of conflict.

The Sample of Preindustrial Societies

The study described in this chapter is designed to produce generalizations about conflict behavior in preindustrial societies, based on data from a worldwide sample of such societies. Drawing such a sample first involves defining the population of the world's preindustrial societies. Critical to testing hypotheses about the functional association among the behaviors and other variables in the sample is the assumption that the societies are sufficiently independent so that any observed relationship we discover is not due to the effects of intercultural contact, or borrowing. This question, known as Galton's problem, stymied systematic cross-cultural studies for some time until researchers developed procedures for either limiting the effects of diffusion or measuring it and incorporating diffusion into their substantive explanations (Dow et al. 1984; Naroll 1973; Ross and Homer 1976).

To address the problems of sampling and diffusion, Murdock and White (1969) developed the Standard Cross-Cultural Sample (sccs). Over the past two decades a large number of primary and secondary studies in cross-cultural research have utilized this sample. Murdock and White first identified 186 linguistically and culturally distinct "sampling provinces" of the world and then selected one society from each for inclusion in the sample, generally because of the quality of its ethnographic coverage. For each society a community was pinpointed historically and geographically, as much as possible, to avoid confounding it with neighboring, but different communities or the same community at different points in time.[1]

The sccs is appropriate for my cross-cultural study of conflict for several reasons: anthropologists recognize its representativeness in careful sampling of the major subregions and cultural groups in the preindustrial world; the sample societies are sufficiently distinct and distant from one another so that diffusion, or Galton's problem, does not chal-

---

1. Although the society is the sampling unit, a specific local community within each society is the coding unit. For the descriptions of the specific focal communities see Murdock and White (1969). The ethnographic reports and other materials on many, but not all, of the societies in the sccs are included in the Human Relations Area Files, a full text archive containing the ethnographic reports on over 350 societies. The indexing system of the Human Relations Area Files allows researchers to search the files on any single society quickly for information on specific questions.

lenge the results; and published codes for these societies are readily available on a large number of economic, social structural, and socialization variables (Barry and Schlegel 1980). My coding efforts, therefore, could focus on political variables. Because of limited resources, the sample used here consisted of the even-numbered SCCS societies, with substitutions from the odd-numbered half in cases where missing data made an even-numbered case of dubious value. In the end, my sample totals ninety societies.[2]

In table 5.1 I show some characteristics of the sample, a profile of the political, social, and economic diversity in the preindustrial societies from throughout the world.[3] The data show that about half the societies are stateless, meaning there is no authority exercised beyond the local community; one fifth are large states. Political authorities are highly differentiated from the rest of the population in about 20 percent of the cases but are virtually nonexistent in about 13 percent. Typical local community size is fewer than fifty persons in 13 percent of the societies and over one thousand in 9 percent, with the median community size between one hundred and two hundred persons, mainly kin. Just half the sample societies are made up of permanent settlements; slightly more than a quarter are nomadic or seminomadic.

Agriculture is the most important economic activity in more than half the societies, but more than one quarter practice no agriculture whatsoever, and even the agricultural societies range from intensive (either with or without the plow), to shifting cultivation (using simple digging sticks). Where agriculture is not the dominant subsistence activity, about 40 percent of the societies rely on domesticated animals as either pastoralists or mounted hunters, and the remainder are foragers who gather, hunt, or fish. Most societies combine several subsistence activities.

Coding Political Conflict

The raw data for a quantitative cross-cultural study are the ethnographic reports of anthropologists, missionaries, travelers, and others.

2. See Ross (1983) for greater detail concerning the sampling and coding procedures and the raw data codes.
3. The Murdock and White sample does include some European preindustrial societies, but the region is nonetheless underrepresented, which reflects the bias of the field of anthropology toward nonwestern societies.

Table 5.1
Characteristics of the Sample

Region

	Number	%
Africa	16	17.8
Circum—Mediterranean	11	12.2
East Eurasia	15	16.7
Insular Pacific	15	16.7
North America	17	18.9
South America	16	17.8
Total	90	100.1

Source: Murdock and Wilson 1972

Levels of Sovereignty

	Number	%
Stateless—local community is highest level	47	52.2
One level above local community	16	17.8
Small state	10	11.1
Large state	17	18.9
Total	90	100.0

Source: Tuden and Marshall 1972

Subsistence Type

	Number	%
Foragers	21	23.3
Domesticated animals	13	14.4
Shifting agriculture	22	24.4
Horticulture	9	10.0
Advanced agriculture	25	27.8
Total	90	99.9

Source: World Cultures 1989; variable 858

Local Community Population

	Number	%
Less than 50	12	13.3
50 to 99	17	18.9
100 to 199	23	25.6
200 to 399	13	14.4
400 to 999	17	18.9
More than 1,000	8	8.9
Total	90	100.0

Source: Murdock and Wilson 1972

Fixity of Settlement

	Number	%
Nomadic	17	18.9
Seminomadic	10	11.1
Rotation	4	4.4
Semisedentary	7	7.8
Horticulture	7	7.8
Permanent settlements	45	50.0
Total	90	100.0

Source: Murdock and Wilson 1972

Intensity of Cultivation

	Number	%
No agriculture	23	25.6
Casual agriculture	6	6.6
Shifting agriculture	25	27.8
Impermanent settlements	8	8.9
Intensive agriculture	28	31.1
Total	90	100.0

Source: World Cultures 1989; variable 232

(Table 5.1 continues)

Table 5.1 (*continued*)

Political Role Differentiation	Number	%
Full-time leaders—high differentiation from the rest of the population	18	20.0
Full-time leaders—moderate differentiation	10	11.1
Full-time leaders—richer than others but not otherwise distinct	11	12.2
Full-time leaders—low differentiation	7	7.8
Leaders exist who are richer than others	18	20.0
Leaders exist who are older and considered wiser	15	16.7
No leader roles	11	12.2
Total	90	99.9

Source: Ross 1983

In a sense the researcher "interviews" the reports about specific areas of interest, in this case, internal and external conflict. The same questions are asked about each society and the answers recorded on a standardized coding form.[4]

Ethnographic reports contain descriptions of specific conflicts, as well as statements which permit judgments about their severity and frequency in a society. Often an ethnographer reports on a few incidents which were either reported to him or her or (less often) observed directly. I used these descriptions to examine conflicts at three levels: between people within a community, between people in different communities of the same society, and between different societies. To indicate the intensity of conflict, coders were instructed to note the importance of violence, the degree to which feuding and bitter factionalism are regular features of the society, the importance of organized raiding, and the degree of disruption to daily life such events produce.[5] Another variable

4. Coders also noted specific page citations where the data relevant to the coding decision were found. In addition, they recorded descriptions of particular disputes or statements about the relative importance or frequency of certain kinds of conflict or conflict management. In addition to questions about internal and external conflict, the coders were also interested in questions about authority and community in these same societies and the full description of all the variables coded is found in Ross (1983). For greater discussion of some of the problems involved in the coding see Ross (1988c) and appendix B below.

5. Rarely are these reports quantitative, but it is nonetheless possible to infer relative frequency using such ordinal categories as frequently, commonly, occasionally, and rarely.

was external warfare, defined as systematic intergroup fighting in which there is the possibility of killing one's opponent. The coders also looked at the acceptability of violence toward members of the local community, toward people in the same society but outside the local community, and toward people in other societies. Finally, societies received scores based on how conflicts are typically managed and the degree to which physical force, joint problem solving (for example, two-party negotiation or mediation), and third-party adjudication are used as conflict management procedures. While these conflict management questions are not a central focus here, analyzing them helped provide a complete picture of the nature of conflict in a community.

Distinguishing between internal and external conflict was not always easy. In the case of large states or chiefdoms, it is relatively simple to make such a distinction given that these units clearly form distinct political and social entities. In the case of stateless societies, however, deciding when two smaller units are best seen as constituent parts of a single society and when they are distinct is not easy, because many such communities consider themselves linked to neighboring communities (and therefore constituting a single society) for some purposes but not others (Brown 1982; Leach 1954; Naroll 1964; Helm 1967).[6] The theoretical literature does not provide a simple test for defining a society like the existence of a common language or intermarriage. Rather, it suggests that frequently group definition is flexible and situational (Barth 1969). For the purposes of the present study, coders were instructed to decide the boundary question from the perspective of the community, as presented by the ethnographer. Disputes with neighboring communities are classified as internal or external war depending on how the people seemed to view the group they were fighting.[7]

The coding process used here recorded forty-one different variables measuring authority, conflict, and community in the ninety societies (Ross 1983). Thirteen are directly relevant to the comparison of

6. Brown (1982), discussing highland New Guinea, points out that although communities may be independent politically (in that there is no higher authority), when there are important exchanges it is often most useful to view them as part of an interdependent system.

7. For more discussion of this problem and some examples of the specific coding decisions, see Ross (1983).

conflict behavior across communities. The measures are close-ended variables with generally three or four coding categories. The coders selected one of the categories and noted the source of the data for a code and any substantive points relevant to the coding decision.

In cases where multiple sources were available for the same society, coders were instructed to score the society for the earliest point in time for which the data seemed reliable. The aim was to minimize the impact of pacification associated with western colonialism on the codes, particularly those which measure the capacity of a community to fight and otherwise act independently vis-à-vis its neighbors.[8] Of course, this dilemma is complex because virtually all societies have some contact with their neighbors. The idea of the pristine society unseen by outsiders prior to European contact is a product of western thought, not social or political reality. Western contact is only one form of outside involvement which may modify social and political relations. Second, there are indirect ways in which western contact affects a society. For example, Ferguson (1992) discusses the uneven availability of trade goods among the Yanomamo and the impact on local rivalries far before there was an outside pacification of the region.

When there were disagreements between the sources for the same society, an attempt was made to resolve disagreements by referring to additional sources or, when necessary, by making judgments about the plausibility of the data from each source.[9] In the final coding, every

8. Ember and Ember (1992), who coded internal and external warfare for many of the same societies in the sample, specify whether or not a society was pacified at the focal time period. As one might expect, the correlation between my scores on warfare and those of Ember and Ember is much higher when looking only at their unpacified cases than for the entire sample (Ember, Ember, and Ross 1992).

9. Naroll (1962) identifies useful data quality control measures. In general, a source is considered superior when the researcher spends a longer time in the field, speaks the local language, focuses on the variable being coded, cites several different sources, or presents other data which are consistent with the data on this variable. In the coding for this study, more common than disagreements between sources were situations where one source discusses a particular domain while another ignores it entirely. Regional experts were sometimes helpful in the selection of data from among multiple sources, a procedure I turned to perhaps a dozen occasions in this study.

variable for each society was scored independently by myself and another coder. The codings were compared, differences were discussed, and a final set of codes was agreed on.[10]

The frequency distributions of the conflict and conflict management variables are presented in table 5.2. Although I was interested in an overall measure of internal and external conflict for each society, there is no single quantitative assessment. Instead, my approach was to develop a number of individual measures for specific aspects of internal and external conflict and then later determine the extent to which these form a common domain. Only then were the variables which were highly related empirically combined to construct composite measures (Campbell and Fiske 1959; Campbell 1988; Ember et al. 1991; Romney 1989).

Measures of Political Conflict

The data in table 5.2 suggest the diversity of conflict behavior in the world's preindustrial societies and provide no support for the argument that they share one characteristic type of conflict. At least one case is coded at each data point on virtually all variables. Some societies are low in local community or intercommunity conflict, while others abound in such struggles. In general terms, conflict is lowest within local communities, moderate between communities of the same society, and highest between communities of different societies. Physical force is used in a good proportion of the disputes in preindustrial societies, and although there are societies where warfare seems to be rare, these are in the minority.

A first step in analyzing these data is to investigate the relationship among the different conflict measures. To what extent are societies in which one form of conflict is high more likely to have high scores on

10. This approach is inconsistent with traditional notions of reliability in two ways: the coders' awareness of hypotheses under consideration and interactive coding, which made computation of reliability coefficients impossible. I used this procedure because I believe that the naïve coder is not always the best coder and that reliability can result from parallel systematic errors (see Bradley 1989). These codes also benefited from the increased understanding and insights that often developed from discussion of each society during the coding process and from attention paid to the sources of disagreements, in particular. For further discussion of this point of view see Ross (1983:171–173).

Table 5.2
Cross-Cultural Measures of Conflict

Number of cases	Percentage of cases	Variable

1. **Local conflict.** At the level of the local community it is neither useful nor easy to distinguish between political conflict in particular and social conflict more generally. The measures of local community and intercommunity conflict assess the frequency or severity of conflict.

Number of cases	Percentage of cases	Variable
4	4.4	1 Conflict in the community is endemic—it seems to be a reality of daily existence. Indicators may be physical violence, feuding, or bitter factionalism
20	22.2	2 Conflict in the community is high. While physical violence, feuding, and factionalism may be present, they are not so high as to be a pervasive aspect of daily life
46	51.1	3 Conflict in the community is moderate. There may be disagreements and severe differences in the community, but they do not generally result in high levels of violence or disruption
20	22.2	4 Conflict in the community is relatively mild or rare
0		9 not codable
Total 90	99.9	

2. **Intercommunity conflict** (between communities of the same society)

Number of cases	Percentage of cases	Variable
25	28.1	1 Endemic (physical violence, feuding, or raiding regularly occur)
23	25.8	2 Moderately high (often involving physical violence)
21	23.6	3 Moderate (tendency to manage disputes in a peaceful manner)
20	22.5	4 Relatively mild or rare
1		9 not codable
Total 90	100.0	

3. **Physical force** (use of force by individuals involved in disputes, not institutionalized force such as police)

Number of cases	Percentage of cases	Variable
34	37.8	1 Often used
32	35.6	2 Sometimes used
24	26.7	3 Rarely or never used
0		4 not codable
Total 90	100.1	

Table 5.2 (*continued*)

Number of cases	Percentage of cases	Variable

4. Compliance with community norms and decisions on the part of individuals in the community

43	50	1 High
31	36	2 Moderate
12	14	3 Highly variable
4		4 not codable
Total 90	100.0	

5. Internal warfare—organized, systematic violence waged by one group in the society against another, individuals acting alone

31	36.5	1 Warfare between groups of the same society is frequent (at least once a year)
14	16.5	2 Common (at least once every five years)
10	11.8	3 Occasional (at least once every generation)
30	35.3	4 Rare or nonexistent
5		9 not codable
Total 90	100.1	

6. External warfare (wars with other societies)

45	53.6	1 Frequent (at least once a year)
13	15.5	2 Common (at least once every five years)
6	7.1	3 Occasional (at least once every generation)
20	23.8	4 Rare or nonexistent
6		9 not codable
Total 90	100.0	

7. Hostility toward other societies. Unlike the warfare variable that measures behaviors, this variable evaluates the feelings toward other societies

28	37.8	1 Extensive—quite bitter feelings exist toward almost all outsiders
18	24.3	2 High—bitter feelings often exist toward outsiders, but not always
17	23.0	3 Moderate—sometimes bitter feelings exist, but there is much differentiation among outsiders
11	14.9	4 Low—little hostility is shown to outsiders
16		9 not codable
Total 90	100.0	

8. Acceptability of violence directed at members of the local community

0	0.0	1 Valued
7	8.1	2 Accepted
18	20.9	3 Tolerated
61	70.9	4 Disapproved
4		9 not codable
Total 90	99.9	

(Table 5.2 continues)

Table 5.2 (*continued*)

	Number of cases	Percentage of cases	Variable

9. Acceptability of violence directed at members of the same society outside the local community

	12	15.6	1 Valued
	28	36.4	2 Accepted
	10	13.0	3 Tolerated
	27	35.1	4 Disapproved
	13		9 not codable
Total	90	100.1	

10. Acceptability of violence directed at other societies

	39	60.9	1 Valued
	16	25.0	2 Accepted
	3	4.7	3 Tolerated
	6	9.4	4 Disapproved
	26		9 not codable
Total	90	100.0	

11. Conflict management. Although the categories are not mutually exclusive, the aim here is to assess a society's dominant mode of dealing with conflicts as they arise

	31	35.2	1 Contending parties are encouraged to find a solution on their own
	27	30.7	2 New parties are easily drawn in and there are strong social pressures for resolving disputes using informal mechanisms
	30	34.1	3 Authorities get involved and work to achieve a settlement
	2		4 not codable
Total	90	100.0	

12. Mediation, negotiation, or arbitration—third-party involvement without binding decision making as in litigation

	57	64.8	1 Often used to settle disputes between members of the society
	19	21.6	2 Sometimes used to settle disputes between members of the society
	12	13.6	3 Rarely or never used to settle disputes between members of the society
	2		9 not codable
Total	90	100.0	

13. Adjudication—binding third-party decisions whether or not societies have formal court systems

	27	30.3	1 Often used
	21	23.6	2 Sometimes used
	41	46.1	3 Rarely or never used
	1		9 not codable
Total	90	100.0	

other measures? To what extent are there patterns among the individual conflict measures which can justify our grouping them into a small number of general indicators?

Composite Measures of Internal and External Conflict

Factor analysis is a statistical technique used to identify an underlying pattern in a large group of variables. For this study, the factor analysis included all political variables coded in the cross-cultural study along with eight from measures of political organization coded by Tuden and Marshall (1972) for the same societies. The results identified five dimensions of political life (Ross 1983). Two dimensions describe the organization of political power and authority, one describes patterns of cross-cutting ties, and two, which are the focus of attention here, measure internal and external conflict and violence (see table 5.3). The variables loading on each factor were then used to form two scales: internal conflict and violence, and external conflict and warfare.[11] Each factor represents the common variation on a particular dimension, and the factor loading is the correlation of each variable with that factor. Variables which load highly on a factor, then, indicate a common pattern underlying it.

Internal Conflict and Violence

The six variables making up the internal conflict and violence scale, in descending order of importance, are as follows: the severity of conflict between residents of different communities in the same society; the acceptability of using violence against members of the same society outside the local community; the frequency of internal warfare; the severity of conflict within local communities in the society; the degree to which physical force is used as a mechanism for dispute settlement; the acceptability of violence against members of the community; and the

11. Each scale consists of the sum of the scores of the variables on each dimension after they have been standardized and multiplied by their squared factor loadings. The raw scores for each of the component variables as well as the scores for each society on these composite scales are found in Ross (1983:186–187). In cases missing data for a variable, the sample mean for that variable is substituted.

Table 5.3
Factor Loadings for Internal and External Conflict Measures

Internal conflict and violence

Intercommunity conflict (2)	.94
Acceptability of violence directed at members of same society outside local community (9)	.90
Internal warfare frequency (5)	.81
Local community conflict (1)	.68
Physical force (3)	.67
Acceptability of violence against members of the local community (8)	.55
Compliance with local community norms and decisions (4)	.52

External conflict and warfare

External warfare frequency (6)	.86
Hostility toward other societies (7)	.69
Acceptability of violence directed at other societies (10)	.64

Note: Variable numbers from Table 5.2 appear in parentheses

variability in compliance with norms and decisions on the part of members of the local community.

The internal conflict and violence dimension distinguishes societies in terms of the level and severity of disputes. Legitimation and frequency of physical violence, feuding, and strong factionalism within and between communities all characterize the high-conflict societies, as does irregular compliance with local community norms and decisions. In these societies, intense conflict is a reality of daily life and organizes activities and perceptions. No phase of daily life—whether it is subsistence activities, the movement of people or goods, the socialization of children, ritual activities, or building a house—fails to be influenced by who are friends and who are foes and where any of them might be at a given time. The Jivaro of Ecuador, whose patterns of conflict are described in the next section, and the Mae Enga of Papua New Guinea, discussed in chapter 6, score high on this dimension.

Societies scoring in the middle of the internal conflict scale, like the Kikuyu of Kenya, have regular conflict, but internal warfare and the use of violence in local disputes is less common. Local Kikuyu communities or ridges contain patrilineal kin, and key decisions are made by elders who meet in council. Cutting across the kinship group is an age organization of males initiated at the same time which links Kikuyu from different communities. Although high levels of hostility sometimes exist between communities and disputes break out within them, the elders are often effective in limiting escalation by offering nonbinding decisions (Middleton and Kershaw 1965:43–49). Warfare between Kikuyu communities occurs occasionally but is limited by age association, intermarriage, and other ritual ties.

In societies low in internal conflict, like the Mbuti of Zaire described in chapter 1, few incidents that could lead to intense conflict actually do. In low-conflict societies, differences which arise are often managed in such a way that rancor, polarization, and outright violence are avoided. Broadly based social identities often link people in the same community and between communities so that common interests are emphasized more than differences. Although conflicts develop, and some evoke strong feelings, the existence of cross-cutting ties leads to acceptable solutions before the dispute gets out of hand and violence escalates.

External Conflict and Warfare

Three variables make up the external conflict and warfare scale: the frequency of external warfare, the degree of hostility toward other societies (not limited to war), and the acceptability of violence directed toward people in other societies. Organized intergroup fighting—warfare—is more central to this dimension than to the internal conflict scale, and this is reflected by the inclusion of the term warfare in the full label for this scale.

Societies scoring high in external conflict are found in all parts of the world, in all sizes, and in different ecological settings. The Buganda of Uganda are a centralized state in a densely populated region of Africa; the Comanche are a Plains Indian society of mounted hunters; the Maori are a Pacific island society that take long ocean voyages to pursue enemies; and the Jivaro are a relatively isolated forest people in Ecuador. The description of three of these four societies in the next section offers a feel for the different dynamics underlying external conflict from setting to setting.

Contact with other societies is moderately related to external conflict, but there are many cases which fail to fit this pattern. External conflict requires more than simply the opportunity to fight outsiders. The !Kung of southern Africa and the Tikopia of Polynesia are both relatively isolated societies low in external conflict, yet there are also isolated groups like the Akwe-Shavante of Brazil (Maybury-Lewis 1967), whose contacts with outsiders are highly conflictual. Conversely, there are societies with frequent contact with outsiders like the Manus of the Pacific, whose external conflict scores are not high. Neither the Lepcha of Sikkim nor the Mbuti are highly isolated, but they have little external warfare. Turnbull (1962) describes the relation between the Mbuti and local agricultural peoples as fraught with tension and latent aggression but not organized fighting.

Internal and External Conflict

There is a moderately high correlation between the measures of internal conflict and violence and external conflict and warfare ($r = .39$; $N = 90$).[12] Although this suggests that conflict, at least in preindustrial societies, tends to generalize across group boundaries, in a good number of cases this is not the case. In chapters 7 and 8 I shall explore the degree to which a society's social organization predicts whether internal and external conflict are at similar or different levels.

Internal and External Conflict in Four Societies

The discussion of internal and external conflict has not yet addressed the dynamics of conflict in specific contexts. In the next few pages, therefore, I describe but do not claim to explain conflict in four societies in order to offer a more concrete sense of the dynamics of the culture of conflict in particular societies. The Jivaro of Ecuador are a small-scale society with no formal leaders in which high conflict and violence against internal and external enemies are common. The next two societies have high levels of external conflict and warfare with low or modest levels of internal conflict. The Buganda are an example of a predatory preindustrial state that grows at the expense of its neighbors, while the Comanche of the American Plains are a band society fighting extensively and effectively with some of its neighbors before finally succumbing to white conquest in the second half of the nineteenth century. In these cases, institutions and practices perpetuate intense or frequent conflict, at least in certain domains. There are also cases in which cultural practices discourage conflict. In the profile of the Lepcha, a remote mountain people of Sikkim, conflict is not severe and organized

12. This is statistically significant at the .001 level.

violence virtually unknown. The cases presented here (as well as the peaceful Mbuti in chapter 1 and the conflictual Mae Enga in chapter 6) suggest the complex ways in which cultural systems of high and low conflict can be organized. They illustrate the need to reject overly simple explanations for conflict that claim to fit all preindustrial societies.

Jivaro: High Levels of Internal and External Conflict

High levels of internal and external conflict characterize life among the Jivaro, a people who live in western Ecuador near the Peruvian border. Although the Jivaro are at the lower end of the scale of political and social complexity, there are other societies at the same level of complexity with different conflict patterns. Their level of complexity alone does not account for their high conflict. Harner (1972) describes a pattern among the Jivaro of extensive feuding, killing, and warfare supported by supernatural beliefs and practices. Deeply held beliefs that enemies may attack at any time provide a fundamental motivation for the organization of daily life and a justification for one's own preemptive aggression.

The Jivaro live in widely scattered houses grouped into informal neighborhoods with a population density of approximately one person per square mile. They have no formal leaders and no authority is exercised above the level of the household. Cooperation, when it occurs in trade, agriculture, hunting, or fighting, is based on the mobilization of personal ties and interpersonal obligations. The household consists of a man, his wives and children, and his married daughters and their husbands until the birth of their first child, after which they are expected to construct their own house, preferably in the same neighborhood. Households move often as game becomes scarce in an area, gardens become overgrown, nearby firewood becomes depleted, or potential enemies become more threatening. Although primary kin ties are the most certain connections a Jivaro man knows, the absence of formal obligations makes counting on them problematic at times. Brothers, for example, compete for the same women, and matrilocal residence rules as well as high mobility mean that brothers are often separated geographically.

A man becomes a leader among the Jivaro by earning recognition as an outstanding killer or shaman (Harner 1972:111). The former gains prestige and social obligations by helping people of his locality eliminate their enemies (Harner 1972:112). By taking a life, a man not only avenges the deaths of others but also gains the spiritual power to be known, respected, feared, and protected. Shamans, like killers, are able to help others attack their enemies.

In the absence of political authority or mechanisms for joint problem solving among disputants, aggrieved individuals can only seek retaliation for antisocial acts against either the alleged transgressors or certain of their close kin.[13] This self-help response involves the mobilization of close kin and loyal allies and invariably includes the use of physical force. Rather than ending a dispute, such action is more likely to increase conflict, for, as Harner points out, there is generally widespread disagreement about whether or not each act was a justified response to a previous act. Just as significant, he notes, is the fact that in many cases, like those involving witchcraft or poisoning, the guilt or innocence of a particular party cannot be demonstrated. Feuds, Harner says, are long standing, and even when one party formally initiates a feud with another, attacks may not occur for several years. Hence the need for Jivaro to remain forever vigilant lest their enemies catch them unaware.

Harner describes organized raiding arising from long-standing feuds among the Jivaro, and warlike raiding for heads and booty which the Jivaro launch against their non-Jivaro speaking neighbors. In each case, individuals mobilize fighting units from among their close kin and neighbors in addition to making sure that they have taken the proper supernatural precautions. The quest for personal glory and spiritual power makes it possible to form war parties which unite otherwise feuding individuals or their kin, although the Jivaro also fear that during travels or battles a man may settle an old score with a rival.

In Jivaro society, like the Yanomamo described in chapter 1, concerns about conflict and violence affect most aspects of daily life. There is little institutionalized cooperation and little interpersonal trust. As a result, individuals, with some assistance from close kin and occasional friends, seek security in personal achievements and the establishment

13. Harner reports that "when a man is fatally poisoned [by a woman], the aggrieved family may not attempt to kill the guilty woman, if they feel that the death of the woman would be inadequate to compensate for the death of a man. In such a case, they assume that the proper sanction is to poison the guilty woman's brother" (Harner 1972:173).

of reputations for aggressiveness. Feuding is pervasive and constant attention to possible threats is necessary for survival.

Buganda: A Predatory State

The Buganda kingdom is a strong, centralized, and aggressive preindustrial state. In the nineteenth century it occupied an area bordering the north side of Lake Victoria for about 150 miles and extending 50 or 60 miles inland (Fallers 1964a). The population included about one million Buganda and another million or so subjects living in tributary states (Fallers 1964b:104). The economic system frees men for wars which are waged annually during the dry season, and the Buganda state is "essentially a military machine designed for the exploitation of its weaker neighbors" (Wrigley 1964:19). Expansion and plunder are critical in keeping the state going. Women, children, and livestock are the critical booty sought by the Buganda and used by the *Kabaka* (head of state) to reward local chiefs and by the chiefs to reward the men under their command.

The exercise of authority in the family, the local chiefdom, and the state is harsh and arbitrary (Richards 1964b:295). Fathers are authoritarian and distant, demanding absolute obedience from children and punishing them severely at times (Richards 1964a). Afterward children are supposed to thank them for showing attention and affection, just as it is expected that parents thank the Kabaka if he finds reason to kill one of their children (Richards 1964a:261–262). Within such a system, a combination of ambition, obedience, and cunning is needed for success, but the legitimacy of competition is accepted by all. Although mother-child and brother-sister relationships are far less authoritarian than the father-child ties (Richards 1964a), fear of those who exercise authority is a central cultural theme.

At each level of the system, authority is maintained both through rewards and through fear. By the early nineteenth century, no effective local power groups could challenge the central authority. Although locally based, patrilineal totemic clans exist, they cannot act independently of the Kabaka, and because their offices may be held by a wide range of persons (thus offering great latitude in choice to higher-ups), no effective opposition to the centralized state authority developed.

Ethnographic reports indicate that before the arrival of the British in the latter part of the nineteenth century, the level of internal conflict was low in Buganda. There are land disputes, which do not seem severe, occasional fighting among rival princes (Roscoe 1911:346), and some fighting between clans (Mair 1934:185). Often disputes are taken to chiefs (Fallers 1964b) or local courts (Mair 1934) for adjudication. Clearly there is a good deal of state-sanctioned violence as well. The control system here, and in such other preindustrial states as the Aztecs, suppresses internal conflict and directs it externally. The Buganda case shows how low conflict can be a product of state control and how the internal order can be predicated on external conquests. Investigation of Buganda society points to the need to consider who benefits from any system of conflict management and to be aware of different factors leading to low levels of conflict.

Comanche: A Warlike Band Society

The predatory state is not the only organization with high levels of external conflict; some nonstate societies also are effective in fighting outsiders. For example, LeVine (1965) and others have suggested that in matrilocal societies like the Mundurucu, the dispersion of related males at marriage enhances internal unity and makes the society more hostile to outsiders. A different dynamic is found in hunting societies like some of the Plains Indian tribes, where hunting and horsemanship skills are also crucial in warfare.

The Comanche of the Great Plains of North America are a band society organized around buffalo hunting and warfare, the most important male activities,[14] both requiring good horsemanship and skill with weapons. Hoebel (1940) and Wallace and Hoebel (1952) describe the Comanche as highly individualistic and nonhierarchical. The Comanche live in bands of varying sizes, and individuals or families sometimes change bands. Upon their marriage a new couple is expected to live virilocally (with the husband's kin), although a man continues to have important obligations to his wife's kin, and children generally develop strong emotional attachments to their maternal grandparents. Brothers are often very close, and sororal polygyny is well known. Not surprisingly, intraband marriage is the preferred arrangement (provided incest taboos are not violated).

14. The Plains Indian pattern of buffalo hunting and warfare developed with the arrival of the horse following the arrival of the Spanish in the New World.

Bands are governed by a council representing all kin groups in the community. The council decides when and where the band moves, undertakes a tribal war, makes peace, seeks an alliance, and selects the time and place of the summer hunt, as well as overseeing community religious services, trade, and allocation of supplies to widows and the needy (Wallace and Hoebel 1952:215). War leaders are younger and more authoritarian than chiefs in time of peace, for success in battle depends upon close coordination and certainty. In theory, anyone can initiate a raid, and a man's ability to do so depends only on his ability to recruit followers.

Prior to the introduction of the horse on the plains, warfare was sporadic and not bloody. The horse provided both a new motive for war and a new means for carrying it out. Warfare became central to daily life and came to provide the basis of rank and status in Comanche society (Wallace and Hoebel 1952:245). Warfare among Comanche bands is unknown and there was long-term peace with the Kiowa to the north after 1790 and with the Cheyennes to the east after 1840. In contrast, wars with neighbors in the other directions (especially the Apache) are common. Some military campaigns are short, whereas others cover hundreds of miles and last several months. The aims of warfare are securing horses and captives (many of whom are integrated into Comanche society), protecting their hunting grounds from encroachment, exacting revenge, and especially attaining individual glory. Although booty is collected, and the war leader has absolute say over its disposition, leaders often keep little for themselves and sometimes give it all away upon returning home (Wallace and Hoebel 1952:267, 272). The social recognition of war honors is institutionalized through the practice of "counting coup"—an individual exploit involving contact with the enemy that is socially and publicly recognized as worthy of distinction (Wallace and Hoebel 1952:246). Although raiding and warfare recognize outstanding individual efforts, the community is involved in decisions regarding war, alliances, and peace making. Important community rituals precede the departure of a war party and greet them upon their return, including displaying scalps which have been taken.

Lepcha: Low Level of Internal Conflict

Although the Mbuti, !Kung Bushmen, or Semai have received much more ethnographic attention in recent years, the Lepcha of Nepal, which Gorer (1938) studied, are an equally important example of a peaceful society. Although the community he describes was under the control of the maharajah of Sikkim and was therefore part of a preindustrial state on the fringes of the British Empire, the area itself was quite isolated. Gorer's analysis makes it clear that the Lepchas' low level of internal conflict is not just a function of outside political authority.[15]

In Zongu, the region of Nepal Gorer studied, there are twelve Lepcha villages in which people often live and work quite some distance from each other. On certain tasks, however, there is extensive cooperation. For Gorer, an outstanding feature of Lepcha culture is its explicit focus on sexual behavior which is detached from such strong emotions as jealousy. Brothers are close and sometimes practice a form of polyandry in which they share the same wife. Younger brothers regularly have their first sexual experiences with an older brother's wife, who may eventually become his own wife upon the older brother's death.

Overt conflicts are relatively few and not very severe on the rare occasions when they occur. Theft is virtually unknown and the last authenticated murder took place two centuries before Gorer's fieldwork in the 1930s. Individuals do, however, fall into arrears on their taxes and seek the help of the community in meeting their debts. Sorcery, practiced in the past, is no longer used. Moving boundary marks in the fields, a potential cause of disputes, had not occurred in the fifteen years preceding Gorer's research. In the only case of community conflict which Gorer (1938:124–126) reports, a man named Tempa, appointed muktair (the direct representative of the hereditary ruler) for half the villages, was accused of unjustifiable use of violence and of being an outsider who did not know the ways of the Lepcha. The mandals (heads of each of the villages) met to discuss the matter, excluding Tempa from any feasts or public gatherings and then petitioned the court, which honored the mandals' request to remove Tempa from office.

No lasting animosity was displayed against Tempa but everybody knows the history and draws the moral; Tempa was angry, but being faced with complete unanimity he could do nothing. Today he is still angry with Tak-

15. The Lepcha are also low in external conflict, but because this society is pacified and partially controlled from the outside I do not emphasize this aspect. Gorer suggests that during the eighteenth and nineteenth centuries when Tibetan and Nepalese tribes invaded the area, the Lepcha did not resist their incursions but retreated to even more remote mountain areas.

neum *youmi* [a senior village official] and the two never visit each other on any occasion; they will, however, eat together in neutral places without quarrelling. This possibility of exclusion is the major Lepcha sanction; the person who is not allowed to go to feasts and is not visited, who is in fact "sent to Coventry," leads a very dull and lonely life; but more than that, if he is not allowed to help other people other people will not help him and it is hard to get through the agricultural and domestic work without help. Similar pressure, it is said, is brought to bear when anybody in authority, whether that authority be hereditary or through Court appointment, shows any tendency to abuse his position. It is a most effective control. (Gorer 1938:126)

Quarreling is so strongly disapproved that it is the responsibility of all to make every effort to prevent disputes or to stop them once they have broken out. An annual ceremony destroys the trinity of devils that causes quarrels (Gorer 1938:139). Gorer reports that if (despite the precautions) a quarrel does occur, a mutual friend is likely to hold a feast for the disputants to try to patch up the trouble; if it persists it is assumed to be a problem involving the supernatural and exorcism is used (Gorer 1938:140). Community officials are likely to become involved as soon as they hear of a quarrel. The gyapon (a village administrative official) visits the parties and tries to mediate the differences. If another meeting is needed, each side brings chi (a local alcoholic drink) and a certain sum of money. These intermediaries take statements from both parties, who are then warned that they will be heavily fined if they cannot resolve their differences. If an agreement is reached, the disputants and mediators feast together, a sermon about the duty of living in peace together is delivered, the fines are returned, and the matter is ended (Gorer 1938:140). Gorer reports two such serious quarrels in the three years preceding his stay in the area.

Gorer expands the notion of aggression to include mastery over the environment—including both objects and ideas—and offers a psychological explanation to account for low levels of aggression among the Lepcha. Socially destructive aggression against others, he hypothesizes, is a function of economic security and leisure, a condition unknown to the Lepcha who are utterly dependent upon cooperation with their neighbors for daily subsistence. The Lepchas suppress in-group aggression through strong social sanctions against quarreling and by "the social arrangements of all sexual relationships so as to exclude jealousy" (Gorer 1938:449).

Gorer concludes with a discussion of the consequences for conflict of the fact that early social relationships among the Lepcha meet the immediate satisfaction of the infant's expressed physical desires. This produces, he suggests, an early extinction of self-assertion connected to a tendency for adults to evaluate others as members of society and not as individual personalities. Low ego development among individuals allows for the suppression of competition and aggression in daily life. "They recognize no social goals which can be achieved at the expense of others, they have no social situations which separate rights and du-ties" (Gorer 1938:451).[16]

Conclusion

In this chapter I have described the worldwide sample of pre-industrial societies, the nature of the data collected about them, and the specific measures of internal and external conflict to be used in the subsequent analysis. The profile of the sample shows the great variation in conflict in the world's preindustrial societies. At the same time, most of the conflict measures cluster into two groups, internal conflict and violence and external conflict and warfare. Furthermore, high and low conflict levels are found in all regions of the world. Although internal and external conflict are positively correlated with each other statisti-cally, the linkages are more important in some cases than in others. The

16. Gorer, an early proponent of national character studies, was quite ready to move from a Freudian interpretation of experiences on the individual level to a social interpretation. For example, he says, "From the point of view of physical well being Lepcha babies appear to experience the minimum of frustration and therefore it would seem that in the first months of life there are few experiences to evoke aggression. But parallel with this gratification of phys-iological appetites there is the considerable physical restraint which the babies endure through passing the majority of their waking hours firmly tied to the back of their guardian, and also the complete lack of encouragement which their elders give to the babies' earlier self-maximizing activities and attempts to acquire body techniques and physical independence... passivity and conformity are con-stantly rewarded. I think it is legitimate to trace a connection between this partial extinction of self-assertion in early childhood and the adult Lepcha's tendency to judge their fellows in their rôle as members of society, and not as personalities. This impersonal attitude to their fellows seems to me the chief operative fac-tor for the suppression of competition and aggression in adult life" (Gorer 1938: 450–51).

profiles of individual societies show ways in which the high or low levels of conflict are tied to a society's cultural practices and institutions. In some cases conflict is primarily with internal foes, whereas in other cases opponents are more likely to be outsiders. Why conflict and violence occur at the particular level and take the form they do is the next subject of inquiry. In chapter 6 I test the social structural and psychocultural hypotheses about conflict, and in chapter 7 I then explore the relationship between internal and external conflict.

6

Cross-Cultural Patterns of
Political Conflict

Cross-cultural quantitative analysis, using a worldwide sample, offers a powerful method for evaluating the general validity of plausible theories. In this chapter I shall present the outcomes of the systematic testing of social structural and psychocultural theories about conflict. Quantitative results are presented; however, the primary focus is on examining their theoretical meaning in such a way that those not versed in statistics can follow the argument.

The statistical analysis offers support for components of the social structural and psychocultural theories, yet each is incomplete when adopted alone. In order to profit from the complementarity of the two approaches, a theory that spells out how and when the structural and psychocultural features of a society shape conflict behavior is necessary. I suggest that the psychocultural dispositions shape a society's overall level of conflict, while the structural features determine whether the targets of aggressive actions will be internal or external to the society or both.

Well-chosen single cases have a long and honorable role in social science theorizing. Although they cannot provide convincing tests for general theories, they are helpful in articulating theories and specifying how the mechanisms underlying general theories work. After presenting the statistical results, I illustrate a theory integrating social structural and psychocultural factors for intense conflict through the case of the Mae Enga of highland New Guinea, first demonstrating compelling aspects of each theory and then suggesting how drawing on both can make for a superior theory of conflict.[1]

1. As Rule (1988) suggests, finding cases which are consistent with par-

This chapter is the first of four presenting data relevant to the theories about conflict spelled out in chapters 3 and 4, leading to the conclusion that conflict behavior is rooted in both the interests and interpretations of disputants. In this chapter I present the basic model; I develop it further in chapter 7 through an analysis of the relationship between internal and external conflict. Then in chapter 8 I examine variations in the model through an analysis of cases which deviate from the statistical model and suggest additional processes that may operate in these cases. In chapter 9 I extend the theory beyond the preindustrial societies in the cross-cultural sample to the cultures of Norway and Northern Ireland.

Cross-Cultural Evidence

My cross-cultural examination of social structural and psycho-cultural theories for political conflict begins with the conflict data from the ninety societies in the Standard Cross-Cultural Sample listed in appendix A. To what extent is the great variation in the conflict behavior of the world's preindustrial societies associated with variation in its structural or psychocultural features? (See figure 6.1 for an outline of the major hypotheses).[2]

The theory proposed here seeks to specify the effect of each independent variable on conflict behavior, not simply alone, but in the context of all the other variables, using a multiple regression model, expressed as follows:

---

ticular theories is a much weaker test of a theory than first specifying the class of cases where a theory ought to fit before examining the evidence. Too many researchers, he notes, begin with a favorite theory and then find evidence consistent with it. We might note that in another common situation, where an explanation is selected after the facts of a case are known, there is often no effort to suggest why the selected explanation is better than plausible alternatives. When the facts are known before an explanation is selected the theory has not been adequately tested; the theory still needs to be evaluated in order to confirm whether it is adequate generally or only in certain kinds of situations.

2. The codes for the political variables are found in Ross (1983), and the socioeconomic and child training variables are found in Barry and Schlegel (1980), a collection of codes originally published in *Ethnology*. Appendix B lists the variables used in the data analysis below and the way in which each is operationally defined.

Figure 6.1
Major Hypotheses Relating Social Structural and Psychocultural Theories to Internal and External Conflict

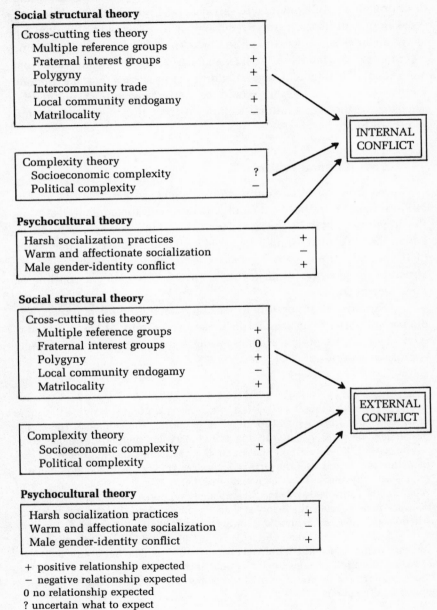

Social structural theory

Cross-cutting ties theory
- Multiple reference groups — −
- Fraternal interest groups — +
- Polygyny — +
- Intercommunity trade — −
- Local community endogamy — +
- Matrilocality — −

Complexity theory
- Socioeconomic complexity — ?
- Political complexity — −

Psychocultural theory
- Harsh socialization practices — +
- Warm and affectionate socialization — −
- Male gender-identity conflict — +

INTERNAL CONFLICT

Social structural theory

Cross-cutting ties theory
- Multiple reference groups — +
- Fraternal interest groups — 0
- Polygyny — +
- Local community endogamy — −
- Matrilocality — +

Complexity theory
- Socioeconomic complexity — +
- Political complexity

Psychocultural theory
- Harsh socialization practices — +
- Warm and affectionate socialization — −
- Male gender-identity conflict — +

EXTERNAL CONFLICT

+ positive relationship expected
− negative relationship expected
0 no relationship expected
? uncertain what to expect

$$Y_{i1} = bX_{i1} + bX_{i2} + bX_{i3} \ldots + E_i, \text{ where}$$

Y_i = society i's score on the dependent variable, internal or external conflict

X_{in} = society i's score on each independent variable

b = the slope of each X term

E_i = society i's error term, or the variance unexplained by the X terms

Because there are many moderate correlations among the independent variables, multiple regression is especially useful in showing how each of the independent variables is related to the dependent variables after the effects of the other independent variables are removed.[3] This procedure produces different and more straightforward results than those obtained from simply looking at the bivariate correlation matrix.[4]

The regression results in table 6.1 support the structural and psychocultural theories of conflict, showing that both structural and psychocultural variables are significantly related to internal and external conflict. In combination the two explain conflict better than either set of variables alone. A closer look shows that low levels of affection, harsh socialization, and male gender-identity conflict increase both internal and external conflict and violence, but that the specific structural factors associated with internal versus external conflict differ. The results suggest that there is a dispositional basis for conflict and violence rooted in early relationships, whereas the selection of internal or external targets

3. Multicollinearity is not a problem here. First, the correlations among the independent variables can produce large standard errors of the regression coefficients but did not in this instance. Second, multicollinearity does not bias the regression coefficient but only increases the standard errors.

4. A few additional comments about the regression model are in order. The regressions presented in table 6.1 were selected from several specifications. Because a number of researchers have suggested important differences between politically centralized and uncentralized societies in their handling of conflict, in addition to the substantive variables, earlier versions included sets of interaction terms for each variable in order to test for systematically different effects in uncentralized and centralized societies (see chapter 3). Interaction terms were specified as the original variable multiplied by a dummy variable (1 = uncentralized; 0 = centralized). If the regression coefficient for an interactive term is large, the original variable has a different impact in the two groups of societies. Societies were coded as centralized if Tuden and Marshall (1972) scored them as having political authority exercised beyond the level of the local community. In cases where the interaction terms produced small regression coefficients, the variable was dropped from the model presented here.

Table 6.1
Internal and External Conflict: Multiple Regressions

	Standardized Regression Coefficient (Beta)	Standard Error of Beta	Pearson Correlation##
Internal conflict and violence			
Mutiple-reference groups scale	−.29**	.11	−.24** (90)
Fraternal interest group strength in uncentralized societies	.22*	.10	.26** (90)
Polygyny	.12	.10	.20* (90)
Matrilocality#	−.07	.10	.05 (90)
Local community endogamy	.01	.10	.04 (90)
Intercommunity trade	.04	.11	.03 (89)
Socioeconomic complexity	.09	.14	.08 (90)
Political power concentration	−.11	.14	−.03 (90)
Affectionate socialization practices	−.31**	.10	−.35*** (89)
Harsh socialization practices	.22*	.10	.33*** (82)
Male gender-identity conflict	.13	.10	.05 (68)
Multiple R = .60** R Square = .36			
External conflict and warfare			
Multiple-reference groups scale in uncentralized societies	.21*	.10	.20* (90)
Fraternal interest group strength	.07	.12	.24** (87)
Polygyny	−.12	.09	.03 (90)
Matrilocality #	.11	.09	.14 (90)
Local community endogamy in uncentralized societies	.43***	.11	.28** (90)
Socioeconomic complexity	.27*	.13	.24** (90)
Political power concentration	−.12	.12	.11 (90)
Affectionate socialization practices	−.39***	.09	−.41*** (89)
Harsh socialization practices	.19*	.09	.30** (82)
Male gender-identity conflict	.32***	.08	.29** (68)
Multiple R = .69** R Square = .47			

N = 90 in the regressions
Means have been substituted for missing data in the regressions
Correlations are for all cases, not just uncentralized societies
When matrilocality is substituted for patrilocality, the value is the same but positive numbers become negative and vice versa
sample size appears in parentheses
*** statistically significant at the .001 level
** statistically significant at the .01 level
* statistically significant at the .05 level

of aggression is shaped by the structural features of a society. The targets may be outside one's society or inside it, or both.

Internal Conflict and Violence

Psychocultural dispositions and weak cross-cutting ties are significantly related to the level of conflict and violence within a society. Specifically, the data show that the more affectionate and warm and the less harsh the socialization in a society, the lower the level of political conflict and violence. Internal conflict is higher in societies with fewer multiple-reference groups and in uncentralized societies with strong fraternal interest groups. In addition, male gender-identity conflict and polygyny are worth including in the model for theoretical reasons, although their coefficients are not statistically significant.[5]

The results do not, however, support the hypothesis that societal complexity has any direct effects on internal conflict. Although the measures of socioeconomic and political complexity used here are strongly and positively related to each other (Ross 1981), when both are included in the regression political role differentiation is negatively associated with internal conflict, whereas socioeconomic complexity is positively related to it, but in neither case is the relationship statistically significant. Political differentiation (which is strongly associated with political centralization) may limit internal conflict through direct control—the peacemaking function of the state—while increasing socioeconomic complexity contributes to conflict, as there is more coveting of what one's neighbor possesses, more inequality in the distribution of valued objects and positions, and a greater capacity to organize aggression collectively (Fried 1967; Otterbein 1968).

Finally, three indicators of cross-cutting ties—matrilocality,[6] in-

5. Theoretical importance, not statistical significance, should always be the criterion for inclusion of a variable in a model (Achen 1982). In the absence of definitive theoretical guides, however, this study has been guided by the magnitude of the standardized regression coefficient and its significance level. Our discussion identifies three kinds of variables: those which are statistically significant and are included, those which are not statistically significant yet are still worth mentioning, and those variables with such low coefficients that they have no significant independent effect on the dependent variable.

6. Substituting patrilocality for matrilocality produces a result with the same value, but the sign is opposite.

tercommunity trade, and intercommunity marriage—have such low coefficients that their effect on internal conflict is negligible. In the case of matrilocality, this finding is particularly striking given the great anthropological attention paid to the impact of residence on conflict (Divale 1974; Ember 1974; LeVine 1965; LeVine and Campbell 1972).[7]

External Conflict and Warfare

Three psychocultural measures—lack of affectionate socialization, presence of harsh socialization, and male gender-identity conflict—are significantly related to the level of external violence and warfare. Structural factors also matter, but in different ways than in the case of internal violence. First, complexity theory is supported since the higher the socioeconomic complexity, the greater the external conflict.[8] Second, cross-cutting ties theory is partially upheld, for when cross-cutting ties are stronger there is more external conflict, but only in uncentralized societies, as centralized societies apparently use other mechanisms to achieve internal unity when confronted by external enemies.

One reason why societies with higher socioeconomic complexity have higher levels of external violence may be that more complex systems have greater resources to mobilize in warfare.[9] Three other factors are likely to be important: the development of occupational specialization, including military experts; the growth of stratification, hierarchy, and inequality; and the maintenance of social and political order and control (Fried 1967). External warfare may develop out of a combination of the increased capacity for fighting, the need for scarce goods, and the

7. Previous studies have focused on warfare, rather than internal conflict, as the dependent variable. Warfare is, however, a key variable on the internal conflict scale. The results presented here may be due to the difference in the dependent variables or to the use of a multivariate model as opposed to the simpler bivariate ones presented earlier.

8. As with internal conflict, there is a slight tendency for the concentration of political power to be negatively related to external conflict when it is included in the regression along with socioeconomic complexity. Although Otterbein (1970) finds that socioeconomic complexity is associated with the growth of military sophistication, he does not find any direct effect on warfare. These results, using different measures than Otterbein, indicate otherwise.

9. To evaluate this argument effectively, we need to know something about the resources of potential and actual opponents, not just the standing of a society on a worldwide scale.

problem of internal instability, as external enemies are seen as threatening internal order and become targets for frustration that cannot be expressed within a society.

Cross-cutting ties theory emphasizes how intrasocietal linkages facilitate external conflict, but the data in the worldwide sample give the theory only weak support and raise the possibility of a different sequence among the variables. Cross-cutting ties theory regards internal unity as having an effect on external conflict: these data suggest that cross-cutting ties are much more related to internal than to external conflict, and that while strong internal ties may make a group more capable of fighting with an external foe, this is not necessarily critical.[10]

The two strongest relationships between cross-cutting ties measures and external conflict hold only for the uncentralized societies in the sample, and in one of these two links the direction of the effect is the opposite of what the theory predicts. The finding that in uncentralized societies the greater the importance of multiple reference groups, the higher the level of external conflict and violence, confirms the theory's prediction. The association between high intracommunity marriage and high external conflict in uncentralized societies, however, does not. I had hypothesized that societies with strong marital links among local communities would be better able and more likely to mobilize fighting forces against external enemies, and therefore engage in less internal, but more external conflict. Perhaps, however, endogamy does not shape external conflict, but rather both endogamy and external conflict are products of a common distrust and suspiciousness of outsiders.[11]

Although several cross-cutting ties measures are not statistically significant in the regression, it is worth noting their relationship to external conflict.[12] Contrary to expectations, polygyny is negatively related to external conflict once the effects of the other variables in the model are taken into account.[13] This contrasts interestingly with the case of

10. Ember and Ember (1971) suggest that external warfare changes residence rules. D. White (1989), using a world-systems framework, argues that external conflict is a key determinant of a variety of internal processes, a topic considered in chapters 7 and 8.

11. In chapter 8 I consider more explicitly other social and political effects of conflict patterns.

12. Fraternal interest group strength, as predicted, makes no real contribution towards explaining external violence.

13. Note that there is virtually no relationship at the bivariate level.

internal conflict, which is weakly but positively associated with polygyny. Certainly this is contrary to what Divale and Harris (1976) see as an integral part of the male supremacist complex, although they refer to internal warfare (where our data support their pattern) more than external warfare. The finding here is perhaps best understood in terms of the difficulties highly polygynous societies have in achieving internal unity, because male competition for women makes it difficult for members to form a cohesive unit against outsiders. Alternatively, polygyny might be seen as a structural "luxury" which societies facing severe outside threats cannot afford.

The effect of matrilocality is easier to explain. When the regression is run without the interaction term for multiple-reference groups, matrilocality is statistically significant. When this term is included, it is not. Theoretically, matrilocal residence is one mechanism for achieving cross-cutting ties, but hardly the most powerful one.[14] Thus, the effect of matrilocality is subsumed in a broader process. Matrilocality is associated with high external conflict due to its creation of linkages among communities, but matrilocality is only one way these ties might be formed.

Summary

The relationship of psychocultural dispositions to both internal and external conflict supports a psychocultural conflict theory which says that dispositions rooted in early experiences shape a culture's style of interactions with others and interpretations of behavior. Psychocultural dispositions are critical to the development and maintenance of the culture of conflict and serve as important supports for institutions and practices which manage conflict in particular ways over time. In societies where early socialization is harsh and physically punishing, when it has little affection or warmth, and when male gender-identity conflict is high, both internal and external conflict and violence are higher. Individuals who have experienced early lack of affection and harsh treatment have much more trouble establishing warm cooperative bonds with others as adults and are more prone to view the behavior of others as hostile and threatening. Projecting threat and aggression onto others—both inside and outside one's society—provides an easy justi-

14. The correlation between matrilocality and the multiple reference groups scale is .17 ($N = 90$), which is barely significant at the .05 level.

fication for one's own violent actions. Finally, although these three dimensions of socialization are conceptually related, according to the results, each makes a statistically independent contribution toward explaining conflict.

If the same dispositional variables are related to internal and to external violence, different structural factors and local conditions are involved in the selection of targets for violence. Cross-cutting ties theory is most clearly supported in the case of internal conflict, where weak overlapping links and strong fraternal interest groups increase internal conflict levels. The case of external conflict offers less support for this theory, however, as the regression coefficients are weaker, the support comes more from uncentralized societies, and several relationships are the opposite from what the theory predicted.

Complexity theory, in contrast, accounts better for external conflict. The literature on complexity and violence may be confused, but these results point to clear associations. Though socioeconomic complexity is positively associated with both forms of conflict, only in the case of external warfare is it statistically significant. Political complexity, measured by the concentration of political power, has weak negative associations with both internal and external conflict, suggesting some capacity for more centralized systems to direct conflicts to targets of their choosing. The results also support the contention that a cross-cultural theory of conflict must account differently for uncentralized and centralized societies (Otterbein 1977; Divale and Harris 1976:531; LeVine and Campbell 1972). Because there is no authority exerted beyond the local level in uncentralized societies, fraternal interest groups, exogamous marriage, and the existence of multiple-reference groups linking local communities of the same society are important in shaping violence in these societies, whereas these same variables are not important in centralized societies.

Finally, one result from the multivariate analysis seems particularly worth highlighting. Matrilocality, which a large number of previous studies identify as a crucial predictor of external warfare, is only weakly related to external conflict once the effect of the other variables in the model is taken into account. Similarly, patrilocality is not significantly related to internal conflict and violence in the multivariate model. The point is not that these residence variables are irrelevant to understanding patterns of conflict and violence but rather that they do not operate in isolation and their effects need to be considered in the context of other

structural and psychocultural variables. Residence rules are not themselves a cause of behavior; they are an indicator of an important underlying process, the establishment of cross-cutting ties, which is clearly
supported in the multivariate analysis. My argument is not that the other
models are invalid—the bivariate correlations are more or less consistent
with earlier findings—but that they are incomplete and therefore biased.

Mae Enga Conflict and Violence[15]

To demonstrate the value of the conflict theory just proposed and
to illustrate the dynamics of the culture of conflict, I shall turn to a well-
known case: Meggitt's (1977) work on warfare among the Mae Enga of
highland New Guinea. Using his material I shall first construct a social
structural explanation for the high level of internal conflict among the
Mae Enga, then offer an alternative explanation for the same phenomenon emphasizing psychocultural factors, and finally suggest how integrating the two approaches provides a better explanation than relying
on either one alone. I think Meggitt's study is a very good one and I
shall dispute none of his facts. It is Meggitt's analysis that interests me,
because his published data (1964; 1965; 1977) on the Mae Enga allow
us to suggest plausible alternative explanations to the one he offers and
to use my own statistical results to propose a broader theoretical framework in which to place his analysis.

The Mae Enga are part of the Central Enga of Enga Province in
Papua New Guinea. Meggitt focuses on the ethnographic description of
Mae Enga warfare and points out that "the assumptions of cultural ecology have informed my ethnographic description . . . [although] as an ethnographer I am not concerned to employ this material to add to the
existing tangle of theories; I leave that to my colleagues" (1977:viii).

His description, while not explicitly linked to theory, provides
abundant support for an explanation for warfare in terms of the Mae
Enga social organization. The crucial units of political organization are
patriclans—clans tracing their linkage through men to a common male
ancestor—residing in fixed territories of about one square mile each. The
clans, the highest decision-making units, but not the larger phratries into
which they are ritually grouped, are exogamous, meaning men marry

15. An earlier, less developed discussion of this case is presented in Ross
(1986c).

women from other clans. There are no villages; rather, homesteads are dispersed throughout clan territory for defense. Although organized fighting can occur within clans, most of Meggitt's analysis concerns fighting between clans of the same or different phratries (1977:13). Population pressure is severe and growing clans easily come into conflict with their neighbors over bordering lands. When warfare breaks out between two clans, each side is likely to recruit allies, offering specific inducements for their participation in the conflict. Allies sometimes come from one's own phratry, but not necessarily, for proximity and recent history seem far more crucial in alliance formation. A war ends when one side is routed, when a stalemate develops, or when pressures from allies convince the warring parties to terminate hostilities. Negotiations between clans for ending the conflict and paying for injuries and deaths can be protracted and complicated and involve tensions not only between the warring coalitions but between clans in the same faction as well.

Meggitt's analysis of war and peacemaking stresses competition for resources (land and population) among clans, the central social and political unit of Mae Enga society. It is the clan that owns land, decides whether or not to participate in fights, takes responsibility for compensation, and provides the core focus of political identification. His evidence is highly supportive of social structural conflict theory and can be restated in its terms.

Mae Enga conflict patterns are fully consistent with the key elements of cross-cutting ties theory: that the absence of strong cross-cutting ties increases severe conflict between groups or communities. Mae Enga clans are classic fraternal interest groups. Related coresident males organize to protect their common interest in land and livestock and to exercise control over women and their offspring. Group interests, defined through localized clans, are central to conflict. Links outside the clan are far less important than those within it. While the ties between a man and his wife's relatives are ritually important and a man will try to avoid fighting his wife's relatives in an interclan battle, such affinal ties do not create permanent bonds between clans.[16] Trade also establishes

16. Meggitt (1965) discusses the importance of ties between a man and his wife's kin. Podolefsky (1984) argues that these ties once served as one mechanism for conflict management in the New Guinea Highlands and that the reduction of intertribal marriage in recent years has been an important factor in

cross-cutting ties among persons in different communities, but the Mae Enga's trade links between neighboring clans are weak since economic specialization and differentiation is minimal.[17]

An account of Mae Enga conflict emphasizing ecological and social structural factors draws attention to the ways in which the organization of society structures group interests and actions. It identifies competition for and defense of land as a primary cause of conflict between clans, and argues that the strong male centered clans are central for defending clan lands and obtaining new territory. Such an explanation for Mae Enga warfare has some limitations, however, in that it is less explicit about how Mae Enga structure gives rise to perceptions—unless we assume that all interests are "objective." If structure creates interests, those interests must be perceived to affect action. How, and when, does this occur? After all, one may easily imagine a variety of interests that are consistent with a particular structure. Why, then, do certain interests become more important than others? Furthermore, while this structural explanation for conflict behavior among the Mae Enga is plausible given its agreement with the ethnographic facts, other explanations are equally consistent and emphasize different elements. Finally, although land shortage seems to be related to warfare here, many societies in the world have land shortages but much less warfare, and areas where land is plentiful are the scene of intense fighting.

One alternative explanation for Mae Enga conflict emphasizes the role of psychocultural dispositions in physical violence. Meggitt's Mae Enga materials permit us to consider in particular how culturally learned behaviors and culturally shared perceptions can account for the frequency of Mae Enga violence in ways that differ from his social structural account. This psychocultural explanation emphasizes the role of images of the self and of others which individuals develop as a consequence of

the resurgence of warfare in the region. Gordon describes Mae Enga society as "moving through phases which alternate between situations of emphasizing corporate group structure and the network of interpersonal relations" (1983:206).

17. Podolefsky (1984) argues that a decrease in intergroup trade weakens ties among groups and is responsible, in part, for the rise in fighting in recent years. But Brown (1982) and Strathern (1974) argue that these exchanges are still quite important. Strathern sees the increasing scale of group relations as creating significant problems. Ross (1993) discusses conflict management failures in New Guinea in greater detail.

socialization involving gender-identity conflict, aggression, and attachment to others. At the center is extremely strong male-female hostility and male feelings of vulnerability, suspiciousness, distrust, and low self-concept, which become the building blocks in a projective system associated with solidarity within clan groups and intense hostility and aggressivity between them.

Male fear of female sexuality is a central organizing principle of Mae Enga daily life, as in other New Guinea societies (Herdt 1987).[18] Men of the same subclan sleep in a men's house from the age of seven or eight and conduct their meetings there. Wives live in the vicinity of the men's house with their unmarried daughters and young sons (Meggitt 1964). Female sexuality is an ever-present threat to men and the Mae Enga have many practices designed to limit its effects (1964:207). Men must take special precautions. Husbands are never with their wives during childbirth. The husband sends his wife special leaves to cleanse herself following the birth so she may return to the gardens. The new mother cannot cook for males for another month, and a husband does not see the child for two to three months for fear it still may have traces of dangerous uterine blood. During a woman's menstrual period she must remain in seclusion in a special hut and can only eat certain "female crops" (Meggitt 1964:207–209). When a boy reaches five years of age or so his father and brothers begin to warn him of the dangers of spending too much time with women and his mother begins to encourage him to spend more time in the men's house and out herding pigs with older boys. Boys who fail to heed these admonitions and who want to remain with their mothers are first ridiculed and then beaten by their fathers (1964:207).

The Mae Enga place many restrictions on women's social behavior to guard against the dangers of pollution. Women are barred from cooking meat on public occasions and from eating meat prepared at a clan cult-house. They may not enter men's houses. While a husband may enter his wife's house, he is careful never to enter the rear sleeping cubicle. Men also believe that a woman's genitals contaminate her skirts so there are rules which prohibit a woman from stepping over objects or from touching them with her skirts. She must not climb on the roof of a house

18. See Ember (1978b) for a cross-cultural discussion of this phenomenon and support for this argument in particular.

lest a male be seated inside; she must never walk over a boy's hair clippings or across the legs of a seated man, across his weapons, or across food. Meggitt notes that:

> Given their beliefs about the essential nature of women, it is hardly surprising that the attitudes of most Mae men towards sexuality reflect unease and anxiety. Men rarely mention sexual matters, menstruation, or childbirth among themselves and would be ashamed to discuss them in mixed company. [Because] ... women are unclean and ... therefore, each act of coitus increases a man's chances of being contaminated; there is also the fear that copulation is in itself detrimental to male well-being ... every ejaculation depletes his vitality, and over-indulgence must dull his mind and leave his body permanently exhausted and withered. (1964:209–210)

Sexual abstinence is the best safeguard against this pollution but has severe disadvantages for a society. Men try to postpone marriage, but young bachelors also seek generalized protection from females through the performance of *sanggai*, rituals intended to both cleanse and strengthen young men. The power of the rituals defends a man against pollution until marriage at which time he needs to learn magic to use before copulating and when his wife menstruates (1964:217).[19]

Central to any psychocultural explanation for Mae Enga aggression is the concept of male gender identity conflict, but we also need to consider how Mae Enga culture deals with the socialization of aggression, affection, and security. In male-dominated cultures like the Mae Enga, where fathers are distant and aloof from their children, frustration develops when young boys must sever especially strong links to their mothers to meet the societal expectations of adult male behavior.[20] One way this separation is attempted is through the bachelor purification cult, a form of initiation rite aimed at facilitating the transition to adulthood (Herdt 1987; Meggitt 1964; Munroe, Munroe, and Whiting 1981: 614–616). Despite cultural attempts to deal with the insecurity and frustration surrounding male gender identity, the solutions are only partial.

19. For an excellent description of this pattern among the Sambia from a more psychological perspective than Meggitt's, see Herdt (1987), who shows very effectively the role of insecurity and distrust in the process.

20. For a somewhat different perspective on male-female relations among the Mae Enga, see Feil (1978), who stresses the shared role of men and women in exchange relations, rather than the view of male dominance found more commonly in Meggitt and others.

Compensatory behavior of bellicosity, aggressive displays, and open fighting are common.

Although Meggitt does not offer abundant specific data about Mae Enga early socialization, his material, as well as other work in the region, is sufficient to support the hypothesis that the Mae Enga share a number of the characteristics with other high aggression societies like the Yanomamo, Somali, or Jivaro. Among the Mae Enga, early relationships fail to promote enduring feelings of warmth and security,[21] which seems to lead to the development of aggressive, uncooperative interpersonal styles of conflict management. Fear of others seems a prominent feature and it is particularly striking that the person a young boy generally feels closest to—his mother—becomes the object to be most feared.[22] There are probably important psychological parallels to the division of the social world into rigidly male and female areas (Herdt 1987). Strong male bonding within the clan occurs with a great deal of projection of fears outward, toward females in general, and males in other clans. The inner fears and anger which threaten the males themselves and the unity of the group are then displaced onto socially acceptable targets through interpersonal and intergroup violence. Shared interpretations of the world as a dangerous place and of specific threatening groups and supernatural forces play a critical role in the Mae Enga culture of conflict.

A psychocultural explanation linking Mae Enga concerns about sexuality with aggression is not how Meggitt chooses to explain male-female relations or warfare. His explanation is rooted in the land needs and social structure of these highland peoples. He argues that because of the rugged territory in which the Mae Enga live, propinquity is significant in both marriage choices and conflict behavior. "We marry the people we fight" is the Mae Enga view, he reports. A man's mother and wife, then, are likely to come from clans which are perennial enemies and responsible for deaths in his clan. This association of adult women

21. The warmest relationship for a young boy is with his mother, a tie that he must sever in order to become a socially effective adult male. Herdt (1987) discusses the psychological aspects of this situation among the Sambia.

22. Herdt (1989) suggests it is important to distinguish between distant and aloof fathers, such as one finds among the Mae Enga, and less distant but emotionally inaccessible fathers in such groups as the Sambia. Although each is associated with cultural complexes involving aggression and fighting as compensatory male behavior, there are also important differences between the two patterns, such as the presence or absence of ritualized male homosexuality.

with enemies, found most powerfully in the equation of sexuality and peril, he says, can be seen in "a chain of homologues . . . traced from extra-clan military threat versus intraclan military protection to feminine pollution versus masculine purity" (1964:218). In a note Meggitt then adds, "As a social anthropologist I am not concerned here to speculate about individual psychological dynamisms operative in such a set of transformations" (1964:224). Such connections would enrich his argument and make it more complete and convincing. An explanation relying on social structural mechanisms alone is insufficient and therefore misleading (compare Koch 1974).

This discussion of Mae Enga conflict points to the distinct strengths and evident weaknesses of social structural and psychocultural theory. Psychocultural theory offers profound insights into the subjective construction of enemies and allies and the ways in which the transfer of feelings across domains can occur. It does not, however, suggest precise targets of aggression or the trust and security that develops within the clan. Although it prepares us to expect high levels of conflict, psychocultural theory tells us little about probable opponents. Here structural theory is much more useful in accounting for clan solidarity, extra-clan hostility, and the role of clan territory in Mae Enga warfare. Structural theory cannot so easily account for the intensity of Mae Enga conflict and its persistence over time. The best explanation for Mae Enga conflict, I suggest, considers it in terms of both social structure and psychocultural dispositions, not one or the other. ·

Conclusion

The statistical models of internal and external conflict and violence and the analysis of the Mae Enga lead me to offer a theory which includes both psychocultural and structural variables. Early social relationships create dispositions toward high or low violence in a society. Structural conditions determine the extent to which the violence is directed at others within the society, at outsiders, or both. Although psychocultural and structural theories of conflict use different language, point to diverse mechanisms, and have dissimilar implications for conflict management, the analysis here points to ways in which each theory is incomplete and to how together they offer a better understanding of the dynamics of conflict than either does alone. Although psychocultural dispositions are excellent predictors of the level of violence associated with a society, they offer little in the way of understanding who argues, contests, and fights with whom, or what triggers particular conflict sequences. Here the structural features of the social, economic, and political system come into play. The culture of conflict is rooted in both of these processes, as is seen generally in the cross-cultural data and more specifically in the Mae Enga case.

From this perspective it is not useful to ask whether structural or psychocultural theory provides the superior explanation for social and political conflict. Each has its particular value. For example, both Greenstein (1967) and B. Whiting (1980) suggest that dispositional variables are likely to be particularly important in matters of great emotional significance to people, questions central to their self-concept, and ambiguous, unstructured situations which engage individuals' personality (or projective systems). Emotional significance produces engagement and investment for individuals, and ambiguity leaves room for interpretation and the imposition of individual inner worlds on hazy, but vital situations.

In crucial but ambiguous settings, collective psychocultural processes are likely to be especially important as individuals seek to answer difficult questions about the meaning of their lives. Groups, after all, provide social support, telling people that they are not alone and that certain answers are right. When achieving certainty is not possible, social consensus and support are important coping strategies. For Whiting (1980), areas such as religion and the interpretation of illness are areas of human behavior producing projective behaviors which are best understood as psychological products. A consideration of conflict and violence also profits from this framework. Conflict situations, often high in emotional significance and ambiguity, allow room for interpretation based on psychological needs. Group support and social dynamics within groups, which begin with perhaps accurate but scanty information concerning a supposedly objective situation, permit projective processes to manifest themselves (for example, Janis 1972).

Interpretive processes, even though they are most often described in psychological terms, are also profoundly cultural. The notion of a culture of conflict draws attention to how people in communities develop and share interpretations rooted in psychocultural dispositions. This approach forces one to consider the common formative experiences and explicit values and practices shared by people growing up together and to appreciate the importance of the common identities, self-concepts, and out-groups which serve as acceptable targets for externalization and projection. The development of the self and the capacity for attachment to others are, at the same time, profoundly individual and social processes. Collective experiences, ranging from the most mundane daily activities, smells, or sounds to the most elaborate sacred rituals, link the individual to his or her community in primordial ways (Volkan 1988). Psychocultural developmental processes determine the content of a person's (or group's) sense of self, specific images of outsiders, and ideas about whom one can or cannot trust in the world. But if these social-psychological perceptions are the raw material out of which conflicts develop, the more concrete realities of social and political organization within one's community and between that community and outsiders give conflict form.

The analysis shows some common psychocultural and different social structural roots of internal versus external conflict in preindustrial societies. But I have said little about the relationship of internal and external conflict to each other. This is the focus of the next chapter.

7

The Relationship Between Internal and External Conflict

An ancient and well-researched controversy in international politics concerns the relationship between internal and external conflict. Most participants in the debate see connections between the two, but there is little consensus on the precise nature of the linkage. Some argue that external conflict can be a forceful mechanism for unifying a previously divided polity; others reverse the causal chain, arguing that leaders of divided groups sometimes seek external encounters as a way of achieving internal unity. Another approach expects consistency between internal and external conflict behavior, arguing that aggressivity inside a polity promotes it externally and vice versa; and a third position suggests that internal and external dynamics are sufficiently independent that there will often be no connection between internal and external conflict.

Nation states provide the basis for almost all the studies in this area. Any general comparative theory of politics, however, must consider the human experience in small-scale preindustrial societies like those we have been examining (Friedrich with Horwitz 1968). Cross-cultural data can be used to examine the old question of the relationship between internal and external conflict in a new light. I shall argue that none of the existing theories is entirely right or wrong; rather, it seems more useful to think about when and how internal and external violence are related, and under what conditions the two forms of violence occur independently.

This examination further explores the general theory proposed in the previous chapter, that a dispositional base determines a society's level of conflict and that structural conditions then direct the conflict toward specific internal and/or external targets. The exploration involves four steps. First, internal and external conflict are used to explain each other by adding them to the models in chapter 6. These results are statistically significant but theoretically unsatisfying. Second, I compare societies where both forms of conflict and violence occur at similar levels (generalizers) with those where they do not (differentiators). Differences between these two patterns of conflict are associated with structural but not psychocultural differences. Third, I contrast differentiating societies that are relatively high in internal conflict with differentiating societies relatively high in external conflict to learn whether, as the theory predicts, they differ in structural but not psychocultural characteristics. Finally, I examine the hypothesis that the "total amount" of conflict associated with a society is related to a society's dispositional but not structural features.

The main focus of the analysis to this point has been on the culture of conflict as a unitary phenomenon emphasizing characteristic ways in which high, medium, and low incidence of societal conflict are organized. Now the results encourage a further refinement, emphasizing that cultural styles of conflict are determined not only by the level but also by the targets of conflict. This is revealed by the fact of variation in conflict between generalizing and differentiating societies, even when both have the same overall level of conflict. To describe these results I use the plural term cultures of conflict because it accurately reflects the existence of cultural variations.

Relating Internal and External Conflict

The most commonly held view is that internal and external conflict are negatively related, either because outside enemies tend to unite a society or because internally divided societies cannot risk outside conflicts (LeVine and Campbell 1972:43–59; Stohl 1980). Underlying most versions of this argument is the drive-discharge or displacement hypothesis, which considers aggression levels somewhat constant and alternative targets of aggression functionally equivalent. In the ethnographic literature, the often-cited relationship among matrilocality, relative internal peace, and external warfare (Ember and Ember 1971; Divale 1974; LeVine and Campbell 1972; Murphy 1957) is explained in these terms.[1] The dispersion of men in matrilocal residence patterns dis-

1. Ember and Ember (1971) explain this relationship among these variables somewhat differently. They argue that if fighting is close to home, parents

courages internal conflict, which would pit male fighters against their close relatives, but it encourages external fighting in order to discharge the tension built up in the society (Murphy 1957).

There is also reason to support the expectation of a negative relationship between internal and external conflict on strategic grounds. Vayda (1961), writing about warfare among swidden (slash-and-burn) agriculturalists, suggests that internal peace serves as a mechanism for external expansion. Sahlins (1961) argues that the ability of segmentary lineage systems to form internal alliances makes them particularly effective in external conflicts.[2] In the international realm, too, many argue that elites use real or alleged outside threats to promote internal unity in situations of domestic stress (for example, Haas and Whiting 1956). Yet in a review of relevant studies in international relations, Stohl (1980) says that only one small study provides empirical evidence for this position. Although there may be occasions where this dynamic is at work, it seems to occur far less generally than many theorists suggest.

Another view is that internal and external conflict are essentially independent. Structural theories of conflict typically hold different forces responsible for each form of violence and predict little connection between the two. Otterbein, for example, looking at a sample of pre-industrial societies, finds no correlation between a society's internal and external warfare scores (1968:286).[3] Rummel (1963) and Tanter (1966) factor analyze a number of domestic and foreign conflict behaviors for 77 nations and produce separate factors for each. When the two forms of conflict are regressed one upon the other, they are only weakly related, and Rummel (1968) strongly argues that each must be explained separately.

The empirical data best support the position that internal and external conflict are positively associated. Psychologically, the argument rests on the mechanisms of generalization and habituation. Individuals and groups develop characteristic behaviors, patterns that are found in relationships both within and outside their society

---

want their sons nearby, while if fighting is only external, division of labor determines residence.

2. Although societies with this structure often have internal conflict as well, both do not occur at the same time. Rather, who one's opponent is at a given time determines with whom one forms an alliance.

3. In a later article Otterbein says that different forms of violent conflict are related (1977:697).

(LeVine and Campbell 1972; Sipes 1975). Empirical research in modern nations has produced a variety of studies showing a positive association between internal and external conflict, at least under certain conditions. A number of people have criticized Rummel and Tanter for consistently interpreting their modest correlation as showing no connection (Stohl 1980), and these critics have shown that domestic stress is often associated with external conflict and warfare (Haas 1965; Hazelwood 1973).[4] When Rummel and Tanter's data were reanalyzed to account for appropriate time lags, the significance of connections between certain dimensions of internal and external conflict increased (Wilkenfeld 1968; Wilkenfeld 1973). Others find that, over time, correlations between internal and external conflict differ by type of political system (Hazelwood 1973; Wilkenfeld 1973; Wilkenfeld and Zinnes 1973). Data on conflict within and between African nations show that domestic and foreign conflict can be highly related to each other (Collins 1973).

Adding Internal and External Violence:
Does It Alter the Model?

The previous chapter presented a multiple regression model of internal and external conflict, using data from ninety small-scale pre-industrial societies, which showed a common set of dispositional variables yet different structural features related to internal and to external conflict. The effect of each kind of conflict on the other one was not considered at that point. The simplest way to consider the connection is to add each form of conflict to the regression model using the other as the dependent variable. The results, shown in table 7.1, reveal that internal conflict is a good predictor of the level of external conflict and that external conflict is an even better predictor of internal conflict. The fact that both variables are significant in the new regressions clearly supports the argument that there is such a thing as a "culture of violence" (Archer and Gaertner 1984; Gurr 1970; Zimmerman 1980), which can be best understood in terms of psychocultural dispositions.[5]

4. Archer and Gaertner (1984) present data suggesting there is a link between domestic crime rates and warfare as well.
5. Weisner (personal communication, 1990) commented that it is hard to socialize people to fight outsiders and that attention to the specific mechanisms

Societies which are psychoculturally predisposed toward violence show more aggression both internally and externally. Teaching a citizenry to fight outside enemies produces more fighters who then have the tendency to use their skills within their society. Similarly, if violence is a mechanism for dealing with internal opponents, why should it not be used with outsiders as well? Yet this argument need not be made solely on psychological grounds. Structural factors are also involved, as for example when fighting, internally or externally, creates stress over the distribution of burdens and benefits, leading to more violence.

When external conflict is regressed onto internal conflict, the sizes of the coefficients for the psychocultural variables are smaller, and the only statistically significant variables remaining are external conflict and weak multiple reference groups (top half of table 7.1). In the case of external conflict, the changes in the equation when internal violence is added are smaller (bottom half of table 7.1). Although these two models show the interrelatedness of internal and external conflict and explain more of the variance than the models in table 6.1, they do not contribute significant insights from a theoretical point of view.

In the case of internal conflict in particular, an identification of the particular mechanisms that cause violence would be far more useful than a model which simply says that societies with high external conflict also have high internal conflict and vice versa. Although the data support the notion of a culture of conflict, they do not explain its underlying dynamics. One formulation suggests that the roots of internal conflict are external to a society and that without outside conflict they would be more likely to be peaceful. While the hypothesis that contact with outsiders can be destabilizing is supported in some situations, there seems to be no good theoretical reason to ascribe a general causal priority to outside conflict as a cause of internal conflict.[6]

---

of socialization for war and secondary socialization and separation would be instructive here.

6. D. White (1989) makes this argument forcefully, if naïvely. Most likely, internal and external conflict have a variety of contingent effects on each other. The thrust of the analysis here is that the structural features of a society are one determinant of the impact of both kinds of violence. Another is, as White suggests, a society's location in the world system, a point considered in more detail in chapter 8.

Table 7.1
Internal and External Conflict: Multiple Regressions Revised to Include Conflict Measures

	Standardized Regression Coefficient	Standard Error of Beta
Internal conflict and violence		
External conflict and warfare	.32**	.12
Multiple-reference groups scale	−.34**	.11
Local community endogamy	.06	.10
Matrilocality#	−.10	.10
Intercommunity trade	.04	.10
Fraternal interest group strength in uncentralized societies	.16	.10
Polygyny	.15	.09
Socioeconomic complexity	.04	.14
Political power concentration	−.05	.14
Harsh socialization practices	.16	.09
Affectionate socialization practices	−.18	.11
Male gender-identity conflict	.05	.10

Multiple R = .65**   R Square = .42

External violence and warfare		
Internal conflict and violence	.23*	.09
Multiple-reference groups scale in uncentralized societies	.23*	.10
Local community endogamy in uncentralized societies	.41***	.10
Matrilocality#	.14	.09
Fraternal interest group strength	.04	.11
Polygyny	−.13	.09
Socioeconomic complexity	.24	.13
Political power concentration	−.07	.12
Harsh socialization practices	.14	.09
Affectionate socialization practices	−.33***	.09
Male gender-identity conflict	.30***	.08

Multiple R = .69**   R Square = .47

*** statistically significant at the .001 level
** statistically significant at the .01 level
* statistically significant at the .05 level
N = 90
Means have been substituted for missing data in the regression
same results when patrilocality is substituted for matrilocality

Generalizers Versus Differentiators

The cross-cultural data show a moderately strong correlation between the internal and external conflict scales ($r = .39$; $N = 90$) indicating that often societies with high scores in one kind of conflict are high in the other, and vice versa. It is also clear, however, that a correlation of this magnitude means that a good number of cases are exceptions to the general pattern. To examine this situation more carefully, I distinguish between societies where internal and external conflict are at about the same level (generalizers) and those where the levels differ, with external conflict high and internal conflict low or vice versa (differentiators). Generalization and differentiation can best be viewed as alternative cultural styles. Among generalizers, behaviors and beliefs are most likely to be similar across domains. In contrast, among differentiating societies, the less common case, internal and external conflict levels differ and we would expect norms concerning appropriate behavior toward insiders and outsiders to vary greatly. One type of differentiating society in the sample is the preindustrial state, such as the Buganda, described in chapter 5. The Buganda, like the Aztecs of pre-Columbian Mexico or the Fon of West Africa, were highly integrated internally and directed their aggression toward neighboring societies who were viewed as objects of conquest. In none of these cases was there significant internal conflict. In predatory states, the key is the ability of the centralized authority to limit the development of local power groups who might fight among themselves. A different route to the same end is found in nonstate societies like the Huron or Papago of North America. Both have high external conflict and are internally peaceful but in neither case is this due to centralized authority. Among the Huron, related males are dispersed through matrilocal residence, and members of the eight clans live in all villages in the society (Trigger 1969). Mobilization of fighting forces to attack outside enemies, particularly the Seneca, is not difficult (Tooker 1964). In contrast, the Papago, who live in much more autonomous, kin-based settlements, are suspicious of one another at times, but without intercommunal fighting. In the face of frequent Apache attacks, the Papago variously flee into the mountains or fight, although warfare is not glorified (Underhill 1939). The differences in these societies' behavior toward and beliefs about insiders versus outsiders are striking.

Generalizing societies, in contrast, are more similar in behavior for each domain. Sometimes nonaggression is found in instances of internal and external conflict, as among the Mbuti (see chapter 1), whereas in other cases high levels of conflict are found in both, as among the Jivaro (see chapter 5). Yet other societies have moderate levels of each, as is the case of the Tiv of Nigeria. The key to understanding generalizing societies is that behaviors and norms in one domain are relevant in others. Generalization is found in societies with very different conflict levels; it does not only occur at the extremes and it is more common than differentiation.

How are the generalizers and differentiators different? Dispositional factors are good predictors of the overall conflict level in a society, I suggest, and the particular structural conditions explain whether the conflict will be internal, external, or both. The differentiators and generalizers, then, should be unlike in structural, not dispositional, ways.

To investigate this question I created a new variable—society's external conflict score subtracted from its internal score—to measure the gap between the two.[7] Generalizing societies have a low score, whereas differentiators have a high one. In the case of differentiators whose external conflict exceeds internal conflict, the score will be negative, whereas when internal conflict is greater than external conflict, the score will be positive. The absolute value of the difference between internal and external conflict scores can be used to measure differentiation versus generalization.

D_i = Absolute Value $[I_i - E_i]$
where D_i = society i's magnitude of differentiation
I_i = society i's standardized internal conflict and violence score
E_i = society i's standardized external conflict and warfare score

The results of rerunning the regression in table 6.1, changing the dependent variable to this newly created magnitude of differen-

7. The specific raw scores for each society on each variable are given in appendix A. Because the range of the two variables differed, I first standardized them. While this gives each variable the same range, I do not suggest that the actual level of internal and external conflict in societies receiving the same score on both measures is the same, an argument that would require both a theoretical elaboration and a level of measurement which I do not make. The measures are, however, useful for ranking the societies in the sample and for providing a rough order of magnitude of each form of conflict. Comparisons between the two measures should, perhaps, be seen as comparisons of ranks rather than of absolute levels.

Table 7.2
Differentiating Versus Generalizing Societies
Conflict and Violence: Absolute Difference (Internal − External Conflict)

	Standardized Regression Coefficient	Standard Error of Beta
Multiple-reference groups scale	.40***	.11
Local community endogamy in uncentralized societies	.32**	.13
Matrilocality #	.22*	.10
Intercommunity trade	.02	.11
Fraternal interest group strength in uncentralized societies	−.21	.11
Polygyny	−.14	.10
Socioeconomic complexity	.24	.15
Political power concentration	−.08	.15
Harsh socialization practices	−.06	.10
Affectionate socialization practices	−.10	.10
Male gender-identity conflict	.07	.10

Multiple R = .58**   R Square = .34

*** statistically significant at the .001 level
** statistically significant at the .01 level
* statistically significant at the .05 level
N = 90
Means have been substituted for missing data in the regression
same results when patrilocality is substituted for matrilocality

tiation measure, are fully consistent with theoretical expectations (see table 7.2). Dispositional variables do not distinguish between the two groups of societies nearly as well as structural ones do. Table 7.2 shows three statistically significant differences between differentiating and generalizing societies, and two other variables, whose regression coefficients are sufficiently large and theoretically interesting.[8] Differentiators, as opposed to generalizers, have greater internal integration and are somewhat more complex. They have more multiple-reference groups linking people in different communities; local community en-

8. As stated in chapter 6, theoretical importance, not statistical significance, should be the primary guide in deciding what variables to include in a model (Achen 1982). Different regression procedures can yield slightly different results. Here if backwards deletion is used, all of these variables are statistically significant (except for polygyny). The regression coefficients are virtually the same, as is the R square, but deleting variables lowers the standard error; hence the regression coefficients become statistically significant.

dogamy is more common among the uncentralized societies; they are more likely to be matrilocal; they show a lower tendency toward polygyny; they have weaker fraternal interest groups within the uncentralized societies; and they have greater socioeconomic, but not political, complexity.

The stronger the multiple reference groups linking people within and between communities in a society, the greater the differentiation between the levels of internal and external violence (see table 7.2). Where there are more multiple-reference groups in a society, targets of aggression will be predictable, with significant structural distinctions between friend and foe. Low local community intermarriage rates and weak fraternal interest groups also characterize uncentralized differentiating societies. A preference for marriage within the local community is perhaps associated with a stronger distinction between insiders and outsiders, and allies and enemies. Fraternal interest groups—related males who are easily mobilized into fighting units—are more likely to generalize aggression across targets, whereas the absence of such groups produces more differentiation.

Residence rules have important consequences for alliance formation and conflict. Matrilocal societies like the Huron tend to be differentiators, whereas patrilocal ones are more likely to be generalizers (LeVine and Campbell 1972:29–42). Coresident male kin (fraternal interest groups) easily form fighting groups in patrilocal societies and defend their interests equally forcefully against opponents from other communities or from other societies. Finally, the results show that the higher the level of socioeconomic complexity, the greater the differentiation, meaning that more complicated systems are more likely to have high levels of either internal or external conflict, but not both. Complexity is associated with greater predictability in the choice of targets, probably a function of greater coordination and control associated with increasing differentiation in social and economic organization.

Societies with High Levels of Internal Conflict Versus Societies with High Levels of External Conflict

A society's structural features, as opposed to its dispositions, predict whether the society is likely to be a generalizer or a differentiator but do not determine whether the higher scoring dimension is external or internal conflict. Next, I shall compare differentiators where levels of external conflict are higher than levels of internal conflict with those where the gap between the two is in the other direction. Once again, structural differences ought to be paramount, if dispositional factors are relevant only to the levels of violence and not to its targets.

The measure employed is the same as above—internal conflict minus external conflict—but this time the actual difference not the absolute value must be used. When the level of internal conflict is high and external conflict is low, a society receives a positive score; when the levels of each form of conflict are approximately the same, it is near zero; and when the level of external conflict exceeds internal conflict, the score is negative.[9]

Structural differences between societies where internal conflict predominates and societies where external conflict is more prevalent appear in table 7.3. Internal conflict is more common than external conflict when there are fewer multiple reference groups and where local community endogamy is low (in uncentralized societies). In addition, higher internal conflict is found in societies where fraternal interest groups are strong and where there is patrilocal residence, polygyny, and lower socioeconomic complexity. In contrast, external conflict is higher than internal conflict when there are strong multiple reference groups, and high local community endogamy (in uncentralized societies). An imbalance in favor of external conflict is also more common in societies that are matrilocal, polygynous, and more complex socioeconomically. This supports the argument that strong cross-cutting ties (except for intermarriage) inhibit internal and enhance external conflict, and the linkage between greater complexity and external conflict.

Greater internal integration means that cross-cutting linkages within a society increase the likelihood of its engaging in external conflict. These data on societies with high levels of external conflict and on differentiators support parts of the argument that internal and external conflict are inversely related. Yet this conclusion holds only with respect to the *relative* amount of each form of conflict, not its absolute level.

9. As internal and external violence are themselves correlated (r = .39), this measure is highly correlated with the one used above to distinguish between generalizers and differentiators (table 7.2), and the two are highly correlated (r = .78).

Table 7.3
Internal Versus External Conflict Societies
(Internal − External Conflict)

	Standardized Regression Coefficient	Standard Error of Beta
Multiple-reference groups scale	−.42***	.11
Local community endogamy in uncentralized societies	−.35**	.13
Matrilocality #	−.17	.10
Intercommunity trade	.02	.11
Fraternal interest group strength in uncentralized societies	.18	.11
Polygyny	.19	.10
Socioeconomic complexity	−.19	.14
Political power concentration	.01	.15
Harsh socialization practices	.02	.10
Affectionate socialization practices	.08	.10
Male gender-identity conflict	−.15	.10

Multiple R = .59**   R Square = .35

*** statistically significant at the .001 level
** statistically significant at the .01 level
* statistically significant at the .05 level
N = 90
Means have been substituted for missing data in the regression
same results when patrilocality is substituted for matrilocality

Finally, because generalizers are far more numerous in the sample than differentiating societies, this pattern of high external and low internal conflict is somewhat rare.

Multiple-reference groups minimize the severity of internal political conflict and enhance the unity of the society when confronted by outside enemies. Although this is not surprising, it is still satisfying to find empirical support in this sample for such an often-cited social scientific proposition. The association with polygyny is probably best explained by male competition over women and the values of male aggressivity associated with such competition (Divale and Harris 1976). The connection between local endogamy and external conflict is more puzzling. It seems reasonable that societies whose members marry within the local community would have the most difficulty establishing internal alliances in order to fight outsiders. But this is not the case, possibly because endogamy is associated with matrilocality, and both are more associated with external rather than internal, conflict (Ember and Ember 1971). One of the consequences of this arrangement is that in order to reside matrilocally, a man does not need to leave the community of his kin.[10]

Predicting Overall Levels of Conflict

The argument under examination here is not only that structural factors distinguish between internal and external conflict societies, but also that dispositional variables will be the best predictors of the overall levels of conflict in a society. To test this final hypothesis, a "total conflict" score was created by adding together the internal and external conflict scores for each society.[11]

Once again the regression results (table 7.4) support the theory. The three psychocultural variables—low affection socialization practices, harsh socialization, and male gender-identity conflict—are the *only* three statistically significant variables related to the total level of conflict in a society.

At the same time, several structural variables, when included in the model, do not achieve statistical significance yet are empirically relevant in distinguishing between societies with high and low levels of conflict. Greater total conflict is found in societies which are more complex socioeconomically, but where political power is less concentrated. A disparity between the technological sophistication and lack of political mechanisms to maintain peace may be relevant here. A second group of variables involves cross-cutting ties. High-conflict societies are more likely to have fewer multiple-reference groups, and, in the uncentralized societies, to have local community endogamy and strong fraternal interest groups. These variables are primarily associated with internal conflict; more refined data might indicate whether they are indicators of low integration or causes of it.

10. If the local community intermarriage rate is deleted from the model, then the coefficient for matrilocality increases and becomes statistically significant. The relationship holds only in uncentralized societies, where there is no binding authority beyond the local community, precisely where the political distinction between internal and external conflict is most ambiguous.

11. The standardized scores for each variable are added together because the raw scores do not have a common metric.

Table 7.4
Total Conflict
(Internal + External Conflict)

	Standardized Regression Coefficient	Standard Error of Beta
Multiple-reference groups scale	−.07	.10
Local community endogamy in uncentralized societies	.23	.12
Matrilocality #	.04	.09
Intercommunity trade	.03	.10
Fraternal interest group strength in uncentralized societies	.14	.10
Polygyny	.01	.09
Socioeconomic complexity	.24	.13
Political power concentration	−.14	.13
Harsh socialization practices	.24**	.09
Affectionate socialization practices	.42***	.09
Male gender-identity conflict	.26**	.09

Multiple R = .67**   R Square = .45

*** statistically significant at the .001 level
** statistically significant at the .01 level
* statistically significant at the .05 level
N = 90
Means have been substituted for missing data in the regression
same results when patrilocality is substituted for matrilocality

Rethinking Internal and External Conflict

The analysis presented here casts new light on the old question of the relationship between internal and external conflict behavior. Although internal and external conflict are on the average positively related in the worldwide sample of preindustrial societies, whether the relationship between the two is positive or negative differs across the cases. There is least support for the position that internal and external conflict are independent of each other some of the time.

I compared generalizing societies (those with roughly the same levels of internal and external conflict) with differentiating societies (those in which one form is much higher than the other) and then compared societies with especially high levels of internal conflict with those with high levels of external conflict. This analysis revealed a number of distinctive structural features in each group but also demonstrated that the dispositional variables were virtually irrelevant. In contrast, when the two conflict measures were combined to produce a total conflict score, psychocultural predictors were much more important than structural ones.

The argument that psychocultural dispositional factors are crucial in determining the level of conflict associated with a society, whereas structural features determine the choice of targets, is supported in terms of the relative size of the standardized regression coefficients and the criterion of statistical significance. Although this conclusion is both parsimonious and provocative, it is also most useful to see the statistical evidence as consistent with a cautious rather than an absolute argument. For the structural features of society to be irrelevant in predicting overall conflict, the coefficients for all of the structural variables would have to be of similar magnitudes but with opposite arithmetic signs in the two regressions in table 6.1; instead we find this to be true with only some of the variables. More common is the pattern where a particular structural variable is important in predicting one form of conflict, and then its coefficient is near zero in the model for the other form. In the case of total conflict (table 7.4), a structural variable may contribute to explaining overall conflict because of its particular impact on either internal or external conflict.

Clarifying what the results allow us to conclude about the relative contribution of each set of explanatory factors does not suggest major weaknesses in the argument. Rather, considering the nature of the data used and the need to evaluate the theory further using data from other political systems as well, the results are as supportive of the theory as could be expected.

Structural features of a society and the interests underlying them do not adequately explain conflict behavior, although they are among the reasons most frequently advanced by both participants and observers. Knowing only the structural arrangements of a society tells one precious little about its overall conflict levels (table 7.4). Psychocultural dispositions are a more rewarding area of inquiry for this question. Given a certain conflict level, however, structural variables are crucial in helping understand whether the disputants are likely to be within the community or external to it. Strong multiple-reference groups and somewhat higher levels of socioeconomic complexity are found in more differentiating societies; the same features make the choice of external targets for aggression more likely.

The organization of the psychocultural environment and of the structure of interests are distinct elements in the culture of conflict—the characteristic ways in which groups and individuals in a society engage in conflict and respond to the actions of others. Although the findings here have been stated mainly in terms of the factors which produce high levels of conflict, they consequently reveal a good deal about cultural systems with low and moderate levels of conflict (Ross 1993). In addition, the exploration of generalizing and differentiating societies shows that the cultural determinants of overall levels of conflict are quite different than those which determine the target of conflict. A key difference may be that differentiating and generalizing societies define group and societal boundaries differently. Generalizers recognize more parallels across domains and, perhaps, tend to define friends and foes more contextually, whereas differentiators make clear distinctions between insiders and outsiders. Cultural styles of disputing, this suggests, may be distinctive in terms of both their level and targets. Rather than a single culture characteristic of high or low levels of conflict, there are additional cultural configurations which mark both the level and style of conflict and which perpetuate it. The theme of cultures (plural) of conflict with distinctive configurations is further developed in the next chapter through an analysis of the societies deviating most from the statistical model of conflict as I suggest additional factors which affect the specific forms that the culture of conflict can take.

8

Variations on a Theme:
Deviant Cases

The analysis of generalization and differentiation suggests the existence of distinct styles of conflict within the worldwide pattern. Another way to consider variation in the general model is through an analysis of particular societies. Inspection of the results of the statistical analyses shows how individual societies—both those that fit the model well and those that do not—obtain the scores they do. The Comanche of North America (see chapter 5) have an external conflict score which is virtually the same as the model predicts. These warriors of the plains live in local bands that cooperate with one another against outsiders although cross-cutting ties between bands are not very strong. Early social relationships are low in affection and warmth but are not especially aggressive. Among the societies where the internal conflict is best predicted are the pastoral Maasai of East Africa (Spencer 1988). Another society that fits the model well is that of the Tikopia, a small island chiefdom with low conflict, strong cross-cutting ties, and socialization which is high in warmth and affection and low in male gender-identity conflict and aggression. If the statistical model offers a general pattern, particular cases help understand individual variations in the culture of conflict. The cases just named all show a close statistical fit with the model. However, much can be learned from cases which deviate from the statistical predictions.

Rule (1988) points out that intensive case analysis is too often self-serving because the cases are selected precisely in order to coincide with a favored theory. Regression analysis helps investigators focus on cases knowing whether they are statistically typical or deviant. The residuals (or standardized error terms) for each society in the model show how well the overall statistical model predicts the actual level of

Table 8.1
Accuracy of Statistical Prediction of Internal and External Conflict

Internal Conflict and Violence

	Worst Fitting Cases		Best Fitting Cases
Society	Standardized Residual	Society	Standardized Residual
Cayapa	−2.74	Eyak	−.01
Lamet	−2.02	Maasai	−.05
Pawnee	−1.97	Gilyak	.15
Riffian	1.76	Azande	.19
Fon	−1.67	Lapp	.20
Semang	−1.60	Huron	−.25
Carib	−1.60	Yokuts	.27
Basseri	−1.47	Warrau	.28
Mapuche	1.44	Aweikoma	.34
Buganda	−1.40	Egyptian	.36

External Conflict and Warfare

	Worst Fitting Cases		Best Fitting Cases
Society	Standardized Residual	Society	Standardized Residual
Cayapa	−2.66	Tiv	.03
Ifugao	−2.25	Comanche	−.03
Lamet	−2.10	Timbira	.04
Mbuti	−1.96	Tallensi	−.05
Mapuche	1.77	Pawnee	.06
Lepcha	−1.58	Warrau	.06
Egyptian	−1.55	Marshalese	−.10
Balinese	−1.47	Aymara	−.10
Gilyak	−1.46	Lozi	−.11
Gheg Albanian	1.43	Yokuts	−.12

the dependent variable for each case. The higher the absolute value of the residual, the worse the fit, and vice versa. A negative residual means that the actual level of conflict is lower than predicted, whereas a positive residual indicates that actual conflict levels are higher than expected. Table 8.1 lists the societies where the fit between the model and the actual data is best and worst for internal and external conflict. In this chapter I first examine differences between societies where the amount of conflict is most under- and overestimated by the statistical model and then present a number of individual cases which diverge most from the model. These deviant cases need not weaken the general argument; rather, they may suggest nuances in the culture of conflict and suggest additional variables which may refine the general model of conflict or operate in selected contexts.

Figure 8.1
Summary Pattern of Deviant Cases: Under- and Overconflicters
Internal Conflict
A. Underconflicters: less internal conflict than expected (overprediction)
　　—more common in East Eurasia and North America
　　—differentiators
　　—women less active politically
B. Overconflicters: more internal conflict than expected (underprediction)
　　—more common in the Circum-Mediterranean and Insular Pacific
　　—generalizers
　　—women more active politically

External Conflict
C. Underconflicters: less external conflict than expected (overprediction)
　　—generalizers
　　—lower contact with outside societies
　　—less emphasis on obedience and self-reliance in socialization
D. Overconflicters: more external conflict than expected (underprediction)
　　—differentiators
　　—higher contact with outside societies
　　—more emphasis on obedience and self-reliance in socialization

Cases That Don't Fit the Model Well: Under- and Overconflicters

In the discussion below, the point of reference is a society's predicted conflict score—not its absolute level of conflict. Cases where the actual level is lower than expected (and hence overpredicted) are called *underconflicters*, while those cases where conflict is more than expected (and underpredicted) are called *overconflicters*. Because over- or underprediction can occur with respect to either internal or external conflict, I will refer to internal and external under- and overconflicters. Figure 8.1 outlines key differences between underconflicters and overconflicters. None of these variations, it must be stressed, involves the structural or psychocultural variables, whose effects have already been built into the statistical model.

Internal Conflict

How do internal underconflicters and overconflicters differ? Comparing those societies having high positive residuals with those having high negative residuals shows only a few systematic differences. Internal overconflicters are more likely in the Circum-Mediterranean and Insular

Pacific but less common in North America and East Eurasia;[1] internal overconflicters are more likely to have a small gap between internal and external conflict levels than the internal underconflicters; and internal overconflicters also have higher levels of female political participation. These last two differences deserve comment.

The internal conflict under- and overconflicters differ in their conflict styles. The underconflicters (where the level of internal conflict is far lower than expected) are differentiators—there is a large gap between internal and external conflict scores. Although the internal underconflicters range from the lowest to the highest external conflict levels, the average gap between the two scores is relatively large, consistent with the argument that external conflict dampens internal disputes (independent of variables already considered in the model). The Buganda and the Fon, for example, are two preindustrial African states with a high level of external conflict which are internal underconflicters; it is plausible that the pressures arising from external warfare and the internal order the militaristic state produces are important in explaining low internal conflict. In contrast, internal overconflicters (internal conflict is higher than expected) are often generalizers (having a much smaller gap between internal and external conflict scores).[2] Among these are societies like the Teda of the central Sahara and the Akwe-Shavante of Brazil that have some of the highest external conflict scores in the sample. One hypothesis is that the institutions and practices associated with intense, prolonged external conflict spill over into internal domains, producing higher levels of internal conflict than would otherwise

1. A separate examination of regional differences (dividing the sample into the main regions of the New World, East Eurasia and the Insular Pacific, and Africa and the Circum-Mediterranean) supports the argument that a society's psychocultural features determine overall conflict levels and that social structural features are crucial for understanding the targets of aggression. At the same time, the importance of specific structural and psychocultural mechanisms varies across regions; only the effects of affectionate socialization practices are consistent across all areas. Gender-identity conflict and weak multiple loyalties increase conflict in the New World, and fraternal interest groups and harsh socialization had a greater impact in the Old World (with some additional differences between Africa-Circum-Mediterranean societies and those in East Eurasia and the Insular Pacific). For the definition of the regions see Murdock and White (1969).

2. The societies falling between the two extreme groups have an in-between score on the absolute difference variable.

be expected.[3] The fact that selective support can be offered for two such contradictory notions—that external conflict is responsible for lower internal conflict levels and that it might account for greater than expected levels—only highlights the absence of a satisfactory general explanation for the relationship between the two types of conflict and suggests the need to further examine significant differences between the groups of deviant cases.[4]

A second, fascinating difference between internal under- and overconflicters is that women are more politically active in the latter group. This finding is surely counterintuitive, for it is in societies high in internal conflict where male pride and dominance might be expected to result in the exclusion of women. One possible explanation for this result draws on the changing character of political alliances in societies with high levels of internal conflict and their need to forge coalitions of support in order to mobilize all potential allies.[5] Women may perform the crucial role of convincing kin in nearby communities to join an alliance against a common enemy and thus serve as the structural go-betweens among potentially hostile and competing groups. From this perspective men cannot afford to exclude women from political life when the price may be loss of potential allies needed for survival. Female political power, as opposed to male authority, is the critical element here. Internal overconflicters may offer women more room for political maneuvering and a role in the alliance formation process as they exploit differences among men. Even in societies which value male domination and control, women may be far more essential to the politics of coalition formation than has been understood. Certainly women are often far more than passive objects of exchanges that solidify linkages among men (Weiner 1976).

A somewhat different view regards the previous explanation as male-oriented and suggests that in low internal conflict situations, women leave politics to the men because the women have better things

3. A causal relationship in the reverse direction, although possible, is not likely given the fact that external conflict has a greater impact on internal conflict than the reverse, found in chapter 7.

4. The argument from chapter 7 is that theoretically, both patterns operate but in different cases, and each has its own dynamics.

5. Portions of this and the next paragraph borrow from Ross (1986b).

to do with their time, but that when the level of internal conflict becomes high, the women feel the need to enter the political arena. When relatively little is at stake, the men sit around and talk, but nothing much of consequence for the women happens. However, if tensions are high and violence is likely to erupt, the women will often bear the brunt of the men's actions; therefore, it is in their interest to get involved. For example, women in a number of societies in the Pacific and elsewhere (Maori, Torajda, Andamese, and Gheg Albanians) actively participate in peace negotiations. Among the Orokaiva (Williams 1930), women have an explicit role as go-betweens and brokers when conflict is severe. The incentive for women to be politically active may be especially high when intercommunity disputes pit a woman's husband and his kin against her father and brothers. Sometimes, as in the case of the Mae Enga of New Guinea (Meggitt 1977), men keep warfare plans to themselves so that the women cannot pass the information along. But the results suggest this case may be an exception; another solution to this problem of divided loyalty is active female involvement in the political process of alliance formation.

External Conflict

Examining the cases where the external conflict data fit the model worst shows a few clear differences between the external under- and overconflicters. External underconflicters have less, whereas the external overconflicters have more contact with outsiders; there is a tendency for the external underconflicters to be generalizers and the external overconflicters to be differentiaters (the reverse of the situation with internal conflict). External overconflicters also tend to emphasize control through obedience and self-reliance in child rearing more than do external underconflicters.

Although the relationship between the nature of errors in prediction and contact with outsiders is not surprising, the causal sequence between external conflict and contact is not evident. Of course contact is a prerequisite for conflict, but it is less clear whether contact leads to the development of conflict-oriented institutions or whether societies that are bellicose in the first place seek outsiders with whom they can do battle.

What is clear is that external underconflicters do not have higher levels of internal conflict as a hydraulic model of conflict would predict.

Rather external underconflicters are generalizers with modest levels of both kinds of conflict. There is, once again, no support for the simplistic idea that external conflict necessarily unifies a society internally or that internal conflict societies cannot "afford" to fight with outsiders. As a group, the external underconflicters have lower absolute levels of internal conflict and are internal underconflicters, whereas external overconflicters are internal overconflicters too. There is much more support here for the idea of a generalizing culture of conflict than for a hydraulic model. The effects of the key parts of such a culture are probably multiplicative rather than additive, reinforcing each other more than the linear model leads one to expect.

Finally, external overconflicters place a greater emphasis on control in socialization, valuing obedience and self-restraint significantly more than the external underconflicters. These qualities are certainly useful in a society for engaging in conflict where successful military activities require hierarchical control and discourage individual initiative.

Five Individual Cases

Examining variations in the theoretical model through specific cases where the model predicts a society's conflict level especially poorly may suggest ways in which the general model should be refined, or may add to our understanding of forces operating in selected contexts. Here no encompassing explanation accounts for the least accurately predicted cases. This means that no single variable was left out of the general model;[6] rather, particular factors may account for unexpected scores in

6. D. White (1989) argues that a society's position in the world system is a critical cause of external conflict which then causes internal conflict making overall conflict a function of a society's position in the world system. To evaluate this hypothesis, however, he uses my measure of a society's contact with other societies with a small sample, rather than his measure of world-system position (because it is not significant statistically). When I added the contact variable to the regression models it produced several results worth noting. First, the higher the level of contact with other societies, the greater the level of external conflict and warfare. There is no effect, however, of contact on internal conflict. Thus, while contact with outsiders is associated with more fighting, it is not related to less internal violence, as may be expected according to displacement theory. When external conflict is the dependent variable, not only is the standardized regression coefficient for contact with outsiders statistically significant and rel-

the individual cases. Thus, examination of specific cases may explain the particular mechanisms at work in certain contexts. In discussing cases with a large gap between the statistical model's predictions and the actual results, I do not ascribe results to miscoded or missing data; instead, I suggest alternative or additional structural or psychocultural mechanisms at work which at least seem consistent with the pattern found in each society (and perhaps a few others).[7] The discussion of five societies shows important local variations in the culture of conflict and the need to consider additional variables in order to explain the failure of the general model in these cases.

Cayapa: Fear of Affiliation

The most dramatic deviation from the general model is the Cayapa, a small-scale society of hunters living in autonomous, dispersed jungle households in highland Colombia and Ecuador. The Cayapa have the greatest gap between their actual and predicted level of both internal and external conflict.[8] The Cayapa are internal and external underconflicters, having a far lower level of conflict than expected (table 8.1).

---

atively large, but three of the variables (socioeconomic complexity, cross-cutting ties in uncentralized societies, and harsh socialization prctices) that are statistically significant in the regression shown in the lower half of table 6.1 are no longer significant when contact is included. In the case of all three variables the regression coefficients are smaller, although the arithmetic signs remain the same (and there is almost no change in the standard errors). But when frequency of external contact is added to the regression in table 7.2 distinguishing between generalizing and differentiating societies, it produces virtually no change in the results, ruling out the hypothesis that generalization is simply a function of opportunity. Clearly the level of intersocietal contact affects conflict patterns, but it would also be useful to locate data on the character of these contacts, which would allow us to better understand the specific dynamic at work. Finally, we should consider not just how contact with outsiders causes conflict, but how conflict patterns (sometimes established within a region) encourage groups to engage in hostile acts toward outsiders.

7. One exception is that of the Lamet, a society in which both external and internal conflict are overpredicted. Data on both harsh socialization practices and male gender-identity conflict are coded as missing, and the fact that the sample mean is assigned in this situation could account for the results. While in this case, poor data probable increased the error terms, in others, the errors may have been lowered.

8. The society with the most under-predicted level of conflict is the Ma-

Altschuler describes harsh Cayapa socialization practices in which young children are alternately rejected and indulged (1965:221). Adults, he continues, are anxious, suspicious of others, and lacking in self-confidence. This pattern and their absence of significant cross-cutting ties may be expected to produce high levels of conflict (especially within Cayapa society), as it does in many other cases. Yet the Cayapa are one of the most peaceful societies in the sample.

The pattern described by Altschuler results in minimal social cooperation (1965:216). There is "a deep-rooted basic anxiety that is manifested by a generalized fear of others, an inability to maintain friendships, low male sex drive, female sexual forwardness and latent male homosexuality" (1965:216). Affiliative behavior can be found only in rudimentary form. "One might almost say that the Cayapa practice a form of avoidance behavior that is extended to all non-kin" (1965:228). Social cohesion, as it exists, is achieved only through heavy use of alcohol when avoidance is not possible (1965:231–232). Groups organize for social action only for a short duration. In this situation, a chief who offers authoritative decisions, according to Altschuler, perfectly complements a people who lack confidence and competence (1965:236).

Although the more common reaction to a psychocultural situation similar to the Cayapa is aggression projected outward, because of their intense fear of others the Cayapa seem to withdraw from social and emotional involvements and turn some of the aggression inward in the form of alcohol dependency. Organized open conflict is rare because the required collective, cooperative actions are absent.

This pattern of social withdrawal, as opposed to overt aggression, is not common, but it is found elsewhere. Briggs (1975), for example, describes a similar pattern among the Utku Eskimos, in which an almost smothering nurturance of infants results in profound fear of affiliation, both intimate and nonintimate, later in life. The result, as with the Cayapa, is a daily existence in which anger, let alone conflict and violence, is rarely expressed but from which collective social action is also absent. Another less extreme example is that of the rural Irish, described by Messenger (1971) and Scheper-Hughes (1979). Here the absence of affection and warmth and distant fathers result in severe problems of

_____

puche of Chile. I do not discuss them here, not because they are unimportant, but because I can offer no good explanation for these results from existing reports.

attachment and intimacy (especially for males); overt conflict is infrequent, although latent conflicts are not hard to find. More common, Scheper-Hughes reports, is widespread alcoholism and the western world's highest rates of schizophrenia (1979:66–70). Again, aggression is turned inward.[9]

Ifugao: Great Isolation

The Ifugao are a stateless agricultural people in the Philippines that Barton studied early in the twentieth century. They are external underconflicters and internal overconflicters. Although it is not of great emotional importance, the effective community among the Ifugao is the village, with groups of villages submitting to a rice chief (Lambrecht 1954:363). There is great fear of others. Families coexist peacefully, but vengeance feuds are common between close villages (Barton 1919:109). Internal fighting is frequent despite the efforts of go-betweens to resolve disputes, and peaceful resolution—when it occurs—seems partially due to the need to defend the community against neighboring communities (Barton 1919:95; Barton 1930:115–116). Ifugao conflict is almost exclusively internal because contact with outsider societies is rare. Interestingly, for other external underconflicters and internal overconflicters, infrequent contact with outsiders does not seem to be a determining factor. Of the ten societies with the most underpredicted external conflict, only the Cayapa share the Ifugaos' extremely low level of contact with outsiders, and among the top ten cases of internal conflict overprediction, only the Shavante are comparably isolated. Clearly, the existence of some situations where isolation lowers the level of external conflict and raises the level of conflict within a society does not provide a general explanation for conflict behavior.

Fon: Concentrated Political Authority

The Fon of Dahomey in West Africa provide another exception to the model. They are internal underconflicters although external con-

9. The rural Irish, included in our sample, have a level of internal conflict significantly lower than expected from our model, although the degree of error is less than it is for the Cayapa and the other societies listed in table 8.1.

flict is at the expected level. The Fon live in an agricultural state ruled by a hereditary royal family. Herskovits (1938) suggests there could be many low-level local disputes, yet he also implies that few conflicts escalate and describes a wide range of local institutions that quickly intervene to settle them. Private vengeance is rigidly repressed (Murdock 1934:574), and Argyle reports that the king and his administrative system effectively prevent internal feuds and wars (1966:126). Also relevant are strong cross-cutting ties found in the kinship and ceremonial groups linking Fon across local communities. Although the patrilineal, patrilocal Fon can be said to have strong, localized fraternal interest groups, they do not fight each other. What is more important is that these units are integrated into the political and social organization of the kingdom and form the core of fighting groups (including all-female regiments) that engage in regular external warfare. Although Fon society limits internal conflict, it was expansionist from the seventeenth century and conducted yearly slave raids well into the mid-nineteenth century (Herskovits 1938:74). Undoubtedly internal integration made the Fon one of the most militarily successful societies in West Africa before the establishment of colonial rule.

Two other large states, the Buganda and the Aztec, and a petty chiefdom with concentrated power, the Burusho, are also internal underconflicters.[10] This pattern is not a general one, however, for there are societies with similarly concentrated power, such as the Lakher and Amhara, which are internal overconflicters, and some like the Azande where internal conflict is at the expected level. If certain forms of political organization are common to internal underconflicters, factors other than concentrated power seem to be involved.[11]

Ethnographic reports give the impression that the Fon effectively limit internal conflicts through a basic acceptance of the state's authority, not due to its power and the threats of its use. In contrast, descriptions of the Buganda and Aztec indicate use of internal force to obtain compliance and limit internal conflict, although some acceptance of the state's authority is also suggested. How to judge the relative importance of coercive power versus legitimated authority as a force producing

10. The Buganda and Aztec also are external overconflicters, but the Burusho are not.
11. Data analysis just as firmly rejects the inverse hypothesis, that in the absence of centralized power internal conflict is more likely to occur.

internal order is, however, a complex question that cannot be resolved with the data available here.

Mbuti: Secure Dependence

Among the underconflicters are several of the most peaceful societies in the sample, including the Mbuti (see chapter 1) and the Lepcha (see chapter 5). Although in these cases the dependent variables are generally accurately predicted to be positive or negative, the model overestimates their level of internal and external conflict.[12]

The case of the Mbuti is particularly useful to consider in detail. For years I have used Turnbull's (1978) essay on nonviolent socialization among the Mbuti to illustrate central psychocultural features of a low-conflict society. Yet when I looked at the Mbuti scores on the two socialization scales, I realized that while they have virtually the highest score on affectionate socialization practices in the sample, the score on harsh socialization practices was just above the mean, far greater than I expected.[13]

I tried to consider why my impression of the Mbuti was at odds with the score on the harsh socialization scale. One code, and its possible meaning, struck me as instructive. The Mbuti are scored high on the measure of the importance of caretakers and companions other than a child's mother, which is consistent with Turnbull's description. Theoretically, this practice is often seen as contributing to weakly developed object ties and interpersonal insecurity. Turnbull, however, does not find this to be the case for the Mbuti. He says that all residents of the community value children highly and feel affection and responsibility for them. An important early lesson for the Mbuti infant is that there are many sources of warmth and affection, just as there are many places

12. Multiplicative effects not reflected in my model may be at work at both extremes.
13. A review of the individual scores of the component variables on the harsh socialization scale revealed that several could be coded differently, at least in light of Montagu's (1978) discussion of Mbuti socialization, which Barry and Paxson (1971) and Barry, Josephson, Lauer, and Marshall (1976; 1977) did not have available when they assigned the codes I used. But this path, I decided, was truly a huge can of worms, for if I questioned these ratings, what about those for other cases where the results didn't quite fit the theory?

where one can feel safe. Multiple caregivers, in Turnbull's analysis, build interpersonal security and trust.[14]

Central to Turnbull's explanation for Mbuti peacefulness is the high level of social trust which the Mbuti develop in their physical and social worlds. These hunter-gatherers are truly in harmony with their surroundings; the rain forest is revered for its protection and generosity; other humans are an essential part of the world for material and spiritual reasons. Yet dependence, whether on the forest or other people, creates no fear. Turnbull's description leads to an expectation of little externalization, projection, and displacement of aggression because the Mbuti lack these intense feelings and achieve secure emotional connections to others. Because of this fundamental trust in others and in their physical surroundings, the Mbuti, who live near each other in camps within their community, hardly avoid disputes altogether; but they do for the most part avoid rapid escalations to violence. There is a tendency toward benevolent misperception when someone makes a mistake. Typically a dispute quickly becomes public and is resolved through discussion and humor, often with much teasing, emphasizing common community membership.[15] Levity in these situations calls on what is shared, and disputants laugh with, not at, each other.

If Mbuti high social trust is part of a projective system where open conflict is not severe, this hypothesis is certainly plausible for several other underconflicters as well. Gorer's (1938) description of the Lepcha (chapter 5) seems to fit this situation, at least in part. Permissiveness and sanction of antisocial behavior produce few instances of open quarreling, let alone violence. Although Gorer does not use the term "social trust," he describes a lack of jealousy and rivalry (particularly with regard to sexual matters) that suggests the absence of a strong basis for projective aggression. The culture of conflict in such situations includes

14. The Mbuti score on the use of corporal punishment and pain infliction is relatively high (3 out of 4). Although Turnbull reports that children are hit if they wander out of their play area, this is done in order to communicate that dangers lurk in the forest and that children cannot go there safely. Turnbull (1978) clearly suggests that this use of physical force is different from situations where it is used in anger, and that even very young children perceive the difference.

15. See Marshall (1961) for a description of humor as a device for conflict resolution among the !Kung.

norms like social trust, as well as practices such as benevolent misperception (Deutsch 1973), allowing the society to avoid bitter disputes.

Teda: The Intersocietal System

Eight of the eleven cases in which the incidence of overall (external plus internal conflict) is most underestimated receive a maximum score on external conflict, and each of these is considerably above the mean on internal conflict as well.[16] These societies are overconflicters and generalizers—for whom psychocultural features are especially important—and yet the model underestimates the overall amount of conflict in each case. This may be due to the model's exclusive focus on the internal characteristics of each society. In these cases, what Waltz (1959) calls the interstate system, referring to international relations, must also be considered. To the extent that high levels of conflict characterize this larger system, the model's underestimation is in part due to its neglect of the regional intersocietal environment.

The Teda people of the central Sahara provide a good case study of this situation. The Iban of Borneo, the Maori of Polynesia, the Riffians of the Maghreb, the Rwala Bedouins of the Arabian Peninsula, and the Gheg Albanians are other similar overconflicters. Like these societies, the Teda are located in a region where conflict and violence are relatively common. The Teda are primarily pastoral, living in groups of fifty to one hundred people in dispersed households. Although nominal chiefs exist, effective authority rests with household heads (Briggs 1960:168–170). Neolocal residence (in which spouses establish residence at a location not determined by the kin ties of either) is favored, so that while local fighting groups develop, they are not necessarily the localized male kin groups described in fraternal interest group theory. Teda society is not integrated by strong cross-cutting ties; there is some concentration of clans by district and the Islamic faith is shared by all, but neither factor creates political units above the level of the local community.

Conflict within Teda groups and between the Teda and outsiders is endemic. Cline (1950:47) finds that personal quarrels (often resulting in death) can be found among men and among women. Individually

16. This estimate results from adding together the standardized residual for internal and external conflict.

initiated actions are crucial in settling disputes, with force frequently used (Cline 1950; Briggs 1958). Raiding neighbors to acquire land is an honorable activity (Cline 1950:25) and blood feuds have a long history (Briggs 1960:178). External warfare is also frequent. The Teda raid caravans passing through their territory, fight regularly with the neighboring Tuareg, and conduct long-distance raids as well. Although Teda identity as such is weak, clans effectively organize fighting groups and suspiciousness of all outsiders is high.

Violence among the Teda, it seems plausible to argue, is part of an intersocietal conflict system characteristic of the region. Although Teda conflict behavior is more or less consistent with their psychocultural behavior, like child rearing practices that have little warmth and affection and tend to be strict, these alone fail to account for the especially high levels of conflict. The Circum-Mediterranean region generally, and parts of the Sahara in particular, have long formed a regional conflict system in which physical violence has played a central role. Although we have no systematic data on the question, Teda conflict levels, from this perspective, could be as much a response to the general modeling behavior and specific responses to the actions of their neighbors as a result of internal characteristics. Waltz's (1959) perspective usefully highlights ways in which a regional system affects a society's conflict behavior, yet he errs in insisting exclusively on the systemic level of analysis (compare Bueno de Mesquita, Siverson, and Woller 1992).

Conclusion

Significant variation within the general model identified in chapters 6 and 7 is explored in two ways, through an examination of the roots of over- and underprediction of conflict and through a consideration of deviant cases. These approaches show that although there is a general link between social structural interests and psychocultural interpretations, on the one hand, and institutions and practices of conflict, on the other, there are important specific variations. The culture of conflict is not just a monolithic force whose manifestations are the same from setting to setting, but also a pattern, internal to each society, which reflects the diverse ways in which particular features come to the fore and interconnect.

Examination of the societies in the sample where conflict levels

deviate most from the statistical model—the under- and overconflicters—shows that the two sets of societies differ in styles of conflict. These
results illuminate the complex relationship between internal and external conflict as well. Internal overconflicters are generalizing societies,
where women are more active politically, whereas internal underconflicters are differentiators and have less female political involvement.
External underconflicters, in contrast, are generalizing societies with less
contact with outsiders, and external overconflicters are differentiating
societies with more external contact and more emphasis on obedience
and self-reliance in socialization.

Two important conclusions follow from this pattern (see figure 8.1
above). First, unlike hydraulic models (which see overall conflict levels
as stable) or theories of the culture of violence (which see aggression as
necessarily reinforcing), generalization is not automatic according to the
results here. Generalization of conflict is related to, but not entirely explained by, contact with outsiders in that levels of external and internal
conflict are more likely to be similar when contact is frequent. Second,
since generalization is found among external underconflicters and internal overconflicters, two different dynamics are probably at work.

Investigating the dynamics of generalization and differentiation
can help us to better understand variations in the culture of conflict.
First, when a society has diverging internal and external conflict levels,
what determines if, and when, the low- or high-conflict pattern is generalized from one domain to the other? Second, in addition to the conflict
pattern, the domain may be relevant. Is the pattern of internal conflict
or external conflict more likely to generalize from one domain to the
other? The data do not offer a direct answer to either of these questions.

I would like to suggest a hypothesis consistent with the results
here: that internal political considerations (whatever they may be) provide the critical point of reference, determining when generalization or
differentiation of internal or external conflict is most likely (recognizing
that generalization is the more likely pattern to develop). It is easiest to
imagine that in an internal overconflict society (figure 8.1, pattern B),
generalization of beliefs and behaviors attached to internal opponents
may be relatively easy to apply to outsiders with whom the society has
no strong bonds. The finding that external underconflict is associated
with generalization (pattern C) is also consistent with a priority placed
on internal dynamics with a generalization of low hostility toward outsiders. Generalization of psychocultural interpretations from internal to

external settings is consistent with the pattern. Likewise, an internal perspective that places a priority on societal survival is consistent with the differentiation found among internal underconflicters (pattern A), as well as among external overconflicters (pattern D). Both D and A can be explained by the community's need for internal unity when faced with an external foe. Here, the importance of internal interests may account for the need to differentiate between internal and external targets. This explanation favors neither internal nor external conflict, nor the process of generalization over differentiation. Rather, it stresses that internal dynamics affects the culture of conflict while allowing for other factors, including survival considerations, driven by outside forces. This is consistent with the broader explanation developed in chapters 6 and 7 that psychocultural processes are associated with generalization and interests with differentiation.

The analysis of individual deviant cases offers further insights into specific structural and psychocultural mechanisms in societies where the statistical model is least accurate. The five factors discussed were fear of affiliation, great isolation, concentrated political authority, secure dependence, and the intersocietal system. Although some of these mechanisms inform the culture of conflict in one or even several deviant cases, they are not factors which alone provide the basis for an adequate general explanation. A variable like the regional conflict system, however, may prove useful in building future theoretical and empirical models of preindustrial societies.

Interests that follow from social structural organization and interpretations rooted in psychocultural dispositions are particularly important in establishing and maintaining a society's culture of conflict. The statistical model in chapter 6 highlights the direct effect of these forces on the level and target of conflict and violence. In addition, however, the examination of the relationship between internal and external violence in chapter 7 and the consideration of deviant cases here emphasize variations in the organization of the culture of conflict within the general model. The exploration of the phenomena of generalization and differentiation of conflict patterns and consideration of societies where correspondence with the statistical model is poor show important variations in the organization of culture.

One of the wider concerns of this project is the utility of the culture of conflict theory—beyond the preindustrial societies used to develop it—to explain conflict in other settings. This is the question I turn to next.

9

Generalizing the Culture-of-Conflict Theory: Northern Ireland and Norway

How can the cross-cultural theory of conflict presented earlier offer insights into settings other than preindustrial societies? Two views of the uses of theory are found in the social sciences today, the "hard science" view and the contextual view. The hard science view emphasizes the testability of a theory's propositions, toward the goal of scientific generalization; the contextual view, in contrast, stresses a theory's ability to illuminate specific cases on their own terms. My view is that each offers useful but different insights. The hard science view points to regularities in human behavior, whereas the contextualist stresses variation in response to particular environments. The hard science perspective minimizes real problems of deciding the truth or falsity of any theory, and too many contextualists cannot say why their explanation is better than another. This chapter first addresses the hard science questions about generalization, and then seeks to use the cross-cultural theory of conflict in a more contextual fashion to discuss two cases outside the preindustrial societies considered so far: contemporary Northern Ireland and Norway.

The first section examines the dynamics of generalization, exploring on the empirical level what replication of the present findings with cases from modern nations would entail and what theoretical limits exist when one generalizes findings from one population to another. The limits to generalization from one group to another depend on the extent to which differences between the two affect the relations being generalized. I argue that there are no such characteristics of modern nations or units within them which make the findings from the cross-cultural study obviously irrelevant.

Having identified no theoretical reasons why the findings from
the preindustrial societies should not be applied to other settings, in the
second part of the chapter, I use the theory to gain insights into two
particular situations. This contextualist use of the theory should provide
new insights into the particular cases.

Applying the cross-cultural theory of conflict to Northern Ireland
and Norway explores two distinct cultures of conflict. The case of Northern Ireland provides the opportunity to examine the persistence of extreme violence and the long-standing inability of two groups to live
together in peace. Norway's situation poses a different question—why
this nation (once filled with fierce warriors) is now a low-violence, low-
conflict society. The cross-cultural theory's explanatory variables provide a significant improvement over previous explanations, most of
which are structural, because the psychocultural dispositions of the
Norwegians and the residents of Northern Ireland are far more critical
for understanding conflict behavior in these societies than is usually
suggested.

Generalization of Findings Beyond a Sample

The hard science view is that the theory of conflict developed in
the cross-cultural study should be tested in other settings—modern nations, local communities, face-to-face groups, or large organizations.
While such a replication is not my immediate plan, I think it is worth-
while to explore briefly what this would entail, thereby illustrating that
such replication is possible and examining possible solutions to some
of the problems it would involve. In testing the theory in new settings,
two important issues need to be addressed: finding the right units of
analysis to use in a test of the theory, and identifying theoretically and
operationally equivalent measures of the psychocultural and structural
variables used in the cross-cultural study.

Because the theory was developed using small-scale societies, it
perhaps should first be tested using units smaller than large nation-states,
as assumptions about the homogeneity of the units on critical variables
may be relevant. Local communities, regions, work groups, industrial
organizations, small states, or ethnic communities may be appropriate
units.

Finding equivalent measures for key concepts in order to test the
cross-cultural theory in modern nations is a challenge all replications

using different populations face. Survey researchers must consider not only whether a question is correctly translated from one language to another, for example, but, more important, whether the affective meanings of the two versions are equivalent. Although some of the specific structural and psychocultural measures used in preindustrial societies are relatively exotic to political scientists, who study modern nations, the concepts underlying the structural variables are usually quite familiar. Socioeconomic complexity, political role specialization, and political power concentration have clear parallels in large nations. Similarly, the notion of cross-cutting ties has been at the core of much political analysis for many years. Although anthropologists pay more attention to residence and kinship rules than do students of modern societies, the measures which are needed must indicate patterns of cross-cutting coalitions, alliances, and sources of integration rooted in a society's social structure. The development of appropriate measures for these concepts at the national, community, or organizational level is not likely to be difficult. The same case can be made for the key psychocultural measures. For example, male gender-identity conflict is certainly a familiar concept in settings beyond preindustrial societies even though we would need to develop measures other than the length of post-partum sexual abstinence or the length of exclusive mother-child sleeping arrangements used in the cross-cultural study. Although I argue that some of the same underlying processes occur in all human groups, the specific indicators must be appropriate in context.

The Logic of Generalization

All empirical research raises the problem of how widely the results from one study can be generalized. None of the conventional answers to this question is definitive. According to sampling theory, for example, when a random sample of a population is properly drawn, results can be generalized to that population within a certain margin of error. Replication of findings in a new sample drawn from the same population also increases confidence in the generalizability of findings. Campbell and Fiske (1959) argue that support for findings increases when the same results are obtained using different methods as well as different measures.

But one must account for situations where the population to which one wants to generalize is not the one on which the first study is based. Strictly speaking, there is no logical reason why findings from a study in population A should hold for population B. This skeptical view questions, for example, the relevance of medical research on monkeys, or learning studies using rats (or American college sophomores) which are then applied to all humans.

In practice, the generalizability of results depends on whether or not differences between the two populations are likely to affect the relationship under study. If no difference is identified between the two populations on critical variables which may plausibly affect the results, then one may cautiously generalize. Thus, medical researchers believe that the similarity in the nervous and immune systems of monkeys and humans makes studies of the effects of new drugs on monkeys applicable to humans. Differences between the two populations such as upper body strength, limb length, or speech skills are not denied but are ignored because there is no plausible reason why these or certain other physical characteristics would produce different reactions to a drug.

Generalization about social behavior across human populations, of course, is more hazardous because social scientists are often unclear about which population characteristics can affect a given relationship. Some generalizations seem safer to venture than others. Cross-cultural psychologists have found many developmental processes, for example, ranging from early psychomotor skills to cognitive functioning, which follow stages identified by Piaget or Kohlberg and seem to occur in the same order, although not always at the same rate, in many human groups. Cross-cultural theorists like Murdock and Whiting have posited a "psychic unity of humankind," meaning that underlying human action in all societies is a common set of emotions, motives, and ways of relating to the world.

Some good candidates for generalization do hold across populations, but to different degrees. For example, Verba, Nie, and Kim (1978) found that socioeconomic status was related to electoral participation in all seven countries they studied, but that the relationship was strongest in the United States and Japan and virtually irrelevant in Austria. Variations reflected the extent to which political parties and other institutions compensated for individual differences in resources. In the end, the researchers concluded not just that Austria differs from the U.S. but that Austrian parties had developed a different pattern of political mobilization than American parties.

Some generalizations are limited to certain populations. Gellner

(1983) argues that the phenomenon of nationalism, for example, is uniquely associated with the rise of industrial society and that its underlying dynamic differs from earlier forms of in-group identification. Differences in the organization of industrial and preindustrial societies, he argues, are entirely different, at least with respect to the establishment and maintenance of group identity and its relationship to the political order.

Other generalizations can be applied to different populations, but in ways that recognize the unique characteristics of each. For example, neo-Marxist theories of conflict are general in predicting that conflict will be a function of the organization of the means of production in all social formations, but specific in identifying the particular dynamics of conflict among hunter-gatherers, pastoralists, sedentary agriculturalists, and members of industrial societies (see, for example, Ferguson 1984; Newman 1983). Generalization across populations, then, depends on the extent to which specific differences in the populations can plausibly affect the relationship under consideration.

Finally, there is the issue of what constitutes evidence for the replication of a finding in a second sample. The weakest of four tests of increasing severity would posit that results are replicated if the sign of a relationship (or a series of relationships) is the same (positive or negative) in a replication. A more rigorous requirement is that the results should be statistically significant in both samples. Third, the magnitude of the relationship would have to be about the same in both populations. The most stringent test would apply to a replication involving a multivariate model, like the one presented in chapters 6 and 7, where the proportion of the variance in each case and the coefficients of each variable would have to be a similar magnitude.

Relevance for Modern Nations

To what extent are the findings from the sample of preindustrial societies relevant to understanding internal and external conflict in modern nations? The answer hinges, in part, on the extent to which we can identify differences between preindustrial societies and modern nations that suggest that a relationship holds in one group but not the other. For example, the cross-cultural study emphasizes the psychocultural roots of conflict, whereas a "realist" view of international politics discounts its importance for modern nations (Morgenthau 1960; Waltz 1959). The realist argues that nations fight because of competition for resources and power, and that although public opinion can be manipulated to generate interpretations of others like those described in the psychocultural conflict theory, the actions of diplomats and other key decision makers are based on a more dispassionate appraisal of the situation. In addition, in small-scale societies like those used in the cross-cultural study, the connection between emotions and action can be far more immediate than in modern nations where multiple layers of institutional bureaucracy intervene.

Yet data about the relationship between disposition and action indicate the relevance of the psychocultural findings in each setting. To counter the realist position there are data on the nature of the motives and actions of modern state officials and the power of institutions to resist popular demands for aggression, two central tenets of the "realist" view of action which have been widely questioned (Jervis 1976; Lebow 1981). The argument that psychocultural dispositions have more immediate effects in small-scale societies points to the need to specify the mechanisms by which these dispositions affect behaviors within complex political institutions. It also suggests that there might be differences in the strength of a relationship between the two settings, rather than in its direction.

Although preindustrial societies and modern nations differ in a number of ways, none of these suggests obvious reasons why the dynamics of conflict would not be similar in each. The social structural and psychocultural dynamics involve mechanisms found in preindustrial and industrial societies and I have no a priori grounds for assuming that these mechanisms do not operate in both settings.[1] What therefore seems most useful is to offer such generalizations, trusting that if they do not seem relevant in modern settings this will become apparent. The insights that may be gained from application of findings from preindustrial settings to modern societies clearly justify the effort.

The cases of Northern Ireland and Norway do not provide a systematic test of the theory in a new setting; rather, the intention here is to examine how this theoretical perspective helps us to understand conflict and conflict management in these two societies. To what extent do structural and psychocultural processes jointly contribute to an expla-

1. It seems more plausible that the magnitude of relations will differ in the two groups of societies—an important question, but not my main focus here.

nation that surpasses an approach based on one or the other alone? In addition, in describing the culture of conflict in these two societies, and the institutions and practices maintained by both psychocultural dispositions and structural interests, I shall suggest why patterns of conflict and conflict management, once established, are so difficult to alter.

Northern Ireland

From its inception as a distinct political unit in 1920, Northern Ireland has been bitterly divided between the dominant Unionist (Protestant) and the minority Nationalist (Catholic) communities. The Protestant majority has insisted, in a variety of ways, on maintaining its "union" with England, Scotland, and Wales in the United Kingdom. The Catholic minority has professed, with varying degrees of enthusiasm, a desire to make the island one nation (Darby 1983).

A History of Protracted Conflict

It is hard to know just how far back to go in order to understand the current conflict in Northern Ireland. English invasions from the twelfth century, expropriation of land, and political domination of the island combined with Scottish immigration, particularly in the north, to turn Ireland into a colonial society (MacDonald 1986). Eventually, the English acceded to demands for Ireland's independence following World War I. The island was partitioned in 1920 into two entities, the Irish Free State and Northern Ireland, and a bitter civil war occurred in the south, which former eventually became the Republic of Ireland, while the six counties of Ulster comprising Northern Ireland obtained home rule within the United Kingdom. The political and economic power of the Protestants and their professed loyalty to the Crown permitted them to maintain a privileged position in the north (See 1986).

Despite intercommunal tension, overt violence in Northern Ireland was low from the mid-1920s until the 1960s,[2] with politeness and avoidance serving as important strategies to minimize overt expression of conflict (Harris 1972; Fitzduff 1992; Wright 1992). The region was self-governing with Protestant domination of political and economic life

---

2. The IRA, which was long outlawed in the Republic, was so ineffective that R. White (1989) says that by 1962 it was virtually inactive.

and widespread discrimination against Catholics in jobs, housing, and political representation (Boyle and Hadden 1985). In the late 1960s, internal tensions erupted in the form of a civil rights movement demanding an end to discrimination against Catholics. The movement achieved startling gains despite violent resistance by Unionist factions who claimed that it was a blatant cover for militant nationalists. Intergroup violence spread as the Protestant Ulster Defense Force (UDF) attacked Catholics' nonviolent demonstrations. Eventually the British sent in army units, which were initially welcomed as protectors by the Catholic community. They failed to restore the peace, as the UDF, which included many supporters of the Reverend Ian Paisley, and the emerging Provisional Irish Republican Army (IRA) fought each other in the name of their religious communities (Lebow 1978; R. White 1989). Soon, however, violent conflict between the IRA and the British army became even more important.

Two events embody the transformation of the struggle from civil rights to competing national and ethnic claims. The first, the internment of suspected IRA activists in August 1971, involved the arrest without warrant of hundreds of Catholics, only a few of whom were found to be legitimately accused. For many Catholics, the event confirmed the claim, most loudly voiced by the IRA, that the British army was acting on behalf of the Unionist government.[3] No Protestants were arrested at the time, and no single event was more responsible for mobilizing anti-British sentiment among Catholics. The second event, in March 1972, was the suspension of Northern Ireland's parliament and the imposition of direct rule from the House of Commons in London. Direct rule—still in place some two decades later—along with the introduction into Northern Ireland of the British army, effectively made the British government and army responsible for the provision of security. The arrests and the imposition of direct rule put an end to the civil rights or reform period and effectively defined the triangular structure of the conflict in the north. Overt conflict between Catholics and Protestants continued unabated, intensified by the reemergence of the overlapping conflict between nationalists, on one hand, and Unionists and the British government, on the other, over the question of the structure of the province

3. R. White (1989) presents data arguing that the internment and murder of Catholics by security forces are the best predictors of the rise of Provisional IRA violence in Derry between 1970 and 1972.

and even its right to exist. Although the peace movement in the mid-1970s raised hopes, optimism was short-lived, intercommunal violence continued, and extremists in both communities continue to have widespread support to this day.

At present there is increasing recognition of the limitations of both the traditional nationalist interpretation of the conflict, which blames the British, and the traditional Unionist view, which faults the Irish for refusing to renounce claims to the area (Wright 1992; Whyte 1990). Instead, a clearer understanding has emerged, that although both British and Irish are important actors in the conflict, the key parties are the inhabitants of Ulster itself (Whyte 1990).[4] This focus draws attention to the internal dynamics of the region in institutionalizing the conflict and perpetuating the political stalemate (Darby 1986, 1990; Whyte 1990).

Cultures in Conflict

A focus on the internal dynamics of the region highlights the lack of consensus between the two religious communities regarding what they consider the major issues at stake and how each group thinks the other views them. One important consequence of these widely differing interpretations of the conflict is that each party sees itself as a threatened (and somewhat powerless) minority (O'Malley 1983). Protestants stress that a unified state would threaten their religious freedom, whereas Catholics point out that they make up only one third of the population of the north and are victims of long-term discrimination. But the divergent perceptions and desires of the players on a range of issues can only partially help analyze the persistence of intractable conflict for they are also evidence of it (Mulvihill and Ross 1989). In addition, as in other complex ethnic conflicts, there are also strong factional differences within each community as well as between them.[5]

The conflict in Northern Ireland is often described in cultural

---

4. O'Malley (1990) makes this point somewhat differently in his moving account of the Catholic hunger-strikers and their families. He concludes that as long as the Catholic community views the British as the all-powerful oppressors, they will be unable to take control of their own fate.

5. Support for the IRA, for example, is somewhat variable within the Catholic community and, in elections in the North, the Social Democratic Labor Party, which opposes the IRA's use of violence and terror, regularly outpolls Sinn Fein, the IRA's political party, among Catholics.

terms. Numerous markers of identity build in-group solidarity and at the same time evoke out-group hostility. Some of these are religious in nature, but many are commonplace objects infused with symbolic meaning: flags (the Union Jack versus the Tricolor), colors (orange versus green), place names (Londonderry versus Derry), and drinks (Bushmill's whiskey versus Paddy's whiskey), to name a few.[6] In the highly polarized world of Northern Ireland, the capacity of virtually any object to develop culturally charged meanings which reinforce communal hostility is striking. Mutual suspicions are, needless to say, strong, and the fact that moderate and extremist factions of one community share many symbolic frames of reference often makes it difficult for members of the other community to differentiate between them. In this setting, to a Protestant any Catholic becomes a potential IRA supporter, and to a Catholic any Protestant seems a likely Paisleyite. Wright (1992:235) calls the two major interpretations of the conflict vigilance (Protestant) and rebellion (Catholic) and says they pervade most understanding of key political events in the region.

McLachlan (1987) emphasizes two additional cultural differences—organization and language. The Catholic community is more hierarchical and centralized, whereas authority in the Protestant community is more dispersed and segmental. Thus, members of each community have their own ways of undertaking collective tasks, and differences in organization produce tension in addition to the central conflict. Second, McLachlan argues that even though both groups speak English, the same words or phrases often take on different meanings, and he suggests that these fundamental cultural differences limit effective communication and understanding in a setting pervaded by distrust.

Why Does the Violence Persist?

The standard explanation for the intractable conflict in Northern Ireland is more structural than psychocultural, emphasizing the division

6. Cairns suggests that the intense conflict may result in cultural expressions of superiority and dominance which then serve to increase the psychological distinctiveness of each group (1982). Volkan (1988), describing similar minor differences in cultural symbols and the intense political meanings which can be attached to them, uses Freud's phrase, "the narcissism of minor differences," to explain the process by which such symbolic expressions come to represent basic differences in identity.

of the region into Protestant and Catholic camps with mutually exclusive interests, few overlapping ties, and historical class differences, as well as persistent discrimination against Catholics in housing and jobs (Whyte 1990; Boyle and Hadden 1985; McFarlane 1986).[7] Protestants and Catholics alike use historical events to justify their positions and to discredit the aggressive claims of the other side. The bitter and divergent accounts of particular events seem to me, however, as much the effect of prior conflict as the cause. After all, the use of history is always selective and patterned. Catholics and Protestants manage to live in peace in many other parts of the world. Furthermore, their social separation and distrust are relative and seem to increase after outbursts of violence, rather than precede them.

Most important, structural explanations for this conflict seem not so much wrong as incomplete, for they never address directly the persistence of intense conflict. This question is central to psychocultural conflict theory, which identifies the dispositions associated with intense feelings of in-group support and out-group hostility. Psychocultural conflict theory can, perhaps, help us understand why countries like Kenya and Zimbabwe at the end of colonial rule, or Nigeria (which in its first decade after independence experienced severe internal conflict) have apparently achieved far more in the area of racial and ethnic reconciliation than the Catholics and Protestants of Ulster.

Structural Elements in the Conflict

Structural theories of conflict assign a causal role to incompatible interests in a community. In a region like Ulster, it is easy to see how differences in access to resources have created privileges that the Protestants want to maintain and that the Catholics seek to share. Structurally, Northern Ireland is a classic divided society in which one social cleavage takes precedence over all others (Boyle and Hadden 1985; Whyte 1990). The absence of cross-cutting ties between the communities that could limit the outbreak and escalation of conflict has been noted by many observers (Cairns 1982; Lipjhardt 1975). Not

7. For example in Lipjhardt's (1975) review article on Northern Ireland in the mid 1970s, he presents ten different images of Northern Ireland, all of which are primarily structural and none of which could be called psychocultural.

only do members of the two communities attend different churches, but they also live in separate areas, often work in distinct places, enjoy different leisure activities, and attend separate primary and secondary schools.[8] The segregated social worlds are reinforced through powerful stereotypes which are rarely modified by evidence to the contrary (Harris 1972). In many ways, the most important social units, especially in Belfast and other cities, are the strong localized male groups that form within each community and perpetrate many violent incidents (Lebow 1978).

Other structural theories identify a group-based notion of interests as a key factor in the persistence of conflict. Realistic group conflict theory (LeVine and Campbell 1972) draws attention to such tangible interests as jobs and housing, and to long-term patterns of communal privilege and deprivation. Biosocial theory points to the kin-like character of each ethnic community[9] and the propensity to defend what are clearly seen as its primordial interests. A complexity theory like cultural materialism identifies group interests created in the earlier colonial system that perpetuate patterns of privilege and deprivation today (MacDonald 1986; See 1986).

Structural factors alone, although clearly critical in understanding Northern Ireland, offer an incomplete explanation of the persistence of the conflict. They do not adequately explain how each side's vital interests come to be decided, nor the intensity of hostility and collective insecurity, nor each community's view of the other as threatening its self-esteem, indeed its very existence (Wright 1992). As Whyte says, "Anyone who studies the Ulster conflict must be struck by the intensity of feeling. It seems to go beyond what is required by a rational defense of the divergent interests which undoubtedly exist. There is an irrational element here, a well of deep unconscious forces, which can only be explained by an appeal to social psychology" (1978:278).[10]

8. Only 4 percent of the children in Northern Ireland attend what are called integrated schools (those which have a significant number of both Protestant and Catholic students).

9. Shaw and Wong (1989) use the term "nucleus ethnic group."

10. Whyte's rejection of an interest-based explanation as adequate is the crucial point here. I am not willing to label unconscious forces irrational, as he does.

Psychocultural Dispositions and Conflict

Psychocultural conflict theory explains conflict in terms of culturally patterned dispositions that shape group identification, assumptions about motivation, and interpretations of social action. Modern psychoanalytic theories such as object relations and self-psychology emphasize how out-group images are rooted in early family contexts, which are then extended to larger social aggregates and become a template for intergroup relations. Psychocultural conflict theory identifies deep-seated threats to survival in ethnic conflicts—formidable barriers to intercommunal conflict management (Horowitz 1985)—that help us to understand how each side in a conflict, as in Northern Ireland or in Israel–Palestine, sees itself as a vulnerable minority.

Although the evidence is indirect, many dispositional elements that the cross-cultural study identifies in high-conflict cultures are also found in Northern Ireland.[11] Male gender-identity conflict and absence of affection and warmth are central in Irish culture, although early socialization does not seem especially harsh. Messenger (1971) and Scheper-Hughes (1979) describe a fear of intimacy, extreme lack of social trust, lack of sociability, great emotional distance between fathers and children; and none of the predispositions needed to deal with political differences in a democratic society are present. Some male bonding occurs in the context of drinking in local pubs (where females are almost never present), but social and emotional withdrawal are also emphasized.[12] The Irish (both in the Republic and in the north) have the highest rate of schizophrenia in the world (Scheper-Hughes 1979:66–74), and there are powerful sexual fears on the part of both men and women. McGoldrick (1982) describes feelings of aggression and a preoccupation with sin and death that are dealt with through social withdrawal and isolation because expressing them within the family context is simply unacceptable. A plausible hypothesis is that aggression is turned toward acceptable targets, either inward (where it becomes schizophrenia and

11. Although the evidence cited below refers to Irish-Catholic, not Protestant culture, there is good reason to see more similarity than difference in terms of the psychocultural dimensions discussed in this section. Both Messenger (1971) and Scheper-Hughes (1979) did their research in the Republic.

12. This is parallel to but not as powerful a pattern as Briggs's (1975) description of the Utke Eskimo.

alcohol abuse) or outward (where it leads to sectarian conflict).[13] The divided social worlds in the cities in the north provide targets for violence both inside and outside each sectarian group, where actions are generally collective and are justified in terms of the defense of the community.

Dispositions identified in other psychocultural explanations are also present. For example, frustration-aggression-displacement theory directs attention toward intra- and intergroup frustrations which are projected onto out-groups (LeVine and Campbell 1972). The Irish experience certainly provides plenty of frustrations for all parties. Social identity theory posits a close linkage between individual and group self-esteem (Cairns 1982) and suggests that threats to group legitimacy can lead to the rapid escalation and persistence of ethnic disputes (Horowitz 1985). In intense ethnic conflicts, like that in Ireland, group legitimacy is continually threatened in public discussions or in constitutional proposals which by appealing to one side's basic needs ignore those of the other (O'Malley 1983). Cognitive and perceptual theory emphasizes the development and use of positive in-group and negative out-group images to attribute motives to out-groups. These images make constructive conflict management difficult and have long played an important role in the Irish conflict (Lebow 1976). Reference-group and other social comparison theories focus on group-based judgments about deprivation and advantage of each community relative to the other.

A psychocultural explanation emphasizes ways in which images of the social world and assumptions about and perceptions of others are central in organizing social and political action. It stresses the importance of shared interpretations of crucial yet ambiguous situations. The

13. Rural Irish communities in the Republic are not very openly conflictual. What seems much more prevalent is repression and the absence of institutional mechanisms for the expression of grievances. Even in the north, many rural communities (although not so much those in the border areas) have little overt conflict. McFarlane (1986) describes how local community ideologies emphasize harmony even in the face of religious divisions, in part by blaming outsiders, hotheads, and special factors for violence when it occurs rather than seeing it as an ongoing part of community life. The point is that even when psychocultural dispositions increase the chances of violence, the structure of a community and social support must also encourage conflict before such acts occur regularly—as in larger, polarized urban communities of the north.

evidence from Northern Ireland is consistent with psychocultural conflict theory. The frustrations, projections, fears of extinction, sense of
low self-esteem, and development of positive in-group and negative out-
group images—identified as basic causes of ethnocentric conflict by this
theory—are all present.

Summary

The culture of conflict in Northern Ireland is an integral part of
the region's persistent intergroup violence. Protestant and Catholic
differences in access to resources are very real, and structural factors
identify ways that they are maintained over time. Focusing on the psychocultural dimension of this conflict introduces a consideration of perceptions and fears behind the interest-based claims each party to the
conflict makes, revealing an important source of the intensity of emotions
and hence their persistence. Deep-seated fears and projective aggression
play a key role in this formulation, for they provide a motivation for
one group's action as a function of aggressive motives attributed to the
other side (Fornari 1975; White 1984; Volkan 1988). The psychocultural
dimension provides a context in which to understand the profound
social and political divisions, not an alternative explanation that stands
by itself. Consistent with the claim that understanding conflict also helps
us understand conflict management, I address elsewhere the question
of strategies of peacemaking in Northern Ireland (Ross 1992, 1993). The
challenge is not only to address the constitution-making aspects of the
conflict, seeking a formula on which the parties can agree, but also to
first find a way to alter the hostile perceptions and mutual fears that
lock the parties into a zero-sum view of any proposals.

Norway: The Peaceful Nation?

In contrast to Northern Ireland, there is relatively little overt violence and conflict in modern-day Norway, a nation that cross-national
studies show to score low on measures of internal violence, strikes,
homicide, and suicide (Galtung 1974; Naroll 1983). The situation in
Norway is relevant to the questions I have been asking because we should
be as interested in successes—referred to by Eckstein as those "solution"
cases, "societies that have managed to deal well with problems that

preoccupy us" (1966:5)—as we are with problem cases (Ross 1993: chapter 3).

The Norwegian case at first seems to have little comparative relevance. This small, prosperous, sparsely populated country, after all, speaks one language, is ethnically homogeneous,[14] does not have prominent class divisions, and is not a major world power. A closer look, however, suggests that some of these factors may be products of the society's capacity to manage conflict in certain constructive ways rather than be the cause. Although there are structural features of Norwegian society associated with low levels of overt internal and external conflict, psychocultural features of Norwegian society must be considered as well. It is not just that Norway is "organized" to avoid severe conflict—avoiding conflict is a deeply held cultural value inculcated through a range of practices in all phases of life.[15] Examining the Norwegian culture of conflict will, I hope, suggest practices that lead to the constructive management of many disputes in Norwegian society and provide insights into the nature of structural interests and psychocultural dispositions in a low-conflict setting.

Norwegian society appears more homogeneous to outsiders than to Norwegians themselves, who are often strongly rooted in local communities, which have regional differences that have been described in racial terms, and whose past linguistic and religious disputes have been bitter at times (Eckstein 1966). Participation in local communities and voluntary associations is very high (Eckstein 1966; Ramsøy 1974). Strong national identification may be due to the fact that Norway was ruled by Denmark until 1815 and then had only limited self-rule under Sweden until 1905.

Norway may score low on measures of internal conflict, but it has fought with outsiders. The Vikings had an aggressive reputation throughout northern and western Europe, although Eckstein says they main-

14. Norway has a small Lapp population that sometimes comes into conflict with the majority (see Eidheim 1969).

15. Eckstein, seeking to understand Norway as a stable democracy, also rejects structural explanations as adequate by themselves. In fact, he says the sharp and persistent divisions in Norway are among those "one would least expect to find in a stable democracy" (1966:67). Although I think his claim about the strength of divisions is unnecessarily exaggerated, his larger point is quite useful.

tained a relatively peaceful domestic society (1966:115).[16] Since independence, however, Norway has been involved in far less external conflict than most other western European nations. Germany invaded and occupied Norway during World War II, but Norwegians formed a united front, refusing in many (often nonviolent) ways to recognize the legitimacy of the puppet regime or to cooperate with it. Perhaps as a result of Denmark's long-term domination, Norwegians remain suspicious of outsiders and voted against membership in the European Economic Community in a 1972 national referendum (Orvik 1975).

An explanation for low incidence of aggression in Norway that is consistent with the structural factors identified in the cross-cultural study may be constructed starting with Norway's social homogeneity. In addition, although Norwegians value individual independence, at the same time they feel a great deal of responsibility for each other's well-being and possess what Naroll (1983) calls large moral nets, meaning many people who can provide support to an individual in times of need. For some this means a rich extended family life; for others, many friends and neighbors are available. Hollos (1974), for example, describes a rural community with isolated farms in which there is a good deal of exchange labor in farming. Although social interaction as such is infrequent and not highly affective, people know that others are available when needed. Extensive involvement in voluntary associations (often characterized by attachments that are more instrumental than emotional) and widespread overlapping networks make it difficult for communities to divide into permanent factions.

The evidence in support of the psychocultural hypotheses in the Norwegian case is also consistent with the general argument I have been making. Early socialization is high in affection, low in aggression, and male gender-identity is not particularly problematic. Norwegian child rearing is often described as warm, indulgent, and kind; physical punishment is rare (Eckstein 1966:160–161). Hollos (1974) describes a high level of maternal nurturance, with little emphasis on discipline or control but with close supervision. Few demands are made of young children

16. Castberg (1954) claims that the Viking warriors represented an aberrant feature of Norwegian culture, not unlike Quisling and other Nazi collaborators—an explanation I do not find satisfactory. The argument that the older Norwegian society represented a historical example of high differentiation (as the term is used in chapters 7 and 8) may be worth exploring in greater detail.

and they engage in a great deal of self-initiated play and exploration of their immediate environment. There is little parental verbal instruction and strong emotion is infrequently expressed. From observations in a more urban setting, Bolton (1984) says there is often high involvement of fathers, an emphasis on peer culture, and little performance pressure on children. In both rural and urban settings, emotional self-control, especially over negative feelings, is stressed (Bolton 1984; Hollos 1974). This is an important theme for adults as well, and, consequently, at times much adult interaction is highly stylized and superficial.

The value placed on not expressing aggression overtly and on exercising self-control that both Bolton and Hollos report is consistent with Sears, Maccoby, and Levin's (1958) findings that lack of aggression is promoted by both low permissiveness and low punishment of children. It is clear that Norwegians learn early in life that overt aggression or even direct confrontation of others is unacceptable. Pressure to conform apparently makes severe punishment unnecessary, for individuals and groups effectively monitor themselves.

Gender identity issues (for males or females) do not seem to be particularly problematic. There is no description in the literature of a need for sons to break their emotional bonds to their mothers, of severe paternal hazing of boys, of compensatory male aggression, or of sexuality as an emotionally charged domain (if anything, the opposite seems more typical). Male-female equality has long been a concern in Norway, and recently there has been increased sharing of tasks between husbands and wives, especially in more urban settings.

An important Norwegian cultural strategy for dealing with aggression is to avoid creating situations where hostility may be inadvertently expressed. In the rural community she studied, Hollos described how family roles are highly structured to separate individuals when tensions might develop (Hollos 1974). A mother-in-law and daughter-in-law who live in the same household stay out of each other's way; father and adult son often engage in the same job in different locations—chopping wood for hours, for example, on opposite sides of the house. Because of the norm against expressing aggression, people who don't like each other sometimes appear together in public and refuse to let this interfere with task performance (Hollos 1974:40). At other times, potential disputants avoid each other (Barth 1952; Ramsøy 1974). Withdrawal and isolation are learned as appropriate ways to handle hostility.

Some authors connect the low Norwegian expression of conflict to a deep collective sense of responsibility (Ramsøy 1974:219–224). Eckstein emphasizes the importance of the noneconomic aspects of relationships as part of the strong sense of community (1966:80–92). The sense of social responsibility is expressed in a variety of ways: in an emphasis on equality and leveling, attentiveness to community norms, conformity, and participation with or without high personal commitment (Hollos 1974:40). There is, simultaneously, great concern for the welfare of others and a certain emotional reserve in personal relations. Tremendous care is taken not to hurt the feelings of others. Directness in interpersonal relations is rare, but cooperation occurs because of mutual attentiveness (Castberg 1954). Hollos describes the use of indirect signals and nonverbal cues to avoid outright commands, even to children. Friendships are highly valued and Gullestad (1984) describes the mutual responsiveness and sensitivities present in friendship groups. Despite their interpersonal sensitivity and reserve, however, Norwegians have little suspicion of public or quasi-public authority, according to Eckstein, and they do not believe that others will take advantage of them. Rather, the community is there for all, if and when it is needed.

Norwegian expressive culture provides few aggressive models. There is little violence depicted on television, no boxing, and films are controlled. For example, E.T. was declared too violent for children under twelve. Newspapers do not sensationalize crime. Few people have guns and even the police are generally unarmed. Finally, low levels of stress in daily life are important to individuals. Lack of noise, low population density, the enjoyment of nature—hiking in the woods, for example—relieve stress. Norwegian values like egalitarianism in sports, the economy, and elsewhere de-emphasize competition and achievement (Bolton 1984; Castberg 1954); safety and health are emphasized.[17]

Decision making and the exercise of authority in Norway are intended to keep overt conflict at a minimum. First, there is an effort in many settings to reach a broad private consensus before deciding upon a matter publicly. Broad-based coalitions are valued and regularly sought, and when consensus cannot be developed matters are often dropped. Conciliation councils—local community institutions on which three citizens serve four-year terms—hear civil cases before disputants

17. The typical Norwegian diet—high fat, low carbohydrate, eaten in four or five meals a day—is linked in some research to low levels of violence as well as stress (Bolton 1984).

go to court, to see if simple mediation may be useful. Connary reports that in this way more than a third of civil cases are resolved quickly and do not go to court (1966:186). Finally, Eckstein argues that Norwegian legalism and formalism remove issues from controversy by standardizing the ways in which tasks are performed (1966:171–172).

Summary

Both the structural and the psychocultural features of Norwegian society contribute to the relatively low level of violence found there and help maintain a culture of conflict which emphasizes the peaceful and constructive management of disputes. The structure of Norwegian society does not give rise to strong opposing interests. In addition, the harmony of the community is stressed through a concern for others and an emphasis on equality. These crucial psychocultural dispositions are rooted in early socialization but are reinforced through a wide range of cultural practices. Interestingly, although Norwegian child rearing is warm, indulgent, and not punitive, adult relationships are perhaps best described as reserved at the interpersonal level, but trusting vis-à-vis the wider community. Although Norwegians seem especially sensitive to what can go wrong in face-to-face encounters, they feel protected by community norms and practices that strongly sanction harmful behavior.

Conclusion

The generalizability of the cross-cultural theory of conflict and violence in settings beyond preindustrial societies requires more support than the two additional cases treated here. Nonetheless, it should be evident that both structural and psychocultural factors combine in Northern Ireland and in Norway to create cultures of conflict which perpetuate high levels of conflict in one case and low levels in the other. An explanation drawing on both is superior to one based on either factor by itself. Although the cross-cultural theory has not been systematically tested in a sample of industrial societies, there is no plausible reason why it should not be relevant in these settings. The burden of disproof is on those who suggest that such generalization is unfounded.

These two cases reinforce the idea that psychocultural conditions are critical in determining the impact of a society's structural features on conflict. In Northern Ireland, the gap in the distribution of privileges between Protestants and Catholics is significant, but it is not as large as that between ethnic groups in other situations where overt conflict has been less enduring and less severe. Only when we consider the particular psychocultural features of Northern Ireland as well as the structural realities can we adequately account for both the persistence and intensity of the conflict. In Norway, the argument is similar, but with the opposite outcome. The psychocultural features of Norwegian society today seem especially important in understanding why potential differences within the society are not translated into severe conflicts, why the social order is inclusive, and why the social and economic system is relatively open. Norwegians, the argument goes, are not prone to distrust of others but do not feel a need for interaction, either. Rather, they seem to have an underlying sense that the community can be counted on at times of real need, but that most of the time autonomy is a virtue. In both Northern Ireland and Norway, cultural practices guide behavior in particular directions and maintain these patterns over time. A society's culture of conflict consists of norms and procedures for dealing with disputes, and these two cases show how they are frequently firmly rooted in both psychocultural dispositions and in societal structure.

A few additional comments are in order on whether the argument offered here pertains mainly to settings where interests and interpretations are narrowly defined and widely shared, or if it can be generalized to large differentiated societies beyond the sample. Skepticism about whether the theory proposed here can be of much use in understanding conflict in large-scale industrial societies rests on an important misconception that underestimates the extent to which there is important social differentiation, if only on the basis of age and sex, even in the smallest, apparently most homogeneous societies. Given modest levels of internal differentiation, a range of competing interests are defined. Thus, the proposition that interests shape conflict behavior and the choice of targets is relevant to simple and complex societies alike. Where small- and large-scale societies differ, however, is in how particular interests are aggregated and how this relates to the definition of allies and enemies. In both small-scale and modern societies, the potential for interest-based internal and external alliances and oppositions exists.

The same basic argument, with slight adjustments, can be made with respect to psychocultural interpretations. Here the main point is to recognize the existence of intrasocietal variation, this time in socialization practices and dispositions, in all societies (Wallace 1962). Management of differences, when they are in direct conflict, and how they play out, is an issue for all cultures. The theory under review here, however, does not suggest that dispositions shape conflict directly, but that they are a critical component in the development of individual and communal cultural interpretations. Social processes are also relevant in the definition, reinforcement, and perpetuation of culturally sanctioned world views. Although conflict-relevant interpretations have a dispositional base, I am not suggesting a simple one-to-one correspondence between dispositions and interpretations. Rather, complex interactions among a host of dispositions and important social processes intervene.

There is no reason, then, to restrict the argument that conflict involves both interests and interpretations to smaller and simpler societies. The specific linkages and dynamics of internal conflict and external conflict may look somewhat different in preindustrial and modern societies, but the significance of interests and interpretations for conflict behavior in each is clear. It is now time to focus on the mechanisms of interests and interpretations, which play a critical role in the development and maintenance of a society's culture of conflict.

10

Interests, Interpretations, and Conflict

In this chapter and the next I synthesize the results from the analysis in the previous four chapters in two ways. Here I focus on the mechanisms of interests and interpretations which underlie the social structural and psychocultural variables associated with internal and external conflict. Integrating the main findings of the study in terms of interests and interpretations points to their significance for understanding and affecting conflict behavior more generally. The final chapter synthesizes the results by examining conflict as cultural behavior, considering the dynamics of the low-conflict society and of constructive conflict and suggesting the conflict management implications of the culture of conflict theory developed here.

Underlying social structural sources of conflict are competing interests, and deriving from psychocultural dispositions are interpretations of social action. Common interests arise among people who live together, interact a great deal, and occupy similar positions in a society's social organization. Structural conflict results when action in pursuit of these interests occurs and threatens the interests of others. Shared interpretations are frames of reference which arise from deeply rooted psychocultural dispositions and explain the motives and intentions of one's own group and of others. Each plays a central role in the dynamics of conflict.

Although structure focuses attention on the apparently concrete interests disputants easily cite, dispositions point to deeper, less conscious, more ambiguous motives of which people are often only dimly aware as they impose a framework from their inner worlds on external events.[1] These motives, which may be felt in intensely personal ways, are relevant here because they are shared with others through social organization. The importance of what is at stake in some conflicts, combined with the uncertainty of outcomes, means that a crucial aspect of conflict behavior is the mutual seeking and providing of support. Precisely because favorable outcomes cannot be assured, consensus and support are emotionally necessary. Through these social processes, conflict behavior becomes invested with interpretive components which are built on emotionally charged shared understandings of the world.

Social scientists of diverse orientations are more likely to explain conflict in terms of social structure than in terms of psychocultural dispositions. Because of Durkheim's dictum that social behaviors should not be explained by reference to psychological processes, many fields avoid all reference to them.[2] My argument, that neither structural nor psychocultural forces alone accounts for cross-cultural differences in conflict behavior, rejects this view. The prominent position I give psychocultural processes is, in part, a counterbalance to what I see as many decades of not-so-benign neglect of these concerns.

In this chapter, I shall first discuss the social structural mechanism of common interests and the psychocultural mechanism of interpretation. Then I consider the importance of the interpretive component of conflict behavior (without labeling all conflict behavior interpretive), emphasizing the social character of interpretive processes. Finally, I suggest that, because interests and interpretations each motivate actions in specific ways, a complete explanation for societal differences in conflict behavior integrates both mechanisms.

1. I am not arguing that all interests are necessarily conscious, for this is often not the case, but I am suggesting that when people describe what a conflict is about, or why they act as they do in a dispute, they almost always cite some interests as a justification, even though additional interests, of which they are less aware, may also be involved.

2. Those who have systematically avoided considering psychological questions are found in all of the social sciences, although it is generally anthropologists and sociologists who cite Durkheim's justification for doing so. Most striking to me is the case of economists, who in micro-level theory make fundamental assumptions about human psychology virtually without interest in examining these empirically.

Social Structural and Psychocultural Mechanisms

Interests and interpretations are the mechanisms which underlie social structure and psychocultural dispositions. I first discuss the interests associated with complexity and cross-cutting ties, which direct conflict in particular ways in preindustrial societies, and then raise the question of interests in other settings. Turning to interpretations, I emphasize those associated with the dispositional variables the data analysis showed to be most important and consider the relevance of interpretations in all social contexts.

Structural Conditions Determine Interests

Social structural conflict theory is rooted in the proposition that shared social positions merge individual and group interests and encourage collective action to advance these interests. Structurally defined interests stimulate the formation of alliances and identify the targets of aggressive actions. Cross-cutting ties and complexity theories link a community's organization to the kinds and intensity of interests found within it. Complexity theory is concerned with the interests located in the resources and capacities at each level of societal development, whereas cross-cutting ties theory focuses on the extent to which groups or individuals have overlapping or exclusive interests at each level of complexity. The interests associated with any specific pattern of organization, according to structural conflict theory, produce characteristic forms of conflict. There may be little association between the social structure of a society and its overall level of conflict and violence, yet the structural conditions determine who fights and who cooperates with whom.

The results of the cross-cultural analysis in chapters 6 and 7 show that greater complexity leads to more differentiation among targets and a tendency to direct conflict outside the society. Several interest-based processes are consistent with this finding. Lee suggests that the evolutionary process leading to the rise of the state externalizes violence instead of controlling or eliminating it (1979:399). Because more complex societies may also possess more resources coveted by others, higher levels of external conflict and warfare may be both defensive (protecting resources) and offensive (acquiring neighbors' assets or launching preemptive attacks).[3] The finding is, in addition, consistent with the argument that societal survival depends on the development of skills associated with warfare and that simpler societies which fail to develop these skills fail to survive (Bigelow 1973). Another reason may be that a higher level of external warfare is a function of the higher level of contact with other societies, rather than any inherent pugnaciousness. Finally, it is plausible that more complex societies are located in intersocietal systems where a high level of conflict is more likely (for some of the reasons already mentioned) so that rather than looking to any single society to explain the pattern, one needs to understand a region's intersocietal system.

Complexity theory emphasizes the interests that emerge with each stage of development. In contrast, cross-cutting ties theory considers the presence or absence of interests rooted in associations extending beyond the local community at any level of complexity. Such ties increase internal integration, making severe internal conflict less likely and severe external conflict more likely. Increased identification, ritual participation, and exchange of people (through migration or intermarriage) and goods within a society serve as brakes on expansion of internal conflict, as people with links to several groups tend to seek to continue to benefit from their ties.

Societies without strong multiple loyalties experience more severe internal conflicts because there are few individuals or institutions who have the power or interest to intervene in disputes. A prototypical case of weak cross-cutting ties among the preindustrial societies studied here is the Mae Enga of New Guinea (see chapter 6), whose strong fra-

3. Cross-cultural studies of warfare, like Otterbein (1970), have tried to distinguish between the frequency of offensive and defensive warfare. I would argue that the categories "defensive" and "offensive" can rarely be applied with much certainty, let alone in a simple dichotomous fashion. The distinction is unclear for several reasons. First, ideological reasons make groups likely to view (and to report) some conflicts as either defensive or offensive. Given the fact that most of our ethnographic data on warfare come from such reports and not direct observation, this is significant. Second, in many disputes all parties are likely to report the same thing—that their own action was defensive and the other side started it. Third, many conflicts involve a series of escalatory sequences, not a single action, and the most accurate judgment is that each party undertook both defensive and offensive actions, which means that the distinction is not very useful theoretically or empirically.

ternal interest groups engage in frequent conflict. In these societies, fraternal interest groups bring related males together, making it easy for them to organize violent actions, either defending their own perceived interests or attacking others. Otterbein (1968) found that the presence of fraternal interest groups predicted internal war in uncentralized societies but not among those which were politically centralized. Our results, using a different sample and different measures, reveal the same findings, that fraternal interest group strength is significantly related to internal conflict only in the uncentralized societies.

At the same time, I suspect that the impact of fraternal interest groups on conflict is much greater than just the cases of internal conflict in uncentralized preindustrial societies. The specific measure used here captures the substantive interests in land and livestock shared by related males in small-scale agricultural societies.[4] In other societies, however, these specific measures (presence of bride-price, patrilineality, and group size) are not necessarily good indicators of organized male interests. Yet I would suggest that the existence of groups of males who defend common interests is quite widespread, although the specific interests, and the organizational forms the male groups take, vary. In other settings, male power groups organize around common residence, religion, ethnicity, occupation, social group affiliation, educational experiences, and sports activities, among others. What is striking is the range of ways in which male bonding occurs and the range of interests served by these exclusive groups. For example, the men's house in highland New Guinea, fraternities in American universities, and male social clubs in London are all institutions which are crucial to the cultivation of their members' interests, although the basis of membership, the specific interests, and how they are pursued are not the same.[5]

4. The measure used here is derived from Paige and Paige's (1981) discussion of fraternal interest groups in stateless societies. The Paiges' argument is based on the defense of economic interests that are highly associated with kinship in certain small-scale societies. Their analysis makes no claim that this pattern is universal even in uncentralized societies; rather, it points to the unique conditions associated with its strength: the existence of important, but immobile resources requiring relatively large and cohesive defense groups.

5. Although I suggest that male interest groups are found in many different settings and have a broad range of interests, I would also say that their existence, strength, and the vigor with which they pursue particular interests varies widely.

Social structural analyses are often more useful in analyzing a conflict once it has started than in predicting where one is likely to develop, because in any community there are always more lines of potential division than can occur at one time, and any single line of cleavage can give rise to more than one set of interests. Although any social classification—age, gender, kinship, ritual affiliation, wealth, or occupation—provides an underlying logic for interest-based organization, the specific events of any conflict often determine which one (or more) of the above will become dominant. In many situations, the hypotheses of social scientists (and other observers) about which lines of social cleavage achieve political significance have proven to be wrong. Lines of cleavage which at first seem firm can turn out to be ephemeral as events unfold.[6] In great part this is because we too readily attribute interests to individuals without first making sure that the actors view the interests as we do (Wildavsky 1991). Assuming that actors necessarily pursue their interests in a rational manner—as both microeconomic and rational choice theory do—avoids understanding how actors actually evaluate their interests and link them to actions.

Many structural analyses make problematic action seem self-evident largely because these analyses are pushed beyond their proper limitations. A critical question few address is why individuals so easily equate their self-interest with that of the group in certain situations. Meggitt's analysis of the Mae Enga of New Guinea (see chapter 6) is an obvious example of this problem. I argue that Meggitt's consideration of Mae ecology and social structure and its role in ongoing violence is never supplemented by a consideration of Mae perceptions. Meggitt makes important (and perhaps correct) assumptions about how the Mae define their core interests but does not specify why they come to define those interests as they do.[7] Only when we consider Meggitt's rich description of socialization to the clan and intense male-female antagonism (1964; 1965) can we begin to understand some of the connections between the structure of Mae Enga society and the heightened perception

6. A dramatic but not uncommon example is the shift in voters from class- to ethnic-based parties as an election campaign heats up. Melson and Wolpe (1970) document this in a Nigerian election.
7. After all, land pressure, clan interests, and long-term survival are rather abstract social constructions built from more empirical observations and socially supported perceptions. Their connections to interests and then to social action are surely more indirect than Meggitt suggests.

of threats, definition of group interests, and we-they distinctions. From this perspective the identification of social structural and ecological factors in conflict is rarely wrong. At the same time, however, explanations for conflict based exclusively on these criteria are often incomplete and therefore misleading.

Psychocultural Interpretations Frame Conflicts for Disputants

Dispositions—learned culturally approved response tendencies—are the basis of the evaluation of the actions of others and guide one's own behavior. They are vital in developing models for action in different situations.[8] The evidence presented in chapters 6 and 7 is that differences between societies in their socialization of warmth and affection, physical aggression, and gender identity determine differences in conflict behavior. Images of the self and others are rooted in earliest socialization and regularly reinforced through a variety of culturally

8. Earlier in this project I considered personality as intervening between socialization and behavior (not unlike the Whitings' framework). Increasingly, however, I found myself rejecting the term, for several reasons. One is that the personality is inherently an individual-level concept and therefore not usefully applied to communities or societies, which are my focus. Second, many socially oriented psychoanalytic theorists do not emphasize (or even utilize) the term, preferring "dispositions" or "object-choices" where earlier formulations would have used the term personality. Third, I have no data on personality, a more abstract configuration than disposition. Fourth, although the idea of personality represents an already created and often fixed combination, it was clear to me that the notion of dispositions refers to more basic elements that can be arranged in different ways and is therefore more suited to an important conflict management concern—changing interpretations of conflict.

Finally, by avoiding the concept of personality I hope to emphasize important differences between my approach and that of earlier national character studies, for which the modal personality was a core concept. My argument does not require any assumptions about homogeneity of personality distributions, which the early wave of national character studies failed to address adequately (Inkeles and Levinson 1968; LeVine 1973; Wallace 1962). The dispositions rooted in early learning do not necessarily correspond directly to a single personality configuration. Early learning may emphasize open expression of aggression in ways which may be consistent with several, although not all, personality configurations. A range of personalities may be compatible with certain behaviors; therefore, personality seems best understood as one mechanism through which dispositions are translated into actions.

sanctioned messages and experiences. Dispositions provide the basis for internal mental representations, which offer standards by which to judge actions, templates for the interpretation of the actions of others, and serve as a guide to one's own behavior. Dispositions learned early in life are relevant not only on the perceptual level; they also involve specific behavioral patterns which serve one throughout life, such as the response to perceived insults, the use of physical aggression, or whom to trust.

Dispositions are vital in understanding why participants react to particular situations as they do. Although participants in conflict have little trouble citing the "objective" basis of differences (for example, insults, theft, or physical attack), an outsider may notice the number of times when the same supposedly provocative action occurs in other settings and is not followed by overt violence. If the same objective conditions produce different responses, an explanation of conflict behavior requires more than the identification of underlying objective conditions (Northrup 1989). It is the *interpretation* of such situations that leads to overt conflict.[9]

Stern's (1985) provocative synthesis of infant behavior observations and psychoanalytic theory emphasizes how early and how effectively humans make socially relevant interpretations based on interactions with significant others in their environment. These judgments form the core elements in an individual's inner model of the external world. Volkan's (1988) analysis of ethnic conflicts suggests two additional elements at work. First, there is often a good deal of similarity in the early social (and often pre-verbal) experiences among members of a group, initially grounded in primary sensations such as smell, taste, and sound, which acquire intense affective meaning and only later come to acquire a cognitive component. Second, Volkan's discussion of the concept of identity makes us aware not only that group members share such experiences but also that those experiences contribute to the developmental task of incorporating group identity into one's own sense of self. Within-group identity formation surely overemphasizes what it is that

9. The term interpretation has been used as a code word for description and story-telling by those who reject systematic comparative analysis. In contrast, I use the term in a wider sense to include peoples' views of their social worlds, but I also want to understand the connection between "objective" situations and interpretations of them.

group members actually share, giving greater emotional weight to the common elements and reinforcing them with an ideology of linked fate.[10] The process is perhaps best viewed as a psychocultural "regression to the mean" which emphasizes shared affective and cognitive elements. Variations from the norm are selectively ignored or negatively reinforced as incompatible with group membership. Individual fears about belonging and connectedness (most acute in late adolescence) lead to selectively purging or weakening of less commonly held beliefs and to stressing others which reinforce attachment to the group.

Individual and group representations which amplify a we-they world view eagerly assign malevolent intentions to others while failing to recognize the existence of similarly rooted motives closer to home. Outsiders become ready objects for the externalization, displacement, and projection of a group's most hostile impulses and deepest fears.[11] Given this pattern, an event, even the simplest fact of daily life, can be easily charged with intense significance as people develop explanations for why it occurred. For example, the attribution of a death to a natural cause, such as a germ or old age, produces a very different community response than when witchcraft or poisoning is implicated.

Although Volkan and other psychoanalytic thinkers say that we-they feelings involving repression, projection, displacement, and externalization are universal, these theorists also propose that there can be important variation in the intensity of these emotions. Severe social conflict is most likely where such processes are most intense. The data analysis in chapters 6 and 7 suggests that perhaps the most important source of such variation is the strength of affectionate socialization practices, which nurture basic trust in the social world and reduce the tendency to attribute hostile motives to others. Absence of affectionate

10. Turner (1988) also has an excellent discussion of the notion of overvaluation of the uniformity within groups.

11. Although the emphasis here is in terms of political community or what in modern settings we would call ethnic groups, Herdt's (1987) detailed analysis of gender identity among the Sambia of New Guinea reveals some of these same features in male-female relationships. Male ideology emphasizes their greater power, but, in fact, much of their elaborate ritual activity is aimed at building up their own strength (which is subconsciously quite insecure and limiting the power of females, who are greatly feared. An important element is, in fact, male insecurity and threat, which is too frightening to be confronted directly and is consequently projected onto females.

socialization practices leads to a situation in which emotional attachment to others is uncertain, fear and frustration are high, and these feelings are easily projected onto outsiders. The association of uncertain male gender identity with conflict is also consistent with the mechanisms outlined above. Insecure identity leads to compensatory behavior that attempts to validate what is uncertain and to attributing to others the hostile impulses arising from deep insecurities. Where male gender identity is more secure, the impulses projected onto others are weaker. Harsh socialization, the third specific variable identified in the data analysis, produces the sense that dealings with others are frustrating and hostile and both models and rewards hostile aggressive behavior.

Contemporary psychoanalytic theory discusses the critical mechanisms underlying the translation of dispositions into actions. Fornari (1975) shows how the universal experience of losing a love object, for example, produces aggression through the process of "the paranoid elaboration of mourning," in which the guilt one feels over the loss is projected onto outsiders who then are attacked as the destroyers of the love object. We all lose love objects through death and other social processes. Human reactions to this loss include guilt (felt or repressed), hostility projected onto others, and the desire to harm others in reaction to one's own repressed rage. There are also important nonpsychoanalytic mechanisms relevant to the conversion of dispositions into actions. One is social learning, which emphasizes modeling of established cultural patterns as a learning mechanism (Bandura 1973). When established ways of dealing with conflict are readily observable and children are encouraged to imitate them, behavior patterns can be learned in ways which do not require any assumptions about underlying psychodynamic processes. Direct instruction or modeling may often provide a sufficient basis for the continuation of certain behavior patterns.

The Interpretive Component of Conflict Behavior

Conflicts are not concerned exclusively with what people do to each other. Conflicts also involve what one group of people think or feel that another group of people are doing—or may try or want to do (Northrup 1989). In an atmosphere of suspicion, not only actions but also assumptions about the intentions and meanings behind actions (or inactions) play a central role. In few conflict situations do events themselves provide clear explanations for underlying motives; rather, individuals must turn to internal frameworks as well. This interpretive element in conflict behavior shapes subsequent action in critical ways.

Conflict behavior is interpretive because of the powerful mixture of emotional salience and situational ambiguity. Salience occurs when what are felt to be important interests are involved. Ambiguity is great when the meaning of actions or intentions is unclear. Disputants often are unaware of these features (especially ambiguity), or how the combination of salience and ambiguity readily involves threat and produces psychic regression with a return to intense, primitive feelings.

The dispositions invoked in such situations shape how participants react to conflicts because they are a critical ingredient in disputants' interpretations of events. Interpretations are social, not just personal, when they are shared with others, in a collective process connecting the experience of the individual and the group, providing social legitimation and support for some interpretations of events and censoring others.

Shared images of the world and plans for action are predicated on a common conception of the difference between one's own group and outsiders. The interpretive processes involved in intense conflict situations emphasize the homogeneity of each party, often using minor objective differences to mark major social distinctions. Outsiders then can serve as objects for externalization, displacement, and projection of intense negative feelings, which are also present but denied within the group.

It is interesting that disputants often resist recognizing the role of interpretive elements, as if it reveals some kind of weakness. Among the most striking examples are professional diplomats and political figures, who consistently argue that their background trains them to discount such factors. When we examine their world views, in fact, it is often obvious that projective elements inform their actions and are not set to one side (Holsti 1967; Jervis 1976; Lebow 1981; Nagel 1991).

Recognizing the role of interpretive factors offers the possibility of attempting to understand and then modify them, rather than accepting their consequences as somehow inevitable. The conflict management process, for example, can seek to address the mutual fears of adversaries in a variety of ways. Making each party aware of the other's intense concerns about what is at stake and the lack of clarity with which the other's actions are perceived can be a first step toward lowering levels of fear and insecurity on both sides. When such fears are brought to the surface and their sources addressed, the prospects for constructive conflict management become brighter.

The more intense the conflict and the longer it persists, I argue, the more likely that the interpretive component is important and that recognizing its role is necessary to achieving a viable settlement. People fight about real interests, be they material or symbolic, but the way they proceed, the intensity of feelings, and the lengths to which disputants go to defend or acquire what they believe is their due are evidence that the pursuit of interests has an important psychocultural component which is not yet well understood.

Psychocultural insights are particularly useful in helping us to understand the intensity of emotions found in so many conflicts. Outsiders can easily devise solutions that resolve differences, yet disputants often remain incomprehensibly unyielding. Why? Often intense conflicts are linked to central elements of group and individual identity, and any satisfactory outcome needs to take these into account. Powerful insecurities and fears feed projection, externalization, and displacement and obscure the consideration of interests, the ostensible focus of the dispute.

My deliberate emphasis on the importance of psychocultural interpretations in conflict is a corrective to general neglect in social science literature found by LeVine (1973). Too many social science accounts of conflict never raise psychocultural questions, let alone evaluate their empirical relevance. One recent example is Boehm's (1984) ethnohistorical study of feuding in Montenegro. He offers a compelling account, emphasizing the role of honor, strategic decision making, and ways in which feuding serves to contain conflict. Feuding is a conflict-limiting strategy for Boehm, who sees its alternative as all-out fighting between groups following a murder. His rational-actor model highlights the self-conscious nature of subsequent strategic choices, so that blood feuds are most likely between two clans of relatively equal size, while in situations of inequality, the weaker group may choose to flee. Boehm's account completely ignores psychocultural explanations for feuding in Montenegro and elsewhere. Yet it seems very plausible that the Montenegrans (and those in other Mediterranean feuding cultures) have certain psychocultural patterns which make it especially difficult to conceive of responses to homicide other than feuding or warfare. The concepts of honor and manly virtue are not just values which shape action by themselves; rather, they are rooted in Montenegrans' basic psychocultural processes of attachment, identification, repression, projection, displacement, and externalization. Data on such dynamics would not necessarily invalidate Boehm's rational-actor analysis but could provide a richer explanation of the underlying mechanisms.

Simply citing Durkheim or Weber's rejection of psychological explanations does not justify ignoring psychocultural processes. Equally without merit is the materialist claim that all psychological processes are epiphenomena and can be explained on the basis of the organization of production or ecological factors. Although there is often a link between psychocultural and material processes, using theory alone to assert that the influence between them is unidirectional fails to consider ways in which the effects of each domain are independent and not reducible to a consequence of the other.

The argument for a more prominent role for psychocultural theory in explanations for conflict and other social behaviors raises the question of what data are required to evaluate these theories effectively. At present, much of the writing in this area emphasizes theory at the expense of evidence, an imbalance that needs to be redressed. In this study I have relied on others' cross-cultural codes of child rearing and the reports of psychoculturally informed ethnographers. This was not always fully adequate, however. For example, I found too little direct data on some critical questions in the ethnographic record and therefore much of what I wrote about world views and interpretations is indirect and inferential. Some ethnographic accounts, however, contain rich psychocultural data or data relevant to psychocultural questions even when these matters are not a researcher's major focus, as is the case with Meggitt's Mae Enga data. And psychoanalytically informed ethnographers such as Herdt can provide particularly rich data and interpretations. In the analysis of Montenegro, for example, a researcher seeking to add psychocultural insights to Boehm's analysis might incorporate useful data from others working in this region. In addition, however, new field data are still needed to better understand the psychocultural dynamics associated with conflict and conflict management.

Conclusion: Linking Interests and Interpretations

This chapter has focused on the mechanisms underlying structural and psychocultural sources of conflict behavior. Whereas interests are crucial to understanding the effect of structure, interpretations underlie psychocultural dispositions. Although I have dwelt more on interpretations to correct what I have seen as a previous neglect of their importance, the argument gives neither interests nor interpretations priority. Each tells us different and important things about conflict behavior.

These two mechanisms have been discussed as if they were autonomous, but a consideration of how interests and interpretations can affect each other leads to conclusions about ways in which social structural and psychocultural processes underlying conflict are interdependent. Individual- and group-based interpretations of social action involve real people and real events. A community's social structure identifies the actors and their interests. Understanding conflict in a community requires learning about how its interests—and the actions taken to pursue them—are understood.

In addition, it is essential to understand that the translation of dispositional tendencies into behavioral patterns is a fundamentally social process; community support for certain types of actions ensures that they will be learned and maintained and disapproval makes them less common. From this standpoint, minor differences in the nature of early relationships and social learning can be greatly magnified by cultural reinforcement. Leaders mobilizing for action often polarize groups by emphasizing differences which are, in fact, quite modest. Patterns of social support and interaction shape perceptions of the group's identity and its differentiation from others, facilitating subsequent mobilization.[12]

Clarifying the content of interpretations can be especially helpful in explaining why some groups (or individuals) are continually embroiled in disputes while others rarely have them. But an understanding of conflict situations only in terms of the interpretations parties ascribe to conflicts is inadequate, for there are important questions which the interpretive mechanisms fail to address. These involve the nature of the parties likely to oppose each other, the justifications each party articulates (to itself and to third parties) for its actions, and the specific agree-

12. This is not incompatible with psychoanalytic processes, as Volkan's (1988) attention to the role of group identification processes in individual development makes clear. His discussion of "the narcissism of minor differences" is particularly relevant here.

ments by which particular disputes can end. Here, interests associated with social structure complement the interpretations arising out of psychocultural dispositions.

Interests and interpretations motivate actions in such different ways that an adequate explanation for societal differences in conflict behavior is one which considers both mechanisms. Resource scarcity, whether absolute or relative, finds expression in group and individual interests. When overt conflict develops and what form it takes when it occurs depend on the relationship among the disputants, their interpretations of each other's motives, and their own fears. An explanation of a cultural pattern of conflict can begin with either the interests or interpretations involved, but to be comprehensive it must at some point consider both elements. For example, high conflict among the Mae Enga (and other highland New Guinea peoples) is surely related to land scarcity, but the intensity and persistence of local fighting is only comprehensible in light of the psychocultural dispositions linking the land to the core of one's identity and rarely remitting trust and security outside the clan.

In every society interests and interpretations are organized in particular ways that reflect and shape its culture of conflict. If the language of conflict in any society emphasizes unique features, my analysis points to important common elements as well, which I shall consider in the next chapter, a discussion of the concept of the culture of conflict.

11

The Culture of Conflict

In closing, I draw on my cross-cultural analysis to develop three insights about conflict. First, the culture of conflict is a useful tool for understanding societal level differences in conflict, emphasizing both how culture shapes conflict behavior and how conflict can be understood as cultural behavior. Second, just as medical diagnoses frequently focus on pathology, social analysis can easily examine only problems. The results of the cross-cultural study provide an opportunity to reflect on the positive lessons from low-conflict societies. Through discussion of low-conflict societies, I hope to suggest how some of their institutions, practices, and norms may be relevant in other settings. Third, the cross-cultural theory of conflict with its emphasis on social structural interests and psychocultural interpretations has important implications for the management of individual disputes. In particular, I suggest that constructive conflict management is most likely when both interests and interpretations are effectively addressed.

Conflict as Cultural Behavior

The culture of conflict is a society's configuration of norms, practices, and institutions which affect what people enter into disputes about, with whom they fight, how the disputes evolve, and how they are likely to end. It is a product of social structural organization and psychocultural dispositions. Culture is an emergent concept, something which appears on the aggregate but not individual level in the sense that a single person cannot have his or her own culture; rather, culture is what is shared by people living in a society. Although any society's culture of conflict has unique features, the analysis here has emphasized a small number of general patterns.

The concept of the culture of conflict is relevant to understanding both conflict and conflict management. Although theories of conflict have many implicit hypotheses about what constitutes effective conflict management, and despite the fact that approaches to conflict management are based on often unarticulated hypotheses about the roots of conflict, theories of conflict and approaches to conflict management are too rarely brought together. The concept of the culture of conflict directs attention to how societal level institutions and practices affect the course of particular conflicts. Despite the fact that different processes operate at the societal and dispute levels, culture links the two.

Culture affects conflict behavior, but conflict can also be viewed as cultural behavior. All conflict occurs in a cultural context. Knowing something about the cultural context in which a conflict occurs tells us a lot about its roots, its likely course, and its management. This study identifies two critical sources of cultural differences in conflict—social structure and psychocultural practices.[1]

Culture is a way of life transmitted (with modifications) over time, and embodied in a community's institutions, norms, and accepted practices. It provides critical tools by which groups and individuals operate in and understand their social worlds. Culture is broadly seen in worldviews that influence action, whereas a social community (less abstract than culture) uses more direct methods to shape the behavior of its members (Price-Williams 1985).

The goals and procedures of community institutions are linked to culturally shared notions of appropriate behavior. In terms of conflict, this refers to shared expectations about how to respond to particular kinds of events, how others in the community are likely to react, and what are reasonable goals and approved ways of pursuing them. Culturally shared rules can guide behavior even in the absence of institutions to enforce them. Even in as basic a conflict as Axelrod's prisoner's dilemma tournament between computer programs, culture is present in the definition of what constitutes winning and in the payoff matrix, and changes in either of these produce different outcomes.

1. This does not deny the effect of individual differences within any cultural community. Group members who are more—or less—assertive, ambitious, or pugnacious in a setting often make a difference.

Conflict is cultural behavior, therefore, because culture shapes so many of its key elements. Conflict can take place outside a culturally shared frame of reference; when it does, the absence of common assumptions makes it especially difficult to contain. In such situations one party may use its own cultural assumptions to try to understand what another has done or is likely to do, often with disastrous results (Cohen 1991). At other times a group decides that an adversary's values and behaviors are completely at odds with its own and therefore behaviors toward it are not subject to any of the inhibitions on within-group conflict.

Culture is critical in the development of in-group and out-group identities, providing the metaphors and associations to distinguish allies and enemies. Through participation in day-to-day events, groups associate affectively salient experiences around which identities coalesce. Critical differences between groups are not found in the objective dissimilarities between such experiences so much as in small disparities that can take on great emotional meaning.

Cultural differences can mark the political polarization of a community and at the same time provide signals that help people to lead their lives with a minimum of overt conflict. In Northern Ireland, Boyle and Hadden note:

Ulster people [do not] spend [all] their time arguing, abusing each other or fighting. On the contrary, they are naturally reserved and wary on first acquaintance. That is because it is important for them to establish on which side someone else stands. When two Ulster people whose communal identity is not self-evident meet, each immediately sets about discovering—without, of course, asking—whether the other is Protestant or Catholic. Since the difference between members of the two communities is not instantly apparent, as it would be in societies divided by race, colour or language, they use a series of more or less accurate cues: surnames . . . ; Christian names . . . ; schooling (perhaps the best test if it can be got at); the 'h' test (Catholics tend to say 'haitch,' while Protestants tend to say 'aitch'); or just the attitudes that may be disclosed on a whole range of sensitive issues. The point of this elaborate process is to enable both parties to avoid saying or revealing something that may prove embarrassing or offensive or may lead to disagreement on some fundamental issue. The desire to avoid having to embark on an argument that both sides know cannot be resolved is as good an indication as any of the stubbornness with which each clings to its basic political beliefs. (1985:58)

Culture shapes how individuals understand their social worlds, how they classify people, evaluate possible actions, and sanction certain responses but not others. Conflict reflects cultural priorities but can also be used to alter them. Culture is also political because its control over the definition of legitimate actors and actions favors certain people and groups.[2]

Generalizing societies (where internal and external conflict are at similar levels) and differentiating societies (where internal and external conflict are at different levels) offer two contrasting cultures of conflict. While more preindustrial societies are generalizers than differentiators, the fact that differentiation is associated with increased complexity and stronger cross-cutting ties means that both cultural styles might occur in many settings. What the data analysis could not address are the conditions giving rise to the development of each style or the dynamics of its perpetuation. The two groups of societies are most readily distinguished in terms of their structural features. However, it is reasonable to expect important psychocultural practices involved in the maintenance of generalization and differentiation as well. This question is worthy of more systematic analysis.

The Low-Conflict Culture

The data analysis in chapters 6 and 7 highlights differences between low- and high-conflict societies. Throughout the discussion, however, there has been greater emphasis on those societies with high levels of conflict because it is easier to account for an existing or problematic phenomenon than an absent one. Yet a low level of conflict is not simply the absence of a high level of conflict. The culture of conflict in low-conflict societies can and should be described and discussed on its own terms. I first discuss low conflict societies, building on the data analysis from the earlier chapters, while noting that in some low-conflict societies, conflict is not dealt with very effectively. For this reason I then introduce the notion of the constructive conflict society, a society defined

2. Conflict that arises over cultural definitions becomes especially important once societies develop any permanent social divisions. The culture of conflict, then, both includes a society's core values at any point in time and reflects prior conflicts that favor some groups and individuals over others.

not in terms of low conflict level, but in terms of conflict management processes which promote integrative solutions that meet the underlying needs of all parties.

High- and low-conflict societies are most clearly distinguished by their psychocultural features, whereas structural features are important when we consider differences between internal and external conflict. A model of the low-conflict society can provide both theoretical and political insights. Theoretically, one seeks to better understand the institutions and practices common to low-conflict communities. Politically, increased discussion of low-conflict communities in a world where the dramatic cases of death and destruction get the lion's share of attention may counter the sense that high conflict is inevitable and suggest how specific distinctive institutions and practices found in low-conflict settings may have relevance elsewhere.

The low-conflict society is not one without disputes and differences, but more often one where differences that arise are managed in such a way that extreme rancor, polarization, and outright violence are avoided.[3] Such a society is most distinctive in terms of the psychocultural features which permit it to develop institutions and practices which handle disputes in certain characteristic ways. The common structural features characteristic of low conflict societies are less obvious, however.[4] Low-conflict societies are not simply those with less wealth and hence fewer resources for people to fight over, for the data analysis found little relationship between overall conflict and measures of wealth or complexity.[5] Nor are low-conflict societies more likely to be centralized,

---

3. I prefer the term low-conflict society to peaceful society for several reasons: it suggests the notion of a continuum rather than a dichotomy and allows that all societies have at least some conflict. In addition, peace is often juxtaposed to war and open fighting whose relative absence I see as just one feature, albeit an important one, of low-conflict societies.

4. Many claims about low- versus high-conflict societies have a tautological character. For example, high conflict is often explained in terms of cultural or ethnic diversity, whereas other cases where the same diversity exists but the level of conflict is far lower are ignored. As already discussed, Northern Ireland's high level of conflict is explained in terms of differences between Catholics and Protestants without regard for the many nations in Europe (and elsewhere) where the incidence of overt Protestant-Catholic conflict is far lower.

5. Under certain conditions there may be a negative relationship between material abundance and conflict, to the extent that the scarcities producing the

powerful states that limit internal fighting, although this has been the case with the Buganda and the Aztecs. Koch (1974) says that conflict among the Jale of New Guinea frequently escalates rapidly because there are no effective third parties to step between the disputants, but the analysis here finds many low-conflict societies that lack these powerful third parties and many cases of high conflict levels despite the presence of third parties.

Psychocultural Conditions

Low-conflict societies have a psychocultural environment that is affectionate, warm, and low in overt aggression, and relatively untroubled by male gender identity conflicts. These patterns, established in early relationships, are likely to produce dispositions facilitating the peaceful resolution of disputes. The low level of overt conflict these dispositions engender means that fewer violent events provide models of appropriate action and the idea that nonviolent action can be efficacious is more strongly reinforced.

A secure self-identity that promotes interpersonal and social trust is probably a crucial disposition in the low-conflict society, and it facilitates the management of conflict in several ways. Secure and trusting individuals are less likely to interpret conflict situations in extreme terms, thus increasing the likelihood of more moderate, less escalatory responses to events.[6] Greater trust means a lower sense of social isolation, less fear of abandonment, and a stronger sense that effective action can make things right. Conflict situations tend not to be viewed in intensely personal terms, facilitating third party involvement in developing solutions, and the acceptance of compromises. Finally, a strong disposition to empathize with (if not necessarily accept) the concerns of others enhances the tendency to work with others toward mutually acceptable solutions (White 1984).

Lest the reader think that I have moved from data-based analysis

---

most violence may be relative rather than absolute. For the past several decades, for example, conflict within third world nations has been greater than conflict in industrialized nations.

6. Deutsch (1973) uses the term "benevolent misperception" to refer to ways in which disputants make assumptions of each other's cooperative motives and good intentions.

to utopia construction, let me hasten to add that these characteristics are relative, not absolute. Disputes in low-conflict societies can certainly be intense and bitter, but the point is that they are less likely to lead to violence and destruction, which then make constructive solutions difficult to achieve.[7] Certainly there can be anger and bitterness accompanied by displacement, projection, and externalization. But in the end, these processes are less intense because conflicts produce less of a threat to the fundamental existence of one's self or one's group.

Structural Trade-Offs

The psychocultural dispositions found in low-conflict societies apply to both internal and external conflict. The structure of societies low in each form of conflict, however, is quite different. Societies with low levels of internal conflict are internally integrated and their extensive cross-cutting ties discourage bitter, enduring disputes. Multiple lines of social cleavage offer alternative sources of identification and attachment, lessening the relative importance of any single social identity.

Strong cross-cutting ties produce a relatively large number of potential third parties who can step between disputants when conflicts arise. These third parties act because their own interests are threatened when a dispute remains unresolved, and they can invoke the interests they share with the disputants or those which affect the wider community, putting the specific issue of contention in perspective.[8] In a dramatic but apt example of this phenomenon, Turner (1957) vividly describes how the Ndembu of Zambia respond to the periodic stress caused by the conflicting principles of virilocal residence and matrilineality through intense ritual activity which unites previously divided individuals and groups. North American Plains Indians also use intense ritual activities at such emotionally charged times as the onset of the

7. Turnbull (1961) describes conflicts among the Mbuti, for example, where intense emotions are expressed; but few of these cases end in violence producing permanent injury and damage.

8. Extremists in polarized societies use this maneuver in reverse whenever they fear that moderates on both sides may be moving toward accommodation. A bombing or some kind of dramatic terrorist action rekindles the sense of threat to each community's existence and creates a climate in which continued public discussion between moderates is not viable.

hunting season to bring together kinship-based and other local groups who could easily come into conflict during the coming months.[9]

Cross-cutting ties lower the intensity of conflict psychologically in addition to affecting interests. The existence of interpersonal or institutional links among groups sharing common interests can make the other's demands seem more reasonable, or at least less threatening. Cross-cutting ties produce nuanced, less extreme images that facilitate a reaction to the substance of a demand rather than to a caricature of its sender, preventing potential adversaries from seeing each other as non-human. Where fraternal interest groups are weak, for example, the contrast between images of one's own kin group and those of others is probably far less than in those societies where such groups are strong.

A parallel psychological question concerns the affective significance accorded such ties in relation to material security and emotional needs. Low-conflict societies not only have greater overlapping ties than high-conflict communities, but these ties are also affectively more important in the low-conflict society. The selective emphasis, de-emphasis, or invention of all social ties (not just kinship) is important. In low-conflict societies, the value of attachment to others may result in relative overvaluation of links beyond the local community, whereas in high-conflict societies the opposite is the case.

But if cross-cutting ties lower the severity of internal conflict, they may embolden a society facing an external enemy (often to the point of foolhardiness). Murphy's (1957) classic description of the internally peaceful yet externally fierce matrilocal Mundurucu of Brazil is a well-known example of this phenomenon.[10] LeVine (1965) offers a second apt case, that of the pastoral Kipsigis of East Africa where kinship and age-based organizations produce widespread social links within the tribe but fierce conflict with outsiders. Not only do strong within-group ties build unity, thus facilitating joint action, but LeVine also suggests that

9. Gluckman (1955) describes rituals of rebellion in which members of a community are permitted, at fixed occasions, to attack the ruler in ways that both vent deeply felt frustration and renew support for existing authority.

10. Although the multivariate analysis (chapters 6 and 7) does not support Murphy's hypothesis that matrilocal and patrilocal societies significantly differ in their levels of internal versus external conflict, it does show that strong overlapping identities are negatively related to internal conflict and positively related to external conflict—as his theory suggests at the general level.

this is associated with highly polarized images which exaggerate insider-outsider differences and justify subsequent aggression.

Societies with low levels of external conflict are less complex socioeconomically and are more isolated. Yet it is hardly desirable that societies should move toward simpler technology or greater isolation in order to lower levels of conflict. Instead, it may be that the best we can do is be aware of how increased complexity increases the likelihood of severe conflict and try to actively guard against its effects.

Increased complexity brings a greater capacity to develop enduring links within and between societies. Strong cross-cutting ties within a society lower internal conflict, and strong ties between groups in different societies can have the same effect on external conflict. The argument for building significant ties between societies is similar to that of Haas (1964), Mitrany (1966), and other functionalists who saw this as the route to European integration. Functional linkages among societies on their own, however, are insufficient to build constructive conflict relationships, yet they can be a crucial ingredient when accompanied by relative equality between the parties, appropriate political leadership (Lindberg and Sheingold 1970), and a conducive psychocultural environment.[11]

The Intersocietal System

In building a model of the low-conflict society, it is important to remember that a prosperous society living with aggressive neighbors in a hard-to-defend location is likely to find itself under attack at some point, no matter what its internal characteristics. As discussed in chapter 8 in relation to the Teda, conflict and cooperation are discussed not only in terms of the properties of the individual states, but in terms of those of the intersocietal system (Waltz 1959; Midlarsky 1975; Zinnes 1980).

For conceptual and political purposes, anthropology created the myth of the isolated (almost pristine) traditional society that could be

---

11. Interaction between groups does not necessarily improve intergroup relations. When scarce resources, threat, and inequality are perceived, for example, interaction can raise rather than lower tension. The most positive changes occur when members of different groups see themselves as pursuing a greater common goal (Sherif et al. 1988).

understood entirely on its own terms. In fact, however, migration, fighting, trade, and other exchanges between nonwestern preindustrial societies were extensive in most of the world long before western colonial contact (Ferguson and Whitehead 1992). Few societies were sufficiently isolated historically that the activities of their neighbors could be ignored. Even the island societies of the Pacific mastered ocean travel and conducted trade and warfare over great distances. Isolation in the precolonial period was relative, not absolute, and perhaps severe only in the most remote Arctic, mountain, or desert areas.

D. White (1989) and others (Divale 1974, for example) examine intersocietal interactions generally, and patterns of external conflict in particular, as a source of changes in a society's internal social organization and level of internal conflict. In a highly speculative analysis, White suggests that a society's location in the world system affects external disputes, which in turn promote internal disputes.[12] From this perspective, low-conflict societies are likely only in certain settings. These communities need either to have relatively peaceful neighbors (as part of a local security system), to be located in an environment where they are not vulnerable to attack or from which flight is a viable option, or to be so much stronger than their neighbors that no one dares attack them.

The finding here that preindustrial societies are much more likely to be generalizers than differentiators is consistent with the argument that regional cultural systems reflect the internal properties of particular societies and patterns of interaction among them.[13] A society's regional context can affect conflict by encouraging changes in internal social organization either through functional adaptation or intercultural borrowing. The plausibility of the hypothesis that changes in interests, dispositions, and internal conflict patterns can develop, in part, as a

12. White's hypotheses about the impact of external conflict and incorporation into the world system on internal conflict merit serious consideration, yet his data analysis—using inadequate measures, questionable procedures, and a tiny sample—does not provide much useful evidence.

13. Divale (1974) suggests that societies with high levels of external warfare, for example, tend to become matrilocal, whereas internal warfare promotes patrilocality. Ember (1974), however, presents convincing data against Divale's hypothesized sequence. Without temporal data I can only speculate about the relationship between changes in socioeconomic complexity, cross-cutting ties, contact with other societies, and external violence.

response to external forces points to the need for more serious investigation of this question in a variety of settings.

The Constructive Conflict Society

The term "low-conflict society," a quantitative label, is certainly useful, yet we need to characterize a society's conflict management style qualitatively as well. Deutsch's (1973) concept of constructive (as opposed to destructive) conflict at the individual dispute level can be fruitfully applied to the societal level as well. Deutsch focuses on the kinds of exchanges between parties in a conflict, the attention given to their concerns, the search for creative solutions to conflicts, and the degree to which conflict management speaks to the needs of disputants—all pertinent questions about the conflict management styles of different societies.

Constructive conflict management is characterized by cooperative processes (not just attention to outcomes) that focus on the ability of different parties to define shared interests and to communicate openly in order to establish empathy between the disputants. An eventual legitimation of both sides' interests and a convergence of points of view results—what Deutsch (1973) calls "benevolent misperception." Communication and perceptions are central explanatory factors in his scheme and are prerequisites for resolving differences of substantive interests. Constructive conflict management, Deutsch argues, is more likely in situations where the power of the parties is relatively equal, although he offers suggestions as to how weak parties can bolster their negotiating position (1973:393–399). Deutsch suggests that third parties may be crucial in developing cooperative conflict procedures and in helping parties to reach constructive outcomes. One indicator of constructive conflict societies is probably that third parties are much more available than in destructive conflict societies. Finally, he argues that it is easier to go from cooperation to competition than the reverse (Pruitt and Rubin 1986). Constructive conflict patterns may be fragile and reestablishing them in a society after a period of intense destructive conflict may be difficult.

The psychocultural dispositions and social structural conditions found in low-conflict societies facilitate constructive conflict management because they enhance effective communication and shared identity leading to the resolution of substantive differences in interests. In societies where the prevailing view of the world is of effective cooperative action, rather than life-and-death struggle, the exchanges and compromises necessary for creative problem solving are far more likely to occur.

High-conflict situations are rarely constructive and are often characterized by an escalation of hostile actions producing a polarized community, a radicalization of leaders, and little room for a middle group between the extremes (Coleman 1957; Pruitt and Rubin 1986:7). Differences of substance, which may be open to negotiation early on, are often transformed into differences of principle which make any compromise feel like defeat. In such situations disputants recognize few constraints on their actions and resort to violence easily.

Low-conflict societies are most likely to have constructive conflict management because the dispositions of disputants are most conducive to creative joint problem solving and open communication. Yet low levels of conflict may occur when power inequalities among the disputants are large and the weaker party is unable to press its case effectively. We have little reason to believe that the constructive conflict management as Deutsch describes it occurs very often in hierarchical societies like the Buganda and the Aztec, where authorities intervene to impose solutions on less powerful disputants. Another low-conflict situation lacking in constructive conflict management is found among the Cayapa (described in chapter 8) and similar societies, where levels of conflict are apparently very low because people are so fearful of interpersonal interaction that they avoid exchanges and interactions needed for creative problem solving. Briggs' (1975) description of conflict among the Utke Eskimo also reveals the dynamics of low conflict in the absence of the constructive conflict pattern. The Utke are so overwhelmed by what first appears to be nurturance—but is really a powerful combination of affection and aggression—that few adults are capable of significant relationships in which powerful emotions are expressed. Overall conflict levels among the Utke are very low, but, as with the Cayapa, this is due not to constructive conflict management but rather to the avoidance of any interaction.[14]

Finally, there are many dispute-level examples of constructive problem solving even in societies not easily characterized by construc-

14. Some of these elements, in less extreme form, are found in the discussion below of the use of fear as a socialization mechanism among the Semai (Ross 1993).

tive conflict management processes. In such situations, it is useful to ask why constructive conflict management is limited to certain contexts and how constructive techniques may be extended to other domains. An initial hypothesis is that such techniques are most likely to occur in societies with moderate, or even moderately high, levels of conflict in small, interdependent, local groups with well-established positive interpersonal relations. Localized kin groups are typical here, but certainly such patterns are found elsewhere, where there is an equation of group and individual interests, or the ability to perceive the short-run group interest as serving the long-run needs of the group.

Both interests and interpretations are important in the description of the culture of conflict in societies characterized by low levels of conflict and constructive conflict management processes. The psychocultural features of these societies make polarization of disputants and rapid escalation of conflict less likely and increase the possibility that the interests of all will be addressed. In such situations, the core identities of participants are rarely threatened directly, making it easier for them to develop some understanding, if not acceptance, of the opponent's demands and to consider compromises and third-party intervention. In these societies, the long-term relationship among disputants is at least as significant as the substantive differences in any specific dispute (what Axelrod [1984] calls the shadow of the future).

Conflict and Conflict Management[15]

The perspective developed here reveals real limitations of some common proposals to improve conflict management. Changes in legal procedures or institutions that manage disputes, for example, are rarely going to be successful in isolation.[16] The proposal that disputants need only "get to know each other better" is similarly doomed. My analysis suggests that changes in conflict management procedures are most

15. The topic of this section is a central theme in Ross (1993), which uses the theory developed here to analyze conflict management.
16. New Guinea provides a striking example of the way change may alter institutions but fail to address underlying psychocultural dispositions or social structural interests. Precolonial warfare gave way to a short peaceful period under colonial rule, which was followed by a return to warfare and violence in the postcolonial period (Gordon and Meggitt 1984). In Ross (1993) I discuss this case as a failure of conflict management.

effective when they are associated with efforts to address both the disputants' substantive interests and underlying psychocultural interpretations.

Interest-based approaches to conflict management emphasize strategies that bridge substantive differences and package outcomes in ways that benefit all. In contrast, psychocultural approaches focus on altering disputants' hostile suspicions as a step toward dealing with substantive differences. Effective conflict management must address both interests and interpretations as significant sources of conflict.

The cross-cultural theory of conflict presented here explains societal-level differences, and has significant implications for understanding differences in the management of individual disputes both within and between societies. The most effective way to address interests and interpretations in order to make conflict management more constructive, of course, varies from context to context. In some cases underlying interests and the social structural conditions which give rise to them take priority; in other cases, increasing the emphasis of addressing disputants' shared interpretations of the world proves the best route to make a society's culture of conflict more constructive.

Current strategies of conflict management address interests and interpretations quite differently, as a brief comparison of joint problem solving and third-party decision making, two commonly used modes of conflict management, reveals. Joint problem solving consists of the principal disputants acting together to resolve a dispute; it can include direct bargaining between the parties as well as decision making with third party assistance, as in mediation, arbitration, or negotiation. In contrast, in methods such as adjudication or administrative decision making, known as third-party decision making, representatives of the wider community invoke shared norms to impose binding decisions on the disputants.

Third-party decision making works on the assumption that differences in interests are real and can be effectively resolved through reference to certain abstract principles like law or community norms without great regard for the larger context of a dispute or how disputants view each other. Focusing on the substantive interests at stake, outside parties, who represent the community's authority (which the disputants accept), decide among competing claims and back their decisions with sanctioned force. As a conflict management strategy, the approach focuses on past behavior more than future action (although this may be involved), and the process addresses the substantive differences among the parties rather than the more subjective background of the conflict.

Joint problem solving, in contrast, emphasizes perceptions and dispositions (such as low levels of trust or threats to identity) as the source of many conflicts, and addresses these subjective elements to create a climate in which creative problem solving can occur. Differences in interests are not denied but are viewed as surface manifestations of the more basic conflict or as symptoms of a dispute as much as the cause. In addition, joint problem-solving strategies focus less on the interests parties have in resolving past differences and emphasize instead their interests in living together in future harmony. Interests, then, are often seen as somewhat flexible and subject to redefinition so that resolving interest differences hinges, in part, on how the parties view each other and themselves. From this perspective, if antagonistic perceptions rooted in deeply held worldviews are altered, resolution of differences in interests may follow.

Each method addresses certain sources of conflict more readily than others: joint problem-solving may overlook the essential role of differences in interests in a conflict and overemphasize the importance of the interpersonal bonds and images created between disputants, especially when large communities are involved. In contrast, third-party decision making sometimes fails to address underlying psychocultural interpretations and may offer "solutions" to a dispute that do little to address its underlying sources.

Assumptions about the psychocultural aspects of conflict are embedded in third-party dispute management strategies, just as assumptions about interests inform joint decision making. What is striking, however, is how poorly developed each of these assumptions is and how they differ from the assumptions made about the same factors in the cases of the other dispute management method. In some cases assumptions about sources of conflict which underlie different procedures appear to contradict each other. Genuinely constructive dispute management procedures address both sets of factors in a comprehensive view that sees structural and psychocultural roots in almost all serious conflicts.

Dispute-Level Lessons

Whereas a societal-level analysis of conflict focuses on dispositional and structural factors in their most general form, at the dispute level it is crucial to identify more proximate manifestations of interests and interpretations to avoid invoking factors that are too remote, mechanical, or reductionistic. Neither social structural interests nor psychocultural dispositions defined at the societal level provide useful answers to such questions as:

Why was a particular interest pursued?

Why did a dispute escalate at the time it did?

Why were certain incompatible demands made by each side?

Why were a certain set of dispute management methods used and with what effect?

How did the interests and interpretations of disputants change in the course of a conflict?

How might the conflict have been managed better than it was?

Explaining the course of particular conflicts means identifying the precise interests and interpretations involved and trying to understand how they connect to more general forces.

This consists of more than just identifying specific interests and interpretations involved in a conflict. Dispute-level analysis of conflict also pays particular attention to the process by which a conflict unfolds, trying to understand its origin, development, and management and examining changes within any dispute. Societal level analysis, in contrast, focuses on continuities across disputes in a society. How, then, can interests and dispositions which are seen as relatively unchanging at the societal level help explain change at the dispute level?

If interests are seen only in terms of the social structural conditions that produce them, then adjusting interests during conflict management seems to be a contradiction, or leads to the idealistic request that parties simply set their interests aside in order to achieve agreement. In many situations, however, the overlap of interests among disputants is frequently greater than initially recognized because disputants have different priorities even when contesting a common concern (Raiffa 1982). Furthermore, the choice for each disputant is almost never between keeping everything or having to share it with others. Rather, it is between what can be obtained through alternative action strategies including noncooperation (Fisher and Ury 1981). Often the latter, in fact, presents unattractive options. Thus, social structural conditions broadly shape interests, but more proximate events modify, reorganize, and prioritize them, and shape what actions are actually taken.

Similarly, although disputants' interpretations of conflict situations are linked to dispositions rooted in early socialization, interpretations in specific disputes are not fully determined by such distant events. For one thing, psychocultural theory identifies how dispositions are subject to change under certain conditions, if and when the fundamental sources of anxiety are addressed.[17] Consideration of more proximate psychocultural data than socialization experiences is necessary in considering specific conflicts. Even if good data on child rearing for major actors are available, we would turn first to data on beliefs and behaviors most clearly associated with the events to be explained. Psychocultural dispositions are important in making sense of conflict and conflict management, and while the cross-cultural theory of conflict ultimately links these to early developmental experiences, more proximate manifestations of psychocultural dispositions are required in order to understand any single dispute.

Rather than altering psychocultural dispositions, constructive conflict management strategies can selectively emphasize specific dispositions, and linkages among dispositions can be reorganized. The mechanisms underlying psychocultural processes involve the invocation of analogies, metaphors, and other connections linking early experiences and images to later experiences. In cultures where there is a high predisposition to define in- and out-groups in dramatically different terms, to see the actions of others as threatening and provocative, or to identify with few beyond one's inner circle, conflict management cannot alter the inner psychic structures. It can, however, provide alternative psychoculturally appropriate analogies, metaphors, and images which may be more compatible with constructive conflict management.

Here I draw on the principle of psychocultural complexity and the notion that the organization of dispositions is as important as the presence of any particular disposition.[18] Therefore, although groups and individuals tend to emphasize certain dispositions, reorganization and changes in emphasis are also possible. Psychocultural dispositions

17. As an individual experience, the change in dispositions shares key assumptions with psychoanalysis.
18. I want to suggest here an approach focused on the *system* of interacting dispositions—in the same way that family systems therapy focuses on the interactions among members of a social system, not the characteristics of any single member in isolation (Bowen 1978).

and interpretations can be incorporated into strategies of conflict management without changing the fundamental worldviews of all parties in a short time—a most unrealistic goal, to say the least. A more modest but achievable aim would be a degree of affective and cognitive reorganization, with results in both being more important than the magnitude of change in either one. Such reorganization could involve an expansion of who is included in the label "we," stress metaphors associated with past cooperative successes, or offer a vision of mutual gain that effectively challenges a current scenario of animosity. When disputants have a long history of hostility, achieving this is difficult, and the involvement of skilled third parties can be especially helpful. Altering participants' interpretations of a situation can be achieved without necessarily addressing their childhood experiences but cannot ignore how culture selectively reinforces dispositions first developed at that stage.

Conclusion

This book has examined conflict and violence cross-culturally and has identified psychocultural and social structural factors which explain both differences in overall levels of conflict and particular patterns of conflict and cooperation. The culture of conflict refers to the complex ways a society's institutions, practices, and norms produce a pattern of conflict. It also includes culturally shared ideas about valued objects and interests, about ways to pursue them, about appropriate responses to the actions of others seeking the same valued items, and about past experiences relevant to understanding conflict behavior.

This concluding chapter has explored two extensions of the argument from the cross-cultural study. Explicit consideration of societies characterized by low levels of conflict and constructive conflict processes will, I hope, deepen awareness of their existence and extend our understanding of their internal dynamics. These societies are not defined simply by the absence of conflict but also by the presence of psychocultural dispositions and structurally defined interests that promote the management of disputes in essentially constructive and peaceful ways. Understanding and analyzing such cases demonstrate that high levels of conflict are not inevitable and that particularly effective practices may be applicable in other settings.

Last, I have considered ways in which the theoretical framework of the cross-cultural theory of conflict also provides a framework for the analysis of the management of individual disputes. Interests and interpretations, I suggest, are important in social conflicts, and effective conflict management needs to address both. Conflict management cannot necessarily alter deeply rooted social structural patterns or change basic psychocultural dispositions in every dispute. It may, however, recognize the role played by underlying interests and dispositions and try to address these directly so that we may in the future manage conflicts more constructively than we do at present.

Appendix A

Societies in the Sample

The 186 societies in the Murdock and White (1969) Standard Cross-Cultural Sample and their scores on a large number of social, economic, and cultural variables are described in Barry and Schlegel (1980). Greater detail about the selection of the ninety societies examined here and other topics regarding the sample is found in Ross (1983).

Table A below lists the societies in the sample and the scores of each society on the critical dependent variables: internal conflict and violence and external conflict and warfare. As described in chapter 5, the scale scores are the sum of the scores on the individual measures after they have been standardized and weighted by their squared factor loadings. The raw data for the individual variables for each society appear in Ross (1983). In cases where the data for an individual variable could be coded for a society, the sample mean was not substituted.

Table A. Societies in the Sample: Internal and External Conflict Scores

	Murdock-White Sample Number	Internal Conflict Score	External Conflict Score
!Kung	2	−3.0069	−3.7179
Lozi	4	−.5901	−.5021
Suku	6	1.5824	−1.4967
Nyakusa	8	3.2710	.2632
Kikuyu	11	.0089	−.4348
Buganda	12	−3.0069	1.2067
Mbuti	13	−3.6571	−3.7179
Tiv	16	2.6209	−.208
Fon	18	−3.2359	.7254
Mende	20	.6416	.2441

	Murdock-White Sample Number	Internal Conflict Score	External Conflict Score
Bambara	22	−1.9880	−.689
Tallensi	23	1.8080	−.0043
Hausa	26	−.8848	.6773
Azande	28	.3311	1.2067
Otoro	30	4.3722	.2441
Shilluk	31	3.8365	−.4348
Maasai	34	4.3722	1.2067
Somali	36	4.2617	1.2067
Amhara	37	2.7946	1.2067
Teda	40	5.8616	1.2067
Riffian	42	5.0533	.7927
Egyptian	43	3.7261	−.3173
Rwala	46	4.2962	.7254
Gheg Albanian	48	2.8747	1.2067
Rural Irish	51	−1.9880	−.3173
Lapp	52	−2.3722	−2.7242
Kurd	57	3.4959	1.2067
Basseri	58	−2.6146	.2121
Gond	60	−4.1167	−1.8097
Santal	62	−4.1121	−2.3412
Burusho	64	−4.5718	.3114
Kazak	65	.2040	1.2067
Lepcha	68	−4.5718	−3.7179
Lakher	70	3.1646	1.2067
Lamet	72	−3.2484	−2.7242
Vietnamese	73	−2.3822	−.3173
Semang	77	−4.5718	−3.2366
Adamanese	79	1.0123	.0465
Negri	82	.7493	.2632
Balinese	84	−4.1121	−2.7242
Iban	85	2.7434	1.2067
Toradja	87	−1.0498	.7254
Tiwi	90	2.8747	−1.0318
Orokaiva	92	3.5639	1.2067
Kapauku	94	3.5639	−1.8097
Manus	96	1.6356	−.9161
Trobriand	98	1.4720	−2.7242
Tikopia	100	−3.2359	−3.7179
Fijian	102	3.7261	.3114
Maori	104	1.2217	1.2067
Samoan	106	2.9938	−.3173
Marshalese	108	1.0252	−1.8097
Yapese	110	3.2710	−1.2483
Ifugao	112	4.8318	−1.8097

	Murdock-White Sample Number	Internal Conflict Score	External Conflict Score
Korean	116	−1.7300	.4289
Ainu	118	1.6579	.7927
Gilyak	119	.1994	−2.7242
Ingalik	122	−.9775	−1.4967
Copper Eskimo	124	1.0098	−2.7242
Saulteaux	127	−2.2356	.7254
Slave	128	.8253	.7927
Eyak	130	−1.3384	−.2692
Belacoola	132	2.1445	−.9161
Yurok	134	.9157	−1.0154
Yokuts	136	−2.1307	−2.0763
Klamath	138	3.9171	.7254
Gros Ventre	140	−4.1121	−.5021
Pawnee	142	−3.2405	.7254
Huron	144	−2.7808	.7254
Comanche	147	.0480	.7254
Chiricahua	148	−4.1167	.2441
Havasupi	150	−4.5718	−.9161
Papago	151	−4.5718	−.5840
Aztec	153	−2.7101	1.2067
Miskito	156	−1.8082	.6773
Cuna	158	−1.5396	−.2692
Goajiro	159	3.4535	−1.9753
Warrau	162	−.9474	−1.4967
Carib	164	−2.5183	−.3173
Mundurucu	166	−3.6571	1.2067
Cayapa	168	−4.5718	−3.2366
Jivaro	169	5.8616	1.2067
Aymara	172	.9142	.9583
Nambicuara	174	.4766	−.4348
Timbira	176	−4.5718	1.2067
Shavante	179	5.4065	1.2067
Aweikoma	180	2.8067	.7927
Abipon	183	5.1045	1.2067
Mapuche	184	3.8365	1.2067
Yahgan	186	−1.6756	−2.7242

Appendix B

Measures and Sources for the Independent Variables

The variables used in the analysis are calculated as described below in table B, indicating the specific source for each. The sources for the raw data for the economic, social structural, and child training variables for societies in the Standard Cross-Cultural Sample have been published in *Ethnology* between 1969 and 1977 and in Barry and Schlegel (1980). The data on the political variables are reported in Ross (1983).

Table B lists each society's scores on the composite independent variables used in the tables in chapters 6 and 7: socioeconomic complexity, strength of multiple reference groups, fraternal interest group strength, harsh socialization practices, and affectionate socialization practices which are not available elsewhere. Scores on the other independent variables are available in the sources indicated.

Multiple reference groups is a scale developed from factor analysis of 36 political variables for the societies in the sample as explained in the text and details of which are given in Ross (1983). This scale is derived from a summation of the scores on each of the component variables, which are first standardized and then weighted by its squared factor loading. The raw scores for each variable, as well as the scale scores, are presented in Ross (1983). The variables used were as follows (with their factor loadings given in parentheses): the extent to which individuals living in different communities of the same society are linked together in politically relevant ways (.64), the strength of in-group ("we") feelings directed beyond the local community (.62), the number of different areas of life in which community decision making (either formal or informal) occurs (.58), the strength of in-group feelings directed toward the local community (.56), the extent to which kinship organizations linking different communities are present and politically important (.53), the extent to which ritual groups linking different communities are present and politically important (.50), and to what extent there is intervention in disputes as they develop and community pressures encouraging settlement (.42).

Local community endogamy is a five-point variable measuring the degree to which marriage tends to be endogamous (as opposed to exogamous) with respect to the local community (Murdock and Wilson, 1972). To measure its effects in uncentralized societies, a society's score on this variable was multiplied by a "dummy variable" coded "1" for all societies with no authority beyond that of the local community and "0" for societies with some authority beyond the local community. This measure of political centralization is taken from Tuden and Marshall (1972).

Matrilocality and *patrilocality* are coded from Murdock and Wilson (1972). Societies are coded as patrilocal if Murdock and Wilson said they were patrilocal or virilocal; otherwise, patrilocality is considered absent. Similarly, matrilocality is scored as present if the society is matrilocal or uxorilocal according to Murdock and Wilson, absent if it is not.

Intercommunity trade is a seven-point measure of the degree to which a community in the society trades for foodstuffs (Murdock and Morrow, 1970).

Fraternal interest group strength is taken from Paige and Paige (1981) and is measured by the presence or absence of bride-price, patrilineality, and a trichotomized measure of the size of effective kin-based political subunits. For 66 of the societies their score is used. For the remaining 24 not in their sample, bride-price and patrilineality are coded from Murdock (1967) and Murdock and Wilson (1972). The size of effective kin groups is estimated using a recoded version of Murdock and Wilson's (1972) community size measure. Our measure is highly correlated with Paige and Paige's for those societies where both scores are available. To measure its effects in uncentralized societies, a society's score on this variable was multiplied by a dummy variable coded "1" for all societies with no authority beyond that of the local community and "0" for societies where some authority is exercised beyond the local community. This measure of political centralization is taken from Tuden and Marshall (1972).

Polygyny is a three-point measure—monogamous, less than 20 percent polygynous marriage, and more than 20 percent polygynous—derived from Murdock and Wilson's (1972) form of family variable.

Socioeconomic complexity is a scale made up of eight different measures which load on a single dimension when factor analyzed and are weighted in the other scales described above. The eight measures are importance of agriculture's contribution to subsistence, importance of animal husbandry, lack of importance of hunting, lack of importance of gathering, the extent to which food is stored, the size of the average community in the society, and the degree of social stratification and cultural complexity. The first five measures are from Murdock and Morrow (1970), the size measure is from Murdock and Wilson (1972), and the stratification and complexity measures are from Murdock and Provost (1973).

Political complexity is measured by a thirteen-variable scale called political power concentration based on factor analysis (Ross, 1983). The crucial variables are: the extent to which leaders act independently in a community, the presence or absence of checks on political authority, the degree of political role differentiation in a society, the importance of decision-making bodies, and the level of taxation. Raw scores on the individual variables and the scale are given in Ross (1983). For more detail concerning sources of political complexity see Ross (1981).

Harsh socialization practices is measured by a scale derived from a factor analysis of socialization measures from Barry and Paxson (1971) and Barry, Josephson, Lauer, and Marshall (1976, 1977) which were appropriate to measure either harshness of socialization, affectionate socialization, or protest masculinity. The variables and their loadings on the harsh socialization dimension were: severity of pain infliction (.69), extent to which corporal punishment is used (.63), the degree to which children are not indulged (.57), the extent to which children are scolded (.51), importance of caretakers other than the mother (.44), the degree to which fortitude is stressed as a value (.37), and the degree to which aggressiveness is stressed as a value (.28).

Affectionate socialization practices is a second scale derived from the factor analysis just cited. The variables loading on this dimension are the degree to which trust is emphasized as a value during childhood (.74), the degree to which honesty is stressed as a value during childhood (.67), the closeness of the father in childhood (.65), the degree to which generosity is stressed as a value during childhood (.53), the degree to which affection is expressed toward the child (.49), and the extent to which children are valued by the society (.34).

Male gender-identity conflict is measured following Whiting and others by the length of abstinence from sexual intercourse by the mother after birth, described as the cultural norm. The seven-point measure is from Barry and Paxson (1971). Whiting also suggests that the nature of mother-infant sleeping arrangements can be used to measure this variable, but the Barry and Paxson (1971) measure of sleeping arrangements is not sufficiently precise to be useful.

Table B. Scores on Composite Independent Variables

	Murdock-White Sample Number	Fraternal Interest Group Strength	Multiple Reference Group Strength	Socio-Economic Complexity	Harsh Social-ization	Affec-tionate Social-ization
!Kung	2	0	−1.020	−5.253	−3.246	2.611
Lozi	4	2	−.452	2.678	−.436	−1.044
Suku	6	1	−.190	.425	9.000	9.000
Nyakusa	8	2	.206	.313	−.400	−.725
Kikuyu	11	2	−.145	1.228	.378	.106
Buganda	12	4	.710	1.781	−1.122	−1.552
Mbuti	13	0	.795	−5.064	.527	2.131
Tiv	16	3	.407	1.788	.527	1.347
Fon	18	4	1.853	3.306	.925	−1.223
Mende	20	2	1.053	2.185	9.000	−.441
Bambara	22	4	1.154	3.812	.104	−.461
Tallensi	23	4	1.049	2.645	−.865	.042
Hausa	26	2	1.465	5.275	.139	−.814
Azande	28	2	1.084	−.169	−.062	−.939
Otoro	30	4	−.492	2.854	−.436	.216
Shilluk	31	3	−1.573	3.092	−.152	−.459
Maasai	34	4	.336	−.411	1.058	−.795
Somali	36	4	1.132	1.578	9.000	−.283
Amhara	37	1	1.150	3.804	1.040	−.939
Teda	40	2	−.307	2.516	.424	−.369
Egyptian	43	4	−1.189	6.445	1.751	−1.739
Rwala	46	4	−1.114	.206	.682	−.599
Albanian	48	2	.026	1.616	−.595	−1.259
Rural Irish	51	2	−2.079	7.038	−.081	.738
Lapp	52	0	−2.384	−.765	−2.714	1.154
Kurd	57	4	−1.232	4.548	1.275	−.701
Basseri	58	3	−.781	.583	.992	−.461
Gond	60	2	.143	−.332	9.000	−.218

	Murdock-White Sample Number	Fraternal Interest Group Strength	Multiple Reference Group Strength	Socio-Economic Complexity	Harsh Social-ization	Affec-tionate Social-ization
Santal	62	2	2.166	.804	−1.673	−.523
Burusho	64	1	−.581	3.692	−1.687	.253
Kazak	65	4	.121	2.977	.748	.324
Lepcha	68	2	−1.844	1.095	−.180	.842
Lakher	70	3	.462	2.661	.129	.257
Lamet	72	2	−1.518	−.507	9.000	−.283
Vietnamese	73	3	−.144	4.672	.027	.976
Semang	77	0	−2.071	−4.826	−1.673	.483
Adamanese	79	0	−2.071	−5.076	−1.439	−.722
Negri	82	9	−1.235	4.618	−1.153	.778
Balinese	84	1	1.496	4.502	−.500	.820
Iban	85	0	−.945	.163	.296	.936
Toradja	87	1	1.778	.349	−1.725	−.346
Tiwi	90	1	−2.044	−4.523	−1.477	.021
Orokaiva	92	2	−1.730	−.533	1.016	.771
Kapauku	94	3	.192	.997	−.430	−1.938
Manus	96	1	−2.227	−.095	1.570	1.984
Trobriand	98	0	−.475	1.816	−1.388	1.258
Tikopia	100	2	1.433	1.765	−.723	1.634
Fijian	102	9	.234	2.185	1.413	−2.400
Maori	104	1	1.480	.000	−.956	.182
Samoan	106	0	−.197	1.766	1.042	−1.136
Marshalese	108	1	−1.240	.635	−.743	.362
Yapese	110	0	−1.017	1.594	.094	−.457
Ifugao	112	3	−2.031	1.965	−.246	−.835
Korean	116	1	−.288	4.817	.915	.226
Ainu	118	0	.547	−3.792	.888	.134
Gilyak	119	2	−1.091	−3.678	9.000	1.433
Ingalik	122	1	−1.291	−2.459	9.000	1.433
Copper Eskimo	124	0	−2.196	−3.520	−.516	.017
Saulteaux	127	1	−1.122	−2.601	−1.983	−.967
Slave	128	0	−2.412	−2.551	−.594	.327
Eyak	130	0	−.295	−3.089	−.449	.021
Belacoola	132	0	−1.088	−2.119	1.456	−.722
Yurok	134	1	−3.211	−3.700	−2.386	−.305
Yokuts	136	2	.147	−1.973	−.177	.871
Klamath	138	0	−2.196	−3.433	1.364	.193
Gros Ventre	140	1	.563	−3.401	.760	1.193
Pawnee	142	0	−1.672	.087	1.751	−.148
Huron	144	2	1.908	1.017	−1.217	.001
Comanche	147	1	−.954	−3.124	−.297	−1.616
Chiricahua	148	0	1.312	−3.237	−.207	1.078

	Murdock-White Sample Number	Fraternal Interest Group Strength	Multiple Reference Group Strength	Socio-Economic Complexity	Harsh Social-ization	Affec-tionate Social-ization
Havasupi	150	0	−1.635	−1.943	−.698	.955
Papago	151	1	.136	−.625	−2.047	.808
Aztec	153	2	2.166	4.682	2.343	.586
Miskito	156	0	−.297	−.824	−.503	−.188
Cuna	158	0	.528	1.521	−.898	−.722
Goajiro	159	2	−1.302	−1.011	2.289	−.441
Warrau	162	0	−1.648	−3.741	−1.523	−.135
Carib	164	0	−2.953	−3.508	1.209	−.305
Mundurucu	166	1	1.480	−2.086	9.000	−.675
Cayapa	168	2	−2.325	−.132	1.016	.061
Jivaro	169	0	−3.211	−1.983	.764	.193
Aymara	172	3	−2.016	2.169	−.245	−1.920
Nambicuara	174	0	−.197	−3.149	−1.490	−.242
Timbira	176	0	.531	−.586	−.939	1.309
Shavante	179	9	−.024	−3.465	.749	−.978
Aweikoma	180	0	−2.271	−5.341	.653	−.978
Anipon	183	2	−2.119	−1.513	−.271	.021
Mapuche	184	2	−1.542	1.413	.175	1.282
Yahgan	186	0	−1.871	−3.933	.449	1.078

Bibliography

Achen, Christopher H. 1982. *Interpreting and Using Regression*. Sage Quantitative Applications in the Social Sciences Series, no. 29. Beverly Hills: Sage Publications.

Adams, Robert McC. 1966. *The Evolution of Urban Society*. Chicago: Aldine.

Adorno, T. W., et al. 1950. *The Authoritarian Personality*. New York: Wiley.

Alcorta, Candace Storey. 1982. "Paternal Behavior and Group Competition." *Behavior Science Research* 17:3–23.

Altschuler, Milton. 1965. "The Cayapa: A Study in Legal Behavior." Ph. D. diss. University of Minnesota.

Archer, Dane, and Rosemary Gaertner. 1984. *Violence and Crime in Cross-National Perspective*. New Haven: Yale University Press.

Argyle, W. J. 1966. *The Fon of Dahomey*. London: Oxford University Press.

Assefa, Hizkias, and Paul Wahrhaftig. 1990. *The Move Crisis in Philadelphia: Extremist Groups and Conflict Resolution*. Pittsburgh: University of Pittsburgh Press.

Avruch, Kevin. 1991. "Introduction: Culture and Conflict Resolution," in Kevin Avruch, Peter W. Black, and Joseph A. Scimecca, eds., *Conflict Resolution: Cross-Cultural Perspectives*. New York: Greenwood Press, pp. 1–17.

Avruch, Kevin, and Peter W. Black. 1991. "The Cultural Question and Conflict Resolution." *Peace and Change* 16:22–45.

Axelrod, Robert. 1984. *The Evolution of Cooperation*. New York: Basic Books.

Bandura, Albert. 1973. *Aggression: A Social Learning Analysis*. Englewood Cliffs, N.J.: Prentice-Hall.

Barkow, Jerome H. 1989. *Darwin, Sex and Status: Biological Approaches to Mind and Culture*. Toronto: University of Toronto Press.

Barkun, Michael. 1968. *Law Without Sanctions: Order in Primitive Societies and World Community.* New Haven: Yale University Press.

Barry, Herbert, III, Lili Josephson, Edith Lauer, and Catherine Marshall. 1976. "Traits Inculcated in Childhood: Cross-Cultural Codes 5." *Ethnology* 15:83–114.

———. 1977. "Agents and Techniques for Child Training: Cross-Cultural Codes 6." *Ethnology* 16:191–230.

Barry, Herbert, III, and Lenora M. Paxson. 1971. "Infancy and Early Childhood: Cross-Cultural Codes 2." *Ethnology* 10: 466–508.

Barry, Herbert, III, and Alice Schlegel, eds. 1980. *Cross-Cultural Samples and Codes.* Pittsburgh: University of Pittsburgh Press.

Barth, Fredrik. 1952. "Subsistence and Institutional System in a Norwegian Mountain Valley." *Rural Sociology* 17:28–38.

———. 1969. *Ethnic Groups and Boundaries.* Boston: Little, Brown.

Barton, R. F. 1919. *Ifugao Law.* University of California Publications in American Archaeology and Ethnology, no. 15. Berkeley and Los Angeles: University of California Press.

Bates, Robert H. 1983. "The Centralization of African Societies," in *Essays on the Political Economy of Rural Africa.* New York: Cambridge University Press, pp. 21–58.

Bernard, Jessie, et al. 1953. *The Nature of Conflict: Studies on the Sociological Aspects of International Tensions.* Paris: UNESCO.

Bigelow, Robert. 1973. "The Evolution of Cooperation, Aggression, and Self-Control," in James K. Cole and Donald D. Jensen, eds., *Nebraska Symposium on Motivation, 1972,* pp. 1–57. Lincoln: University of Nebraska Press.

Boehm, Christopher. 1984. *Blood Revenge: The Enactment and Management of Conflict in Montenegro and Other Tribal Societies.* Philadelphia: University of Pennsylvania Press.

Bolton, Ralph. 1984. "Notes on Norwegian Non-Violence." Paper presented to the Annual Meeting of the Society for Cross-Cultural Research, Boulder, Colo.

Bowen, Murray. 1978. *Family Therapy in Clinical Practice.* New York: Jason Aronson.

Bowlby, John. 1969. *Attachment and Loss.* Vol. 1, *Attachment.* New York: Basic Books.

———. 1973. *Attachment and Loss.* Vol. 2, *Separation: Anxiety and Anger.* New York: Basic Books.

Boyd, Robert, and Peter J. Richerson. 1985. *Culture and the Evolutionary Process.* Chicago: University of Chicago Press.

Boyle, Kevin, and Tom Hadden. 1985. *Ireland: A Positive Proposal.* Harmondsworth: Penguin Books.

Bradley, Candice. 1989. "Reliability and Inference in the Cross-Cultural Coding Process." *Journal of Quantitative Anthropology* 1:353–371.

Briggs, Jean L. 1975. "The Origins of Nonviolence: Aggression in Two Canadian Eskimo Groups," in Waren Muensterberger and Aaron Esman, eds., *The Psychoanalytic Study of Society* 6:134–203. New York: International Universities Press.

Briggs, Lloyd Cabot. 1960. *Tribes of the Sahara.* Cambridge, Mass.: Harvard University Press.

Broch, Tom, and Johan Galtung. 1966. "Belligerence among the Primitives." *Journal of Peace Research* 3:33–45.

Bronfenbrenner, Urie. 1960. "Freudian Theories of Identification and Their Derivation." *Child Development* 31:15–40.

Brown, Paula. 1982. "Conflict in the New Guinea Highlands." *Journal of Conflict Resolution* 26:525–546.

Brown, Roger. 1986. "Ethnic Conflict," in *Social Psychology,* pp. 531–634. 2d ed. New York: Free Press.

Bueno de Mesquita, B., R. M. Siverson, and G. Woller. 1992. "War and the Fate of Regimes: A Comparative Analysis." *American Political Science Review* 86:638–646.

Burton, Roger V., and John W. M. Whiting. 1961. "The Absent Father and Cross-Sex Identity." *Merrill-Palmer Quarterly* 7:85–95.

Cairns, Ed. 1982. "Intergroup Conflict in Northern Ireland," in Henri Tajfel, ed., *Social Identity and Intergroup Relations,* pp. 277–297. Cambridge: Cambridge University Press.

Campbell, Donald T. 1975a. "On the Conflicts Between Biological and Social Evolution and Between Psychology and the Moral Tradition." *American Psychologist* 30:1103–1126.

———. 1983. "Two Distinct Routes Beyond Kin Selection to Ultrasociality: Implications for the Humanities and Social Sciences," in D. L. Bridgeman, ed., *The Nature of Prosocial Development: Theories and Strategies,* pp. 11–41. New York: Academic Press.

———. 1988. *Methodology and Epistemology for Social Science: Selected Papers.* Ed. Samuel E. Overman. Chicago: University of Chicago Press.

Campbell, Donald T., and D. W. Fiske. 1959. "Convergence and Discriminant Validation by the Multitrait-Multimethod Matrix." *Psychological Bulletin* 56:81–105.

Caporael, Linnda, Robin M. Dawes, John M. Orbell, and Alphons J. C. van de Kagt. 1989. "Selfishness Reexamined: Cooperation in the Absence of Egoistic Incentives." *Behavior and Brain Sciences* 12:683–739.

Castberg, Frede. 1954. *The Norwegian Way of Life.* London: Heinemann.

Chagnon, Napoleon. 1967. "Yanomamo Social Organization and Warfare," in Morton Fried, Marvin Harris, and Robert Murphy, eds., *War: The Anthropology of Armed Conflict and Aggression,* pp. 109–159. Garden City, N.Y.: Natural History Press.

———. 1983. *Yanomamo: The Fierce People.* 3d ed. New York: Holt, Rinehart and Winston.

Cline, W. 1950. *The Teda of Tibesti, Borku and Kawar.* General Series in Anthropology. 12:1–52.

Cohen, Raymond. 1990. *Culture and Conflict in Egyptian-Israeli Relations.* Bloomington: University of Indiana Press.

————. 1991. *Negotiating Across Cultures: Communication Obstacles in International Diplomacy.* Washington, D.C.: United States Institute for Peace.

Cohen, Ronald. 1975. "State Foundations: A Controlled Comparison," in Ronald Cohen and Elman R. Service, eds., *Origins of the State: The Anthropology of Political Evolution,* pp. 141–160. Philadelphia: ISHI Press.

Coleman, James S. 1957. *Community Conflict.* New York: Free Press.

Collins, John N. 1973. "Foreign Conflict Behavior and Domestic Disorder in Africa," in Jonathan Wilkenfeld, ed., *Conflict Behavior and Linkage Politics,* pp. 251–293. New York: David McKay.

Colson, Elizabeth. 1953. "Social Control and Vengeance in Plateau Tonga Society." *Africa* 23:199–211.

Connary, Donald S. *The Scandinavians.* London: Eyre and Spottiswoode.

Darby, John. 1983. *Ireland: Background to the Conflict.* Syracuse: Syracuse University Press.

————. 1986. *Intimidation and Control of Conflict in Northern Ireland.* Dublin: Gill and Macmillan.

————. 1990. "Northern Ireland: The Persistence and Limitations of Violence," in Joseph V. Montville, ed., *Conflict and Peacemaking in Multiethnic Societies,* 151–159. Lexington, Mass.: Lexington Books.

Deutsch, Morton. 1973. *The Resolution of Conflict: Constructive and Destructive Processes.* New Haven: Yale University Press.

Devereux, George. 1967. *From Anxiety to Method in the Behavioral Sciences.* New York: Humanities Press.

Divale, William T. 1974. "Migration, External Warfare and Matrilocal Residence." *Behavior Science Research* 9:75–133.

Divale, William T., and Marvin Harris. 1976. "Population, Warfare and the Male Supremacist Complex." *American Anthropologist* 78:521–538.

Dow, Malcolm M., et al. 1984. "Galton's Problem as Network Autocorrelation." *American Ethnologist* 11:754–770.

Durbin, E. F. M., and John Bowlby. 1939. *Personal Aggressiveness and War.* New York: Columbia University Press.

Easton, David. 1959. "Political Anthropology," in Bernard J. Siegel, ed., *Biennial Review of Anthropology,* pp. 210–262. Stanford: Stanford University Press.

Eckstein, Harry. 1966. *Division and Cohesion in Democracy: A Study of Norway.* Princeton: Princeton University Press.

Eidheim, H. 1969. "When Ethnic Identity is a Social Stigma," in Fredrik Barth, ed., *Ethnic Groups and Boundaries.* Boston: Little, Brown.

Ember, Carol R. 1974. "An Evaluation of Alternative Theories of Matrilocal Versus Patrilocal Residence." *Behavior Science Research* 9:135–149.

————. 1978a. "Myths About Hunter-Gatherers." *Ethnology* 17:439–448.

————. 1978b. "Men's Fear of Sex with Women: A Cross-Cultural Study." *Sex Roles* 4:657–678.

————. 1980. "A Cross-Cultural Perspective on Sex Differences," in Ruth

H. Munroe et al., eds., *Handbook of Cross-Cultural Human Development*, pp. 531–580. New York: Garland.

Ember, Carol R., Melvin Ember, and Marc Howard Ross. 1992. "Replication and Generalization in Cross-Cultural Research." Paper presented to the Annual Meeting of the Society for Cross-Cultural Research, Sante Fe, N. Mex.

Ember, Carol R., et al. 1991. "Problems of Measurement in Cross-Cultural Research Using Secondary Data." *Behavior Science Research* 25:187–216.

Ember, Melvin, and Carol R. Ember. 1971. "The Conditions Favoring Matrilocal Versus Patrilocal Residence." *American Anthropologist* 73:571–594.

———. 1992. "Resource Unpredictability, Mistrust, and War." *Journal of Conflict Resolution* 36:242–262.

Fabbro, David. 1978. "Peaceful Societies: An Introduction." *Journal of Peace Research* 15:67–83.

Fairbairn, W. R. D. 1954. *An Object-Relations Theory of Personality*. New York: Basic Books.

Fallers, Lloyd A. 1964a. Introduction, in Lloyd A. Fallers, ed., *The King's Men: Leadership and Status in Buganda on the Eve of Independence*, pp. 1–15. London: Oxford University Press.

———. 1964b. "Social Stratification in Traditional Buganda," in Lloyd A. Fallers, ed., *The King's Men: Leadership and Status in Buganda on the Eve of Independence*, pp. 64–116. London: Oxford University Press.

Feierabend, Ivo K., and Rosalind L. Feierabend. 1971. "The Relationship of Systemic Frustration, Political Coercion, and Political Stability," in John V. Gillespie and Betty A. Nesvold, eds., *Macro-Quantitative Analysis: Conflict, Development, and Democratization*. Beverly Hills: Sage Publications.

Feierabend, Ivo K., Rosalind L. Feierabend, and Betty A. Nesvold. 1969. "Social Change and Political Violence: Cross-National Patterns," in H. D. Graham and Ted Robert Gurr, eds., *Violence in America: Historical and Comparative Perspectives*. New York: Praeger.

Feil, D. K. 1978. "Women and Men in the Enga *Tee*." *American Ethnologist* 5:263–79.

Ferguson, R. Brian. 1984. "Introduction: Studying War," in R. Brian Ferguson, ed., *Warfare, Culture and Environment*, pp. 1–81. Orlando: Academic Press.

———. 1990. "Explaining War," in J. Haas, ed., *The Anthropology of War*, pp. 26–55. Cambridge: Cambridge University Press.

———. 1992. "A Savage Encounter: Western Contact and the Yanomami War Complex," in R. Brian Ferguson and Neil L. Whitehead, eds., *War in the Tribal Zone: Expanding States and Indigenous Warfare*, pp. 199–227. Sante Fe, N. Mex.: School of American Research Press.

Ferguson, R. Brian, and Neil L. Whitehead, eds. 1992. *War in the Tribal Zone: Expanding States and Indigenous Warfare*. Sante Fe, N. Mex.: School of American Research Press.

Fisher, Roger, and William Ury. 1981. *Getting to Yes: Negotiating Agreement Without Giving In.* Boston: Houghton Mifflin.

Fitzduff, Mari. 1992. "Move Sideways to Progress? Mediation Choices in Northern Ireland." Paper presented to the first meeting of the Ethnic Studies Network, Portrush, Northern Ireland.

Fornari, Franco. 1975. *The Psychoanalysis of War.* Bloomington: Indiana University Press.

Freud, Anna. [1937] 1966. *The Ego and the Mechanisms of Defense.* New York: International Universities Press.

Freud, Sigmund. [1914] 1963. "On Narcissism: An Introduction," *General Psychological Theory,* pp. 56–82. New York: Macmillan.

———. [1917] 1963. "Mourning and Melancholia." *General Psychological Theory,* pp. 164–179. New York: Macmillan.

———. [1922] 1959. *Group Psychology and the Analysis of the Ego.* New York: Norton.

———. [1930] 1962. *Civilization and Its Discontents.* New York: Norton.

———. [1932] 1963. "Why War?" in *Character and Culture.* New York: Collier Books.

Fried, Morton. 1967. *The Evolution of Political Society.* New York: Random House.

Friedrich, Carl J., with Morton Horwitz. 1968. "The Relation of Political Theory to Anthropology." *American Political Science Review* 52:536–545.

Galtung, Johan. 1974. "Norway in the World Community," in Natalie Rogoff Ramsøy, ed., *Norwegian Society.* New York: Humanities Press.

Gellner, Ernest. 1983. *Nations and Nationalism.* Ithaca: Cornell University Press.

Gibbs, James L., Jr. 1963. "The Kpelle Moot: A Therapeutic Model for the Informal Settlement of Disputes." *Africa* 33:1–11.

Gluckman, Max. 1955. *The Judicial Process Among the Barotse of Northern Rhodesia.* Manchester: Manchester University Press.

Gluckman, Max, ed. 1969. *Ideas and Procedures in African Customary Law.* London: Oxford University Press.

Goldschmidt, Walter. 1976. "Comment on Campbell: Biological Versus Social Evolution." *American Psychologist* 81:355–57.

Gordon, Robert J. 1983. "The Decline of the Kaipdom and the Resurgence of 'Tribal Fighting' in Enga." *Oceania* 53:205–223.

Gordon, Robert J., and Mervyn J. Meggitt. 1984. *Law and Order in the New Guinea Highlands: Encounters with Enga.* Hanover, N.H.: University Press of New England.

Gorer, Geoffrey. 1938. *Himalayan Village: An Account of the Lepchas of Sikkim.* London: M. Joseph.

Greenberg, Jay R., and Stephen A. Mitchell. 1983. *Object Relations in Psychoanalytic Theory.* Cambridge, Mass.: Harvard University Press.

Greenstein, Fred. 1967. "The Impact of Personality and Politics: An Attempt to Clear Away the Underbrush." *American Political Science Review* 61:629–641.

Gruter, Margaret, and Roger Masters. 1986. *Ostracism: A Social and Biological Phenomenon.* Special issue of *Ethology and Sociobiology.* New York: Elsevier.

Guetzkow, Harold. 1955. *Multiple Loyalties: A Theoretical Approach to a Problem in International Organization.* Princeton: Center for Research on World Political Institutions.

Gullestad, Marianne. 1984. *Kitchen-Table Society.* Oslo: Universtitetsforlaget.

Gulliver, P. H. 1979. *Disputes and Negotiations: A Cross-Cultural Perspective.* New York: Academic Press.

Guntrip, Harry. 1968. *Schizoid Problems, Object-Relations, and the Self.* New York: International Universities Press.

———. *Psychoanalytic Theory, Therapy, and the Self.* New York: Harper Torchbooks.

Gurr, Ted Robert. 1968. "A Causal Model of Civil Strife: A Comparative Analysis Using New Indices." *American Political Science Review* 62:1104–1124.

———. 1970. *Why Men Rebel.* Princeton: Princeton University Press.

Gurr, Ted Robert, ed. 1980. *Handbook of Political Conflict.* New York: Free Press.

Gurr, Ted Robert, and Raymond Duvall. 1973. "Civil Conflict in the 1960s: A Reciprocal Theoretical System with Parameter Estimates." *Comparative Political Studies* 6:135–170.

Haas, Ernst. 1964. *Beyond the Nation-State.* Stanford: Stanford University Press.

Haas, Ernst, and Alan Whiting. 1956. *A Dynamics of International Relations.* New York: McGraw-Hill.

Haas, Michael. 1965. "Societal Approaches to the Study of War." *Journal of Peace Research* 4:307–323.

Harlow, Harry, and Margaret K. Harlow. 1962. "Social Deprivation in Monkeys." *Scientific American* 207:136–146.

———. 1965. "The Effect of Rearing Conditions on Behavior," in John Money, ed., *Sex Research: New Developments.* New York: Holt, Rinehart and Winston.

Harner, Michael. 1972. *The Jivaro: People of the Sacred Waterfalls.* Garden City, N.Y.: Natural History Press.

Harris, Marvin. 1974. *Cows, Pigs, Wars and Witches: The Riddles of Culture.* New York: Random House.

———. 1979. *Cultural Materialism: The Struggle for a Science of Culture.* New York: Vintage Books.

Harris, Rosemary. 1972. *Prejudice and Tolerance in Ulster.* Manchester: Manchester University Press.

Hayano, David M. 1974. "Marriage, Alliance, and Warfare: A View From the New Guinea Highlands." *American Ethnologist* 1:243–253.

Hazelwood, Leo A. 1973. "Externalizing Systemic Stress: International Conflict as Adaptive Behavior," in Jonathan Wilkenfeld, ed., *Conflict Behavior and Linkage Politics,* pp. 148–190. New York: David McKay.

Helm, June, ed. 1967. *Essays on the Problem of Tribe: Proceedings of the American Ethnological Society.* Seattle: University of Washington Press.

Herdt, Gilbert. 1987. *The Sambia: Ritual and Gender in New Guinea.* New York: Holt, Rinehart and Winston.

———. 1989. "Father Presence and Ritual Homosexuality: Paternal Deprivation and Masculine Development in Menanesia Reconsidered." *Ethos* 17:326–370.

Herskovits, Melville J. 1938. *Dahomey: An Ancient West African Kingdom.* 2 vols. New York: J. J. Augustin.

Hibbs, Douglas. 1973. *Mass Political Violence: Cross-National Causal Analysis.* New York: Wiley.

Hoebel, E. Adamson. 1940. *The Political Organization and Law-Ways of the Comanche Indians,* pp. 1–149. Memoirs of the American Anthropological Association, no. 54.

Hollos, Marida. 1974. *Growing Up in Flathill.* Oslo: Universitetsforlaget.

Holsti, Ole R. 1967. "Cognitive Dynamics and Images of the Enemy: Dulles and Russia," in David J. Finlay, Ole R. Holsti, and Richard R. Fagen, eds., *Enemies in Politics,* pp. 25–96. Chicago: Rand McNally.

Horowitz, Donald. 1985. *Ethnic Groups in Conflict.* Berkeley and Los Angeles: University of California Press.

Howard, Michael. 1983. *The Causes of Wars.* Cambridge, Mass.: Harvard University Press.

Inkeles, Alex, and Daniel Levinson. 1968. "National Character: The Study of Modal Personality and Sociocultural Systems," in Gardner Lindzey, ed., *Handbook of Social Psychology.* Vol. 2. Reading, Mass.: Addison-Wesley, pp. 977–1020.

Janis, Irving L. 1972. *Victims of Groupthink.* New York: Houghton Mifflin.

Jervis, Robert. 1976. *Perception and Misperception in International Politics.* Princeton: Princeton University Press.

Jervis, Robert, Richard Ned Lebow, and Janice Stein, eds. 1985. *Psychology and Deterrence.* Baltimore: Johns Hopkins University Press.

Kernberg, Otto. 1975. *Borderline Conditions and Pathological Narcissism.* New York: Jason Aronson.

Kertzer, David I. 1988. *Ritual, Politics, and Power.* New Haven: Yale University Press.

Knauft, Bruce M. 1988. "On Reconsidering Violence in Simple Societies." *Current Anthropology* 29:624–635.

Koch, Klaus-Friedrich. 1974. *War and Peace in Jalemo: The Management of Conflict in Highland New Guinea.* Cambridge, Mass.: Harvard University Press.

Kriesberg, Louis. 1982. *Social Conflicts.* Englewood Cliffs, N.J.: Prentice-Hall.

Kroeber, Alfred, and Clyde Kluckholm. 1952. *Culture: A Critical Review of Concepts and Definitions.* Cambridge, Mass.: Harvard University Press.

Laitin, David. 1986. *Hegemony and Culture: Politics and Change Among the Yoruba.* Chicago: University of Chicago Press.

Lambrecht, Francis. 1953–54. "Ancestors' Knowledge Among the Ifugaos and Its Importance in the Religious and Social Life of the Tribe." *Journal of East Asiatic Studies* 3:359–365.

Leach, Edmund. 1954. *Political Systems of Highland Burma: A Study of Kachin Social Structure.* London: Bell and Sons.

Leacock, Eleanor. 1982. "Relations of Production in Band Society," in Eleanor Leacock and Richard Lee, eds., *Politics and History in Band Societies,* pp. 159–170. Cambridge: Cambridge University Press.

Lebow, Richard Ned. 1976. *White Britain and Black Ireland: Influence of Stereotypes on Colonial Policy.* Philadelphia: ISHI Press.

———. 1978. "The Origins of Sectarian Assassination: The Case of Belfast." *Journal of International Affairs* 32:43–61.

———. 1981. *Between Peace and War.* Baltimore: Johns Hopkins University Press.

Lee, Richard Borshay. 1979. *The !Kung San: Men, Women, and Work in a Foraging Society.* Cambridge: Cambridge University Press.

LeVine, Robert A. 1965. "Socialization, Social Structure, and Intersocietal Images," in Herbert Kelman, ed., *International Behavior: A Social Psychological Analysis,* pp. 43–69. New York: Holt, Rinehart and Winston.

———. 1973. *Culture, Behavior, and Personality.* Chicago: Aldine.

LeVine, Robert A., and Donald Campbell. 1972. *Ethnocentrism: Theories of Conflict, Ethnic Attitudes and Group Behavior.* New York: Wiley.

Levinson, David, and Martin J. Malone. 1980. *Toward Explaining Human Culture: A Critique of the Findings of Worldwide Cross-Cultural Research.* New Haven: HRAF Press.

Lewis, Oscar. 1966. *La Vida: A Puerto Rican Family in the Culture of Poverty—San Juan and New York.* New York: Random House.

Lichtenberg, Joseph D. 1983. *Psychoanalysis and Infant Research.* Hillsdale, N.J.: The Analytic Press.

Lindberg, Leon, and Stuart Scheingold. 1970. *Europe's Would-Be Polity.* Englewood Cliffs, N.J.: Prentice-Hall.

Lipjhardt, Arend. 1975. "The Northern Ireland Problem: Cases, Theories and Solutions." *British Journal of Political Science* 5:83–106.

Lipset, Seymour Martin. 1959. "Some Social Requisites of Democracy: Economic Development and Political Legitimacy." *American Political Science Review* 53:69–105.

MacDonald, Michael. 1986. *Children of Wrath: Political Violence in Northern Ireland.* New York: Basil Blackwell.

Mack, Raymond W., and Richard Snyder. 1957. "The Analysis of Social Conflict: Toward an Overview and Synthesis." *Journal of Conflict Resolution* 1:212–248.

Mahler, Margaret S., Fred Pine, and Anni Bergman. 1975. *The Psychological Birth of the Human Infant: Symbiosis and Individuation.* New York: Basic Books.

Mair, Lucy. 1934. *An African People in the Twentieth Century.* London: Routledge and Kegan Paul.

Mansbridge, Jane, ed. 1990. *Beyond Self-Interest.* Chicago: University of Chicago Press.

Masters, Roger. 1964. "World Politics as a Primitive Political System." *World Politics* 16:595–619.

Maybury-Lewis, David. 1967. *Akwe-Shavante Society.* Oxford: Oxford University Press.

McFarlane, Graham. 1986. "Violence in Rural Northern Ireland: Social Scientific Models, Folk Explanations and Local Variation(?)," in David Riches, ed., *The Anthropology of Violence,* pp. 184–203. Oxford: Basil Blackwell.

McGoldrick, Monica. 1982. "Irish Families," in Monica McGoldrick, John K. Pearce, and Joseph Giordano, eds., *Ethnicity and Family Therapy,* pp. 310–339. New York: Guilford Press.

McLachlan, Peter. 1986. "Northern Ireland: The Cultural Bases of the Conflict." *Conflict Resolution Notes* 4:21–23.

Meggitt, Mervyn. 1964. "Male-Female Relations in the Highlands of New Guinea." *American Anthropologist* 66:202–224.

———. 1965. *The Lineage System of the Mae Enga of New Guinea.* New York: Barnes and Noble.

———. 1977. *Blood Is Their Argument: Warfare among the Mae Enga Tribesmen of the New Guinea Highlands.* Palo Alto: Mayfield.

Melson, Robert, and Howard Wolpe. 1970. "Modernization and the Politics of Communalism: A Theoretical Perspective." *American Political Science Review* 65:161–171.

Merton, Robert. 1957. *Social Theory and Social Structure.* New York: Free Press.

Messenger, John. 1971. "Sex and Repression in an Irish Folk Community," in Donald S. Marshall and Robert C. Suggs, eds., *Human Sexual Behavior.* New York: Basic Books.

Mitchell, Stephen A. 1988. *Relational Concepts in Psychoanalysis.* Cambridge, Mass.: Harvard University Press.

Middleton, John, and Greet Kershaw. 1965. *The Kikuyu and Kamba of Kenya.* London: International African Institute.

Midlarsky, Manus I. 1975. *On War: Political Violence in the International System.* New York: Free Press.

Midlarsky, Manus I., and Stafford T. Thomas. 1975. "Domestic Social Structure and International Warfare," in Martin A. Nettleship et al., eds., *War, Its Causes and Correlates,* pp. 531–548. The Hague: Mouton.

Mitrany, David. 1966. *A Working Peace System.* Chicago: Quadrangle Books.

Montagu, Ashley, ed. 1978. *Learning Non-Aggression.* New York: Oxford University Press.

Morgenthau, Hans J. 1960. *Politics Among Nations: The Struggle for Power and Peace.* 3d ed. New York: Knopf.

Muller, Edward N. 1972. "A Test of a Partial Theory of Potential for Political Violence." *American Political Science Review* 66:928–959.

———. 1980. "The Psychology of Political Protest and Violence," in Ted Robert Gurr, ed., *Handbook of Political Conflict*, pp. 69–99. New York: Free Press.

Mulvihill, Robert, and Marc Howard Ross. 1989. "Theories of Conflict, Conflict Management and Peacemaking in Northern Ireland." Paper presented at the National Conference on Peacemaking and Conflict Resolution, Montreal, Canada.

Munroe, Robert L., Ruth H. Munroe, and John W. M. Whiting. 1981. "Male Sex-Role Resolutions," in Ruth H. Munroe, Robert L. Munroe, and Beatrice B. Whiting, eds., *Handbook of Cross-Cultural Human Development*, pp. 611–632. New York: Garland.

Murdock, George Peter. 1934. "The Dahomeans of West Africa," in *Our Primitive Contemporaries*, pp. 551–595. New York: Macmillan.

———. 1949. *Social Structure*. New York: Free Press.

———. 1967. *Ethnographic Atlas*. Pittsburgh: University of Pittsburgh Press.

Murdock, George Peter, and Diana O. Morrow. 1970. "Subsistence Economy and Support Practices: Cross-Cultural Codes 1." *Ethnology* 9:302–330.

Murdock, George Peter, and Caterina Provost. 1973. "Measurement of Cultural Complexity." *Ethnology* 12:379–392.

Murdock, George Peter, and Douglas R. White. 1969. "Standard Cross-Cultural Sample." *Ethnology* 8:329–369.

Murdock, George Peter, and Suzanne F. Wilson. 1972. "Settlement Patterns and Community Organization: Cross-Cultural Codes 3." *Ethnology* 11:254–295.

Murphy, Robert F. 1957. "Intergroup Hostility and Social Cohesion." *American Anthropologist* 59:1018–1035.

Nader, Laura, and Harry F. Todd, eds. 1978. *The Disputing Process: Law in Ten Societies*. New York: Columbia University Press.

Nagel, Jack. 1991. "Psychological Obstacles to Administrative Responsibility: Lessons of the MOVE Disaster." *Journal of Public Analysis and Management* 10:1–23.

Naroll, Raoul. 1962. *Data Quality Control: A New Research Technique*. New York: Free Press.

———. 1964. "On Ethnic Unit Classification." *Current Anthropology* 5:283–312.

———. 1973. "Galton's Problem," in Raoul Naroll and Ronald Cohen, eds., *A Handbook of Method in Cultural Anthropology*. Garden City, N.Y.: Natural History Press.

———. 1983. *The Moral Order: An Introduction to the Human Situation*. Beverly Hills: Sage Publications.

Newman, Katherine S. 1983. *Law and Economic Organization: A Comparative Study of Preindustrial Societies*. Cambridge: Cambridge University Press.

Northrup, Terrell A. 1989. "The Dynamic of Identity in Personal and Social Conflict," in Louis Kreisberg, Terrell A. Northrup, and Stuart J.

Thorson, eds., *Intractable Conflicts and Their Transformation*, pp. 55–82. Syracuse: Syracuse University Press.

O'Brien, Conor Cruise. 1986. "Ireland: The Mirage of Peace." *New York Review of Books*. April 24, 1986, pp. 40–46.

Olson, Mancur. 1965. *The Logic of Collective Action*. Cambridge, Mass.: Harvard University Press.

O'Malley, Padraig. 1983. *The Uncivil Wars: Ireland Today*. New York: Houghton Mifflin.

———. 1990. *Biting at the Grave: The Irish Hunger Strikes and the Politics of Despair*. Boston: Beacon Press.

Otterbein, Keith. 1968. "Internal War: A Cross-Cultural Comparison." *American Anthropologist* 70:277–289.

———. 1970. *The Evolution of War*. New Haven: HRAF Press.

———. 1973. "The Anthropology of War," in John J. Honigmann, ed., *Handbook of Social and Cultural Anthropology*, pp. 923–958. Chicago: Rand McNally.

———. 1977. "Warfare as a Hitherto Unrecognized Critical Variable." *American Behavioral Scientist* 20:693–710.

Otterbein, Keith F., and Charlotte Swanson Otterbein. 1965. "An Eye for an Eye, a Tooth for a Tooth: A Cross-Cultural Study of Feuding." *American Anthropologist* 67:1470–1482.

Paige, Karen Ericksen, and Jeffrey M. Paige. 1981. *The Politics of Reproductive Ritual*. Berkeley and Los Angeles: University of California Press.

Podolefsky, Aaron. 1984. "Contemporary Warfare in the New Guinea Highlands." *Ethnology* 23:73–87.

Price-Williams, D. R. 1985. "Cultural Psychology," in Gardner Lindzey and Elliot Aronson, eds., *Handbook of Social Psychology*, pp. 993–1042. 3d ed. New York: Random House.

Pruitt, Dean G., and Jeffrey Z. Rubin. 1986. *Social Conflict: Escalation, Stalemate and Settlement*. New York: Random House.

Raiffa, Howard. 1982. *The Art and Science of Negotiation*. Cambridge, Mass.: Belknap Press.

Ramsøy, Natalie Rogoff, ed. 1974. *Norwegian Society*. New York: Humanities Press.

Richards, Audrey I. 1964a. "Authority Patterns in Traditional Buganda," in Lloyd A. Fallers, ed., *The King's Men: Leadership and Status in Buganda on the Eve of Independence*, pp. 256–293. London: Oxford University Press.

———. 1964b. "Traditional Values and Current Political Behavior," in Lloyd A. Fallers, ed., *The King's Men: Leadership and Status in Buganda on the Eve of Independence*, pp. 294–335. London: Oxford University Press.

Romney, A. K. 1989. "Quantitative Models, Science and Cumulative Knowledge." *Journal of Quantitative Anthropology* 1:153–223.

Roscoe, John. 1911. *The Buganda: An Account of Their Native Customs and Beliefs*. London: Macmillan.

Rose, Richard. 1971. *Governing Without Consensus: An Irish Perspective.* Boston: Beacon Press.

Ross, Jennie-Keith. 1975. "Social Borders: Definition of Diversity." *Current Anthropology* 16:53–72.

Ross, Marc Howard. 1981. "Socioeconomic Complexity, Socialization, and Political Differentiation." *Ethos* 9:217–247.

——. 1983. "Political Decision Making and Conflict: Additional Cross-Cultural Codes and Scales." *Ethnology* 22:169–192.

——. 1985. "Internal and External Violence: Cross-Cultural Evidence and a New Analysis." *Journal of Conflict Resolution* 29:547–579.

——. 1986a. "A Cross-Cultural Theory of Political Conflict and Violence." *Political Psychology* 7:427–469.

——. 1986b. "Female Political Participation: A Cross-Cultural Explanation." *American Anthropologist* 88:843–858.

——. 1986c. "The Limits to Social Structure: Social Structural and Psychocultural Explanations for Political Conflict and Violence." *Anthropological Quarterly* 59:171–176.

——. 1988a. "Why Complexity Doesn't Necessarily Enhance Participation: Exit, Voice and Loyalty in Pre-Industrial Societies." *Comparative Politics* 21:73–89.

——. 1988b. "Studying Politics Cross-Culturally: Key Concepts and Issues," Presidential address delivered to the Society for Cross-Cultural Research. *Behavior Science Research* 22:105–129.

——. 1988c. "Some Comments on the Quality and Reliability of Political Decision Making and Conflict Codes and Scales." *World Cultures* 5, no. 1.

——. 1991. "The Role of Evolution in Ethnocentric Conflict and Its Management." *Journal of Social Issues* 47:167–185.

——. 1992. "Ethnic Conflict and Dispute Management," in Austin Sarat and Susan Silbey, eds., *Studies in Law, Politics and Society,* pp. 107–146. vol. 12. Greenwich, Conn.: JAI Press.

——. 1993. *Managing Conflicts Constructively: Interests, Interpretations and Disputing in Comparative Perspective.* New Haven: Yale University Press.

——. forthcoming. "Managing Ethnocentric Conflict: Competing Theories and Alternative Steps Towards Peace." *Journal of Conflict Resolution.*

Ross, Marc Howard, and Elizabeth L. Homer. 1976. "Galton's Problem in Cross National Research." *World Politics* 29:1–28.

Rule, James B. 1988. *Theories of Civil Violence.* Berkeley and Los Angeles: University of California Press.

Rummel, Rudolph J. 1963. "Dimensions of Conflict Behavior Within and Between Nations." *General Systems Yearbook* 8:1–50.

——. 1968. "National Attributes and Foreign Conflict Behavior," in J. D. Singer, ed., *Quantitative International Politics: Insights and Evidence.* New York: Free Press.

Russell, Elbert W. 1972. "Factors of Human Aggression: A Cross-Cultural Factor Analysis of Characteristics Related to Warfare and Crimes." *Behavior Science Research* 7:275–312.

Sahlins, Marshall. 1961. "The Segmentary Lineage: An Organization of Predatory Expansion." *American Anthropologist* 63:322–345.

Schafer, Roy. 1968. *Aspects of Internalization.* New York: International Universities Press.

Schattschneider, E. E. 1960. *The Semi-Sovereign People.* New York: Holt, Rinehart and Winston.

Scheper-Hughes, Nancy. 1979. *Saints, Scholars, and Schizophrenics: Mental Illness in Rural Ireland.* Berkeley and Los Angeles: University of California Press.

Scott, James. 1972. "Patron-Client Politics and Political Change in Southeast Asia." *American Political Science Review* 64:91–113.

Sears, R. R., E. E. Maccoby, and H. Levin. 1958. "The Socialization of Aggression," in E. E. Maccoby, T. Newcomb, and E. L. Hartley, eds., *Readings in Social Psychology,* pp. 350–358. 2d ed. New York: Holt, Rinehart and Winston.

See, Katherine O'Sullivan. 1986. *First World Nationalisms: Class and Ethnic Politics in Northern Ireland and Quebec.* Chicago: University of Chicago Press.

Service, Elman R. 1975. *Origins of the State and Civilization.* New York: Norton.

Shaw, R. P., and Y. Wong. 1989. *The Genetic Seeds of Warfare: Evolution, Nationalism, and Patriotism.* Boston: Unwin and Hyman.

Sherif, Muzafer, et al. 1988. *The Robbers Cave Experiment: Intergroup Conflict and Cooperation.* Middletown, Conn.: Wesleyan University Press.

Shils, Edward, and Michael Young. 1953. "The Meaning of the Coronation." *Sociological Review* 1:63–81.

Snidal, Duncan. 1991. "Relative Gains and the Pattern of International Cooperation." *American Political Science Review* 85:701–726.

Sipes, Richard G. 1973. "War, Sports and Aggression: An Empirical Test of Two Rival Theories." *American Anthropologist* 75:64–86.

Slater, Phillip E. 1977. *Footholds.* New York: E. P. Dutton.

Slater, Phillip E., and Dori A. Slater. 1965. "Maternal Ambivalence and Narcissism: A Cross-Cultural Study." *Merrill-Palmer Quarterly* 11:241–259.

Spencer, Herbert. 1961. *The Study of Sociology.* Ann Arbor: University of Michigan Press.

Spencer, Paul. 1988. *The Maasai of Matapato: A Study of Rituals of Rebellion.* Bloomington: Indiana University Press.

Spotnitz, Hyman. 1976. *Psychotherapy of Preoedipal Conditions.* New York: Jason Aronson.

Stern, Daniel N. 1985. *The Interpersonal World of the Infant.* New York: Basic Books.

Steward, Robert A. C., and Kenneth J. Jones. "Cultural Dimensions: A

Factor Analysis of Textor's 'Cross-Cultural Summary.' " *Behavior Science Research* 7:37–81.

Stohl, Michael. 1980. "The Nexus of Civil and International Conflict," in Ted Robert Gurr, ed., *Handbook of Political Conflict*, pp. 297–330. New York: Free Press.

Strathern, Andrew. 1974. "When Dispute Procedures Fail," in A. L. Epstein, ed., *Contention and Dispute*, pp. 240–270. Canberra: National University Press.

Swanson, Guy E. 1960. *The Birth of the Gods: The Origin of Primitive Beliefs*. Ann Arbor: University of Michigan Press.

Swartz, Marc J., Victor Turner, and Arthur Tuden. 1966. Introduction, in Marc J. Swartz, Victor Turner, and Arthur Tuden, eds., *Political Anthropology*, pp. 1–41. Chicago: Aldine.

Tajfel, Henri. 1981. *Human Groups and Social Categories*. Cambridge: Cambridge University Press.

Tanter, Raymond. 1966. "Dimensions of Conflict Behavior Within and Between Nations, 1958–1960." *Journal of Conflict Resolution* 10:41–64.

Textor, Robert. 1967. *A Cross-Cultural Summary*. New Haven: HRAF Press.

Thoden van Velzen, H. U. E., and W. van Wetering. 1960. "Residence, Power Groups and Intra-Societal Aggression." *International Archives of Ethnography* 49:169–200.

Tooker, Elizabeth. 1964. *An Ethnography of the Huron Indians. Bulletin of the Bureau of American Ethnology*, no. 190, pp. 1–183.

Trevarthen, Colwyn, and Katerina Logotheti. 1989. "Child in Society and Society in Children: The Nature of Basic Trust," in Signe Howell and Roy Willis, eds., *Societies at Peace: Anthropological Perspectives*, pp. 165–186. London: Routledge.

Trigger, Bruce G. 1969. *The Huron*. New York: Holt, Rinehart and Winston.

Tuden, Arthur, and Catherine Marshall. 1972. "Political Organization: Cross-Cultural Codes 4." *Ethnology* 11:436–464.

Turnbull, Colin. 1961. *The Forest People*. New York: Doubleday/Anchor Press.

———. 1978. "The Politics of Non-Aggression," in Ashley Montagu, ed., *Learning Non-Aggression: The Experience of Non-Literate Societies*, pp. 161–221. New York: Oxford University Press.

Turner, John C. 1988. *Rediscovering the Social Group: A Self-Categorization Theory*. Oxford: Basil Blackwell.

Turner, Victor. 1957. *Schism and Continuity in an African Society*. Manchester: Manchester University Press.

Turney-High, Hugh H. 1949. *Primitive War*. Columbia: University of South Carolina Press.

Underhill, Ruth M. 1939. *Social Organization of the Papago Indians*, pp. 1–280. Columbia University Contributions to Anthropology, no. 30.

Valentine, Charles. 1968. *Culture and Poverty: Critique and Counter-Proposals*. Chicago: University of Chicago Press.

Vayda, Andrew. 1961. "Expansion and Warfare among Swidden Agriculturalists." *American Anthropologist* 63:346–358.

Verba, Sidney, Norman Nie, and Jae-On Kim. 1978. *Participation and Political Equality: A Seven-Nation Comparison.* Cambridge: Cambridge University Press.

Volkan, Vamik D. 1988. *The Need to Have Enemies and Allies: From Clinical Practice to International Relationships.* New York: Jason Aronson.

Wallace, Anthony. 1962. *Culture and Personality.* New York: Random House.

Wallace, Ernest, and E. Adamson Hoebel. 1952. *The Comanches: Lords of the South Plains.* Norman: University of Oklahoma Press.

Waltz, Kenneth. 1959. *Man, The State, and War.* New York: Columbia University Press.

Weiner, Annette. 1976. *Women of Value, Men of Renown: New Perspectives in Trobriand Exchange.* Austin: University of Texas Press.

West, Mary Maxwell, and Melvin J. Konner. 1976. "The Role of the Father: An Anthropological Perspective," in Michael E. Lamb, ed., *The Role of the Father in Child Development,* pp. 185–216. New York: Wiley-Interscience.

White, Douglas. 1989. "World System Explanations of War Viewed from the Community Level." Typescript.

White, Ralph K. 1984. *Fearful Warriors: A Psychological Profile of U.S.– Soviet Relations.* New York: Free Press.

White, Robert. 1989. "From Peaceful Protest to Guerrilla War: Micromobilization of the Provisional Republican Army." *American Journal of Sociology* 94:1277–1302.

Whiting, Beatrice B. 1965. "Sex Identity Conflict and Physical Violence: A Comparative Study." *American Anthropologist* 67, pt. 2: 123–140.

———. 1980. "Culture and Social Behavior: A Model for the Development of Social Behavior." *Ethos* 8:95–116.

Whiting, Beatrice B., and John W. M. Whiting. 1975b. *Children of Six Cultures: A Psycho-Cultural Analysis.* Cambridge: Harvard University Press.

Whiting, John W. M. 1974. "A Model for Psycho-Cultural Research." Annual Report. American Anthropological Association.

Whiting, John W. M., and Irwin L. Child. 1953. *Child Training and Personality.* New Haven: Yale University Press.

Whiting, John W. M., Richard Kluckhohn, and Albert S. Anthony. 1958. "The Function of Male Initiation Ceremonies at Puberty," in E. E. Maccoby, T. M. Newcomb, and Eugene L. Hartley, eds., *Readings in Social Psychology,* pp. 359–370. 3d ed. New York: Holt, Rinehart and Winston.

Whiting, John W. M., and Beatrice B. Whiting. 1975a. "Aloofness and Intimacy Between Husbands and Wives." *Ethos* 3:183–207.

Whyte, John. 1978. "Interpretations of the Northern Ireland Problem: An Appraisal." *Economic and Social Review* 9:257–282.

———. 1990. *Interpreting Northern Ireland.* Oxford: Oxford University Press.

Wildavsky, Aaron. 1987. "Choosing Preferences by Constructing Institutions: A Cultural Theory of Preference Formation." *American Political Science Review* 81:3–21.

———. 1989. "Frames of Reference Come from Cultures: A Predictive Theory," in Morris Freilich, ed. *The Relevance of Culture,* pp. 58–74. New York: Bergan and Garvey.

———. 1991. "Why Self-Interest Is an Empty Concept Outside of a Social Context: Cultural Constraints on the Construction of 'Self' and 'Interest.' " Typescript.

———. 1992. "Indispensable Framework of Just Another Ideology? Prisoner's Dilemma as an Antihierarchical Game." *Rationality and Society* 4:8–23.

Wilkenfeld, Jonathan. 1968. "Domestic and Foreign Conflict Behavior of Nations." *Journal of Peace Research* 5:56–69.

———. 1973. "Domestic and Foreign Conflict," in Jonathan Wilkenfeld, ed., *Conflict Behavior and Linkage Politics,* pp. 107–123. New York: David McKay.

Wilkenfeld, Jonathan, and Dina A. Zinnes. 1973. "A Linkage Model of Domestic Conflict Behavior," in Jonathan Wilkenfeld, ed., *Conflict Behavior and Linkage Politics,* pp. 325–356. New York: David McKay.

Williams, F. E. 1930. *Orokaiva Society.* London: Oxford University Press.

Winnicott, Donald W. 1953. "Transitional Objects and Transitional Phenomena." *International Journal of Psycho-Analysis* 34:89–97.

———. 1965. *The Maturational Process and the Facilitating Environment.* New York: International Universities Press.

World Cultures, Electronic Journal. 1989.

Worsley, Peter. 1986. "The Superpowers and the Tribes," in Mary LeCron Foster and Robert A. Rubinstein, eds., *Peace and War: Anthropological Perspectives,* pp. 293–306. New Brunswick, N.J.: Transaction Books.

Wright, Frank. 1992. *Northern Ireland: A Comparative Analysis.* Dublin: Gill and Macmillan.

Wright, Quincy. 1942. *A Study of War.* 2 vols. Chicago: University of Chicago Press.

Wrigley, C. C. 1964. "The Changing Economic Structure of Buganda," in L. A. Fallers, ed., *The King's Men: Leadership and Status in Buganda on the Eve of Independence,* pp. 16–63. London: Oxford University Press.

Yngvesson, Barbara. 1976. "The Atlantic Fisherman," in Laura Nader and Harry F. Todd, eds. *The Disputing Process: Law in Ten Societies,* pp. 59–85. New York: Columbia University Press.

Young, Frank. 1965. *Initiation Ceremonies: A Cross-Cultural Study of Status Dramatization.* New York: Bobbs-Merrill.

Zigler, Edward, and Irwin L. Child. 1969. "Socialization," in Gardner

Lindzey and Elliot Aronson, eds. *Handbook of Social Psychology*. 2d ed. Reading, Mass.: Addison-Wesley.

Zimmerman, Ekkart. 1980. "Macro-Comparative Research on Political Protest," in Ted Robert Gurr, ed., *Handbook of Political Conflict*, pp. 167–237. New York: Free Press.

Zinnes, Dina A. 1980. "Why War? Evidence on the Outbreak of International Conflict," in Ted Robert Gurr, ed., *Handbook of Political Conflict*. New York: Free Press.

Index